Man and Woman in Biblical Perspective

Contemporary Evangelical Perspectives Series

James B. Hurley

Man and Woman in Biblical Perspective

Academie Books
Grand Rapids, Michigan
Zondervan Publishing House

MAN AND WOMAN IN BIBLICAL PERSPECTIVE
Copyright © 1981 by James B. Hurley

ACADEMIE BOOKS is an imprint of Zondervan
Publishing House, 1415 Lake Drive, S.E.,
Grand Rapids, Michigan 49506

Library of Congress Cataloging in Publication Data

Hurley, James B.
    Man and woman in Biblical perspective.
    Reprint. Originally published: Leicester: Inter-Varsity Press, 1981.
    Bibliography: p.
    Includes indexes.
    1. Women in the Bible.   2. Women in Christianity.   3. Men (Christian
theology)—Biblical teachings.   4. Sex role—Biblical teaching.   I. Title.
BS680.W7H87   1981   261.8′344   81-2975
ISBN 0-310-42731-2   AACR2

All scripture quotations, unless otherwise noted, are taken from the HOLY
BIBLE: NEW INTERNATIONAL VERSION (North American Edition).
Copyright © 1973, 1978, 1984, by The International Bible Society. Used by
permission of Zondervan Bible Publishers.

Printed in the United States of America

86 87 88 89 90 91 92 93 / 16 15 14 13 12 11 10 9 8

to
Phyllis
my best friend
my love
my wife
who has walked with me
step-for-step, shoulder-to-shoulder
for thirteen years

to Jamie
who thoughtfully serves God

to Andrew
who loves to hear God's Word

and

to our third child
whom I can feel
but have not yet
seen

Soli Deo gloria

Contents

Preface

More than a decade ago I stood with a group of ministers in South Dakota, discussing difficult passages of Scripture. 'My problem', said one, 'is not the doctrinal or the historical passages, but some of the practical ones which we side-step. Do we really believe and obey Scripture? What do you do about 1 Corinthians 11 and veils?' I felt unhappy with the idea of side-stepping a biblical command because it seemed strange . . . yet the idea of my wife veiling herself *did* seem strange. My questions led to study of that text and that in turn led to my asking more questions about the rationale behind the Bible's teachings about the relationship of men and women. In the end my questions and study resulted in a doctoral thesis and in this book dealing with role relations among the people of God.

I am an evangelical Christian. I receive the Bible as the written Word of the living God whom it proclaims and whom I have come to know and to worship. Because the Holy Spirit spoke through men who lived in specific historical settings and spoke specific languages, I believe that our deepest study of the Bible must consider the language, history, and thought forms of the human authors. The Bible is worthy of the closest and most searching academic study. Such study should result in more profound understanding, which should in turn result in more profound obedience.

In my study I have tried to handle the biblical text in a manner which is academically responsible. I have also tried to maintain a receptive and obedient stance before the Word of my God. I am sure that the conclusions which I have reached will not meet with universal favour. It is my hope that even those who do not agree with me regarding the nature of the teaching of the Bible will feel

14

that I have tried to deal honestly and fairly both with the Scripture and with the views of others.

No man infallibly interprets God's Word. John Calvin's attitude should be an example for us all. With regard to his own conclusions he said, 'I have said what I can say. Others may be able to say more. Let us all beware lest we say more than that which God has said. . . .' It is my hope that the material in this book will be of help to God's people and foster further discussion and learning. I look forward (with a certain amount of fear and trembling) to hearing directly from others whose insight and understanding can help me to extend mine. Either the publisher or Reformed Theological Seminary, 5422 Clinton Blvd., Jackson, MS 39209, USA will ensure that I receive any such insights as may be offered.

No man is an island. This little saying holds true in many areas. It is my cheerful duty to acknowledge with grateful thanks a few of the multitude of persons who have contributed to this book. Without their help, it could not have been. Credit belongs to them, although they should not be held responsible for my views.

Foremost must be my wife Phyllis, who is my most penetrating critic and my best friend. For thirteen years her intellectual gifts have honed and, in the best sense, challenged my thinking. Her life with me and her care for our children have constantly encouraged and taught me, and frequently pressed me to consider anew what it means to be a servant of Christ, a husband, and a father.

Another who has taught me that theology and life must be compassionately joined is Francis Schaeffer. The wedding of the intellectual and the human, of theology and life which has been so evident in him throughout the twenty years of our relationship has been a constant reminder and encouragement to me.

Acknowledgment is also due to my sons Jamie and Andrew. Both have shown maturity beyond their years in understanding and accepting that Daddy must sometimes be glued to the typewriter. They have willingly surrendered many hours to this project.

The writing of this book was made possible by the granting of sabbatical leave by Westminster Theological Seminary and Florida Theological Center. Financial assistance for this project, or assistance in procuring it, was provided by the MacClelland Foundation and, through a Trust, the Universities and Colleges Christian Fellowship of Great Britain. I am grateful to each.

Research and writing are not carried out in a vacuum. I am deeply indebted to the Trustees and staff of Tyndale House, Cambridge for access to their fine research library, without which my task would have been immeasurably more difficult. My writing at Tyndale House was made easier by the provision of a typewriter by Mr and Mrs Michael Fiske.

Particular thanks are to Mr Daniel De Lange and Mr Richard Postmus for their tireless preparation of a computer programme to handle the indexes and for the provision of computer time.

A variety of people have contributed to the development and expression of my thoughts. I am especially grateful to Richard T. France of Tyndale House, George W. Knight of Covenant Seminary, J. P. M. Sweet and C. F. D. Moule of Cambridge University, Linette Martin of London, and my former colleagues in the Department of Biblical Studies at Covenant College for their willingness to listen to and thoughtfully offer a critique of various aspects of my work. Their professional comments, both agreements *and* *disagreements*, have improved my work. I am also indebted to Dorinda Beale, Victor and Margaret Kerr, Marie Trotter, Lucille Walbridge Jansen and Cathy Van Winkle for reading and criticizing the manuscript and to Laura Bell for typing the final manuscript and several generations of editorial corrections of it.

Introduction

THE PROBLEM

'It's one thing to believe that a man rose from the dead or that he could change water to wine. Those things were long ago and are so foreign to me that I can accept them. It is a lot harder to accept that my wife needs to go around veiled and meekly to accept any crazy thing which I decide. It almost seems that she is put down by the Bible.'

Many Christians are facing the sort of tension expressed here. Faith in the God who works miracles can be undercut by the problems we face as we try to understand what he is calling us to do in the mundane arena of life. I am glad that the husband whom I have quoted did not really understand what the Bible says about the relation of husbands and wives. The problem with which he wrestled, however, is a serious one which confronts us in many forms as our twentieth-century culture moves farther and farther from the cultural patterns and thought forms of the times in which the books of the Bible were written.

Is it possible for the Bible to speak to our social customs? Society changes all the time. The Bible does not. It is therefore fair to ask whether the Bible is becoming more and more out of date and whether an effort to live a 'biblical' life-style is not in fact an effort to put the clock back a couple of millennia. Each generation of Christians must think through for itself the application of biblical faith to its own life situation. The solutions of past generations are useful, and will often be adopted, but they must be reconsidered at points of cultural change. This book discusses one such point – a point at which there is much controversy in the twentieth century: the relation of women and men.

The twentieth century has seen a revolution in the relation of women and men. Women have been 'liberated' from the status of 'second-class' citizens. Not since a first-century rabbi named Jesus taught women about the Jewish faith has so dramatic a change in roles been introduced. The changes introduced by that rabbi, who was God as well as man, were joyfully received by some, hated by others, and wrongly understood by still others. The New Testament records of the early church show that the relationship of man and woman continued to be controversial after Jesus' death and resurrection. The changes which have come in our century have produced similar results. Some have joyfully received them; some have hated them; some are confused about what is going on in the discussion of women's liberation, women's rights, and the like.

Within the Christian church there has been much discussion of the roles which the sexes should play. Does the Bible make distinctions between the sexes? How does the place which women were given in the church compare with that which they had in the Old Testament and in the Jewish culture (Judaism) of Christ's day? Should we make distinctions today? What did Paul mean when he said that in Christ there is no more 'male nor female' (Gal. 3:28)? How does that square with his insistence that women may not 'teach or . . . have authority over a man' (1 Tim. 2:12)?

Such questions have practical implications for the Christian church and for Christian marriages. Shall we have women pastors? Should the husband be 'head' of the home? Should women teach in Sunday school? Are men superior beings? Such are the questions addressed by this book.

MY APPROACH TO THE PROBLEM

This book is written from an evangelical perspective. I accept the Bible as the Word of God, written. Because the words of the Bible are indeed God's as well as those of the human authors of the various books which compose it, they are worthy of the closest attention and demand our obedience. Because they are the words of men who lived in given historical situations, as well as those of God, we must make every effort to appraise them in their historical context in order that we may understand them properly. Any who have wondered, as I have, why Jesus illustrated the difficulty with which the rich enter the kingdom of heaven with the difficulty of getting a camel through the eye of a needle will know the joy of discovering the meaning of a man's words within their historical context. I will never forget the sense of understanding and insight which I felt when I discovered that the 'needle's eye' is the small night-entry door in a Near Eastern city gate and that camel caravans entering at night had to remove the valuable goods from the camel's backs to get them through to the safety of the city. The Bible was indeed written in specific social and historical settings.

My conviction that an understanding of its context will enhance our understanding of the Bible has influenced the structure of this discussion of the roles of women and men. The first chapter looks at the role of women in Israel's neighbours, Assyria and Babylon, during the Old Testament period. Chapter 2 is devoted to an examination of Israel herself. Chapter 3 is devoted to the role of women in Judaism and in Graeco-Roman culture at the time of Christ. Their place in the ministry and teaching of Jesus fills chapter 4. He contrasts sharply with the cultures of the day and provides the foundation on which the early church built. Chapters 5 to 8 examine the role of women in the life and teaching of the apostolic church. Modern debate on the role of women in the Christian life has centred on these materials, and in particular on the teaching of Paul. The debated passages are considered in detail in chapters which examine basic apostolic attitudes to women and to marriage, relations between marriage partners, the role of women in worship, and the role of women in church offices. A concluding chapter summarizes the observations and conclusions of the book and offers specific guidelines for the application of its findings to concrete situations. A few examples are given to show how the guidelines may be applied.

Most people do not have opportunity to consult original sources on Assyrian, Babylonian or Judaic times. I have made an effort to provide substantial amounts of texts from such sources, in the hope that each reader will thus be able to interact directly with the period under discussion and to form personal conclusions based upon first-hand observation. Biblical passages are quoted at length for similar reasons. Quotations are taken from the New International Version (NIV), with occasional changes to make the meaning of the Greek or Hebrew more clear.

A final word is in order concerning the way in which the text of this book is set out. This book is intended to present a careful examination of the relevant biblical texts within the context of their day and to discuss their relevance to the present. I have written for the proverbial interested layperson, concerned pastor and theological student rather than for the scholarly community in the strictest sense of the word. I have accordingly tried to make a positive statement concerning the biblical text as I understand it. I have tried to avoid identifying views which I discuss with specific authors who hold them because I have not devoted much space to detailed interaction with the writings of others. It would be unfair to criticize them without more fully developing their thought. The bibliography at the back of this book is intended to provide interested readers with material for further study.

1
Women in Old Testament times

When we try to imagine life in an earlier age, we are likely to project our own customs backwards in time (Surely people always did it the way we do it. What other way is there?) or to create a fantasy from the bits of information which we have (Didn't all cowboys carry revolvers and shoot like Roy Rogers?). But societies differ in the way they do things. They also differ in the roles which they assign to men and women. A look at the roles of women in some of the cultures which surrounded ancient Israel will help us to understand the role of women in the Old Testament and to overcome the vast differences between our twentieth-century Western society and that of the ancient Near East.

In this chapter we shall look briefly at the role of women in Assyria and Babylon before taking a more detailed look at the role of women in Israel. Our survey will not be exhaustive. It is intended to provide twentieth-century readers with useful information from which to develop an accurate picture of the past. Most people are unfamiliar with the ideas of the Old Testament period and with the ways in which those ideas were expressed. Our discussion therefore includes a substantial number of quotations from original sources which should provide insight into the thought patterns and ideas of the period.

I shall look at the role of women in Old Testament times through the eyes of law codes from that period. The Law Code of Hammu-rabi (1792–1750 BC) describes the role of Babylonian women at about the time of Abraham's departure from Ur. A similar Middle Assyrian Law Code (1450–1250 BC) describes the role of Assyrian women at the time of Moses and the exodus. Our look at women and men in Israel will be guided by the legal and narrative portions of the Old Testament.

A. NUCLEAR FAMILY VERSUS TRIBE

Before considering the actual content of the Babylonian and Assyrian laws, it is worth commenting on the role of the family as
opposed to the individual in ancient Near Eastern society.
Twentieth-century Western culture focuses attention upon the
so-called 'nuclear family' consisting of father, mother and children,
with other blood relationships seen as only a backdrop. In the
ancient Near East the situation was very different. 'Nuclear' units
were closely tied in with other family units to form a clan or tribe.
Persons were seen as members of such groupings rather than as
individuals related to them. It is within this framework that the
blood-feud, for instance, is to be understood. If a member of one
clan kills a male member of another, vengeance will be sought
through another murder. The person killed in retaliation, however, need not be the offender; any male member of his clan will
do. The murder is seen as an attack by one clan upon another. It
is an attack upon a clan's resources as well as an attack upon an
individual.

The senior male of the clan functioned in many cases as head
of the whole and could be called upon to render judgment in cases
involving even distant relations. His function as judge and head
had direct consequences for relations with other clans. The patriarch functioned as spokesman and representative, often making
decisions for the whole group. Correspondingly, his decisions had
to take others into view. In situations which were more urban and
less tribal, the patriarchal functions might be more limited; a father
might, for instance, speak only for his wife or wives, concubines,
slaves, sons and their families and unmarried daughters.

Business arrangements and marriages usually involved substantial amounts of the family wealth and the interests of the clan had
to be considered. Fathers negotiated marriages for both male and
female children, who were frequently still infants or children at
the time. Even when the parties were adults the arrangements
frequently involved the father and even the brothers, all of whom
were seen as interested parties.

Financial involvements in marriages became a significant issue
at the death of a husband or at the dissolution of a marriage.
Bridal gifts and dowries represented substantial portions of a clan's
assets. The personal assets of the widow and her potential as
worker could be lost to the clan if she remarried and entered

another clan by remarriage. Ancient law codes reflect a serious concern for just conservation and distribution of such resources.

The importance of the clan and its dual role as a family and a legal unit have implications for the significance of offences within the family. If a son were to reject the authority of his father, his decision would violate not only family customs but also civil obligations. Respect for parents was thus more than a matter of private morality. The position of the father, husband or patriarch as legal spokesman for his tribe naturally affected the marriage relation as well. The husband's authority over his wife and family was a matter of civil law.

In the law codes women and children are considered largely in terms of jurisdiction, 'ownership' and financial obligation. Civil codes necessarily treat relationships in a way which seems formal and cold. Actual relationships between spouses and between parents and children were no doubt warmer and more affectionate.

Our study of the legal and narrative parts of the Old Testament will illustrate this point.

B. BABYLONIAN CULTURE: *c.* 1775 BC

Abraham left Ur in about 1800 BC. Hammurabi was, at about that time, king of Babylon. One of his concerns was the orderly setting out of a legal structure for his kingdom. One of the treasures of the students of the ancient Near East is the Code of Hammurabi,[1] a copy of which has been discovered at Susa. A look at some of its laws relating to women reveals much about the status of women in Babylonian culture.

1. Marriage and divorce

Among the Babylonians marriage was contracted by a man or, especially if he were a minor, by his father with the father of the prospective bride, who was generally still a child. It involved a dowry and gifts of various sorts and might also involve a contract. The contract was of considerable importance as its terms affected the rights of the wife if her husband were to die. A widow was supported by her sons and enjoyed either a financial settlement from the estate or the financial returns from a share of it until the

[1] The best English treatment and translation of the Code is to be found in G. R. Driver and J. C. Miles, *The Babylonian Laws* (hereafter *Babylonian Laws*) (Oxford, 1952).

time of her death or remarriage. At the time of her death, the children of the family inherited the father's estate, unmarried daughters evidently inheriting as well as sons. A widow was fully able to select a new partner, but if that entailed leaving the clan she could not take material resources except her dowry with her.[2] The same privilege of choosing a new partner was accorded women after certain divorce cases.

The liberty to terminate a marriage at will was the prerogative of the husband alone. He was required to 'give [his wife] money to the value of her bridal gift and . . . make good to her the dowry'. In the absence of a bridal gift, a set payment of 'divorce-money' was given her.[3] A woman could not divorce her husband without bringing suit in a court of law. In such cases she refused him intercourse and had to demonstrate that she had 'kept herself chaste and has no fault, and (that) her husband is given to going about out (of doors in a dissipated fashion and with other women), and so has greatly belittled her'. If successful, she might take her dowry and return to her father's house. There was no penalty for him. If, however, the investigation proved that she had been going out and had been wasting the household money, thereby belittling him (by making him an object of scorn), she was executed by drowning.[4] It would seem that his behaviour was an affront to her dignity while false accusation, wasting of resources, or immodest behaviour on her part constituted a capital offence. In cases where he initiated charges that she was going out and wasting the household money, her conviction permitted him either to divorce her without divorce-money or to reduce her to the status of slave-girl.[5]

Cases of infidelity within marriage centred, as was common in the day, upon the wife. Illegal sexual relations with a married woman was a capital offence. Willing adultery resulted in the drowning of both partners, unless the husband chose to spare the wife, in which case the king spared the man involved, thereby maintaining a parity of punishment.[6] Rape of a married woman resulted in the execution of the rapist.

This brief survey shows that Babylonian women were legally subordinate to their fathers and to their husbands. They were

[2] For an extended discussion of the segments of the Code pertinent to marriage, cf. *Babylonian Laws*, 2, pp. 245–275, 334–341.

[3] 138–140; *Babylonian Laws*, 1, p. 55.

[4] 142–143; *Babylonian Laws*, 1, p. 57.

[5] 141; *Babylonian Laws*, 1, pp. 55, 57.

[6] 129–130; *Babylonian Laws*, 1, pp. 51, 53.

clearly, however, not simply chattels. They enjoyed rights of inheritance alongside sons and brothers. Upon the death of a husband or after certain sorts of divorce a woman was entitled to marry any man 'after her heart'. As we have seen, women were not on a par with their husbands in the area of divorce. Whereas husbands needed no reason to divorce their wives, wives had to demonstrate wanton behaviour on the part of their husbands which had resulted in their own public disgrace.

2. Women in social life

There are many questions which a twentieth-century reader would like to ask of Hammurabi's legal scribe. In his laws we are given almost no information about the structure of households and little about women's role in society. There does seem to have been some sheltering of women and the laws do presume that most women who inherit will ask either a brother or an appointed manager to handle their estate, indicating perhaps that women were not prepared to handle such things. Conversely, however, the widow was entitled to manage her estate alone, implying her right to engage in commerce.

Further light is shed on the matter by tablets of the period. An extensive series of tablets representing the correspondence of Iltani, the wife of King Aqba-hammu, who was a contemporary of Hammurabi, reveals that women were sometimes deeply involved in the life of society.[7] Iltani was in correspondence with a variety of persons ranging from servants to her brothers and sisters. Her documents show that she was personally involved in all manner of trade and commerce, dealing in servants, goods, money and the like. The letters not only make extensive reference to slave-girls being sent to various places, but also indicate women involved in wool-working, textile manufacture and laundering. The women mentioned are servants or subjects and thus it is impossible to generalize to the population at large, but it would seem that the cloistering of women (keeping them indoors in a harem) was not necessarily a universal practice. Indeed, it would have been financially impossible for most persons of that time to cloister their women. We may assume that, while careful measures were taken to guard the women from attack and from shame, they were

[7] The correspondence is presented in S. Dalley, C. B. Walker and J. D. Hawkins, *The Old Babylonian Tablets from Tell al Rimah* (British School of Archaeology in Iraq, 1976). Of particular value with respect to women are tablets 22, 81, 96, 106, 120, 134 and 293.

necessarily involved in various social and commercial activities which would take them outside the home. This would be especially true in rural areas.

3. Women in religious life: priestesses

If we turn to the religious sphere we are given a bit more light. The Code of Hammurabi devotes no space to regulations for priests but does contain a lengthy set regulating various sorts of priestesses. Political resistance evidently prevented his regulating the priests as he did the priestesses.[8] The laws make it clear that there was a complex hierarchy of priestesses and devoted women but reveal nothing of priestly life. The priestesses ranged from royalty to the daughters of poor free men. Records from the period show their fathers dedicating them and sometimes providing for their well-being. Iltani, wife of Aqba-hammu, had a sister who was a priestess at Babylon in just such a state. It further appears that some priestesses managed to acquire and to administer a substantial amount of personal wealth and that that property was at their personal disposal.

The text of the laws does not give a clear picture of the social roles of the various classes of priestesses, although it makes clear that at least some of them, the highest classes, were cloistered. The implication seems to be that among Babylonian priestesses, as among Near Eastern cultures generally, women of the richer classes were sometimes cloistered. There is no indication in Hammurabi's code as to which, if any, of the classes of priestesses were cultic prostitutes nor is there indication of the relation between priests and priestesses. It is generally assumed that Babylonian worship paralleled similar worship in other places and did include cultic prostitutes, women through whose body a male worshipper might commune with the deity.

The Code of Hammurabi thus reveals a culture in which women enjoyed inferior legal rights. There is no indication that they were considered inferior beings as such. It appears that widows and priestesses enjoyed a greater degree of liberty and legal privilege than most other women, having no husband over them. The Assyrian laws, to which we now turn, will provide more detail in certain areas and reveal the harsher Assyrian view of societal relations in general.

[8] *Babylonian Laws*, 2, p. 359.

C. ASSYRIAN CULTURE: 1450–1250 BC

Excavations at Assur between 1903 and 1914 brought to light nine tablets containing Assyrian laws which have subsequently been assigned to a date somewhere between 1450 and 1250 BC, approximately to that of Israel's exodus from Egypt. They therefore provide a useful Semitic comparison to the Mosaic legislation.[9] The Assyrian laws are markedly more harsh than either those of Babylon or the Old Testament.

1. Marriage and divorce

Assyrian marriage, as Babylonian, was typically contracted by a man or his father with the father of the intended bride. Neither the (typically) youthful bride nor the under-aged husband necessarily had any say in the arrangements. As in Babylon a series of gifts and a dowry were exchanged and a contract was often drawn up. The contract was of vital importance to the woman. The Assyrian divorce law reads as follows: 'If a man divorces his wife, if (it is) his will he shall give her something; if (it is) not his will, he shall not give her anything; she shall go forth empty.'[10] Unless a woman had a marriage contract specifying benefits in case of divorce, she could be sent away with only her dowry and private property, without any divorce money. There was no provision by which a woman might divorce her husband. The Assyrian code is also harder on the woman if she is widowed. While an Assyrian wife who is left without provision must be supported by the sons, she may not inherit a portion of the estate, nor may a daughter inherit a portion of her father's estate. The rights of a widow to remarriage are parallel to those accorded by the Babylonian documents.

An interesting insight into the essential view of marriage in both Babylon and Assyria may be gained by considering the situation of a wife whose husband is away. In cases of proven desertion, a tablet certifying her status was issued. In other cases, such as

---

[9] The date of the exodus has received much attention in critical scholarship. Virtually all scholars, however, will accept the 200-year time-span of the dating of the Assyrian laws as roughly corresponding to that of the exodus. Conservative evangelical scholars and critical liberal scholars have more substantive conflicts concerning the date of the material contained in the Mosaic Pentateuch. I assume the earlier conservative dating of it at the time of Moses as correct. Those who do not do so will necessarily perceive the Assyrian laws as a less direct parallel with respect to time.

[10] 37, as rendered in G. R. Driver and J. C. Miles, *The Assyrian Laws* (hereafter *Assyrian Laws*) (Oxford, 1935), p. 405.

disappearance without adequate provision for her security, the wife had to wait a specified period of time before remarrying. If it turned out that husband had been prevented from returning by reasons beyond his control, he could reclaim his wife from her new husband by filing a claim and providing an appropriate substitute for her.[11] Sons from the second marriage were considered property of their father and remained with him upon the departure of their mother. Clearly the Babylonian law places the legal interests and preferences of the husband and father before those of his wife and children.

The tendency to view women and others from the perspective of the clan and of the adult male owner/father/husband is perhaps even more clear in the criminal segments of the code. Adultery is treated as an offence against a husband's property and can be committed only by or with a married woman. A man accused of adultery could clear himself by swearing that he did not know that the woman was married. In a society which officially recognized prostitutes, the sexual act itself was not legally significant. Thus sexual relations with unmarried women, even by married men, were not construed as adultery. Adultery was viewed as the violation of a husband's rights. The woman in such cases was punishable by her husband 'as he will'. Punishments could range from verbal rebuke to disfigurement to dismemberment to execution.[12] In judicial cases in which the parties were found guilty a range of penalties is offered the husband, with the proviso that his wife and the adulterer must be similarly treated:

if the woman's husband puts his wife to death, then he shall put the man to death; (but) if he has cut off his wife's nose, he shall make the man a eunuch and the whole of his face shall be mutilated. Or if he has allowed his wife to go free, the man shall be allowed to go free.[13]

It is always the husband who is the offended party. This legal contemplation of the male right and property offence becomes yet more clear in cases dealing with the 'ravishing' of an unmarried girl. The law states that in such cases,

---

[11] Driver and Miles provide a lengthy discussion of divorce and support of deserted wives in conjunction with their discussion of 37, 38 and 36, 45 in *Assyrian Laws*, pp. 250–270.

[12] 14; *Assyrian Laws*, p. 389.

[13] 15; *Assyrian Laws*, p. 389.

28

the father of the virgin shall take the wife of the ravisher of the
virgin (and) give her to be dishonoured. . . . The father shall
give his daughter . . . as a spouse to her ravisher. . . . If the
father does not please (to do so) he shall receive 'the third' for
the virgin (in) silver (and) give his daughter to whom he
pleases.[14]

The 'ravishing' of the virgin damages the clan's financial resources because the girl will no longer receive a bridal gift upon
marriage. The clan has also been insulted by the wrong use of one
of its women. In a clear application of the *lex talionis* (equivalent
punishment) the guilty man is required to pay the bridal gift and,
if the father so desires, to take the girl, who might otherwise not
be taken by anyone as a bride. The wrong use of the virgin is
compensated for by the prostitution of the offender's wife by a
member of the offended clan. This legal prescription deals with
the offending and offended parties – the men or clans involved.
Both the daughter ravished and the wife prostituted are passive
with respect to the law. It is worth noting that once again it is not
the sex act itself but rather its context which defines its legal status.
Thus, the prostituting of the offender's wife is morally approvable.
Within Assyrian and Babylonian culture, as distinct from Israelite
culture, sex was not regulated by religious belief but was rather
regulated by civil law as a matter of property or guardianship
rights.

2. Women in social and religious life
The Assyrian laws include a discussion of veiling customs for
distinguishing prostitutes and slave-girls from married women,
concubines, and single women of high birth. The code stipulates
that

women, whether married or [widows] or [Assyrians] who go
out in the [public] street must not have their heads
uncovered. . . . A harlot shall not be veiled; her head must be
uncovered. He who sees a veiled harlot shall arrest her. . . .
Slave-girls shall not be veiled, and he who sees a veiled slave-
girl shall arrest her. . . .[15]

[14] 55; *Assyrian Laws*, p. 423.
[15] 40; *Assyrian Laws*, pp. 407, 409.

Veils were a sign of rank and dignity. A married woman or woman of rank suffered no civil penalty for being unveiled. A harlot, if convicted, lost her clothes to the man who arrested her, was beaten fifty stripes with rods, and had pitch poured over her head, the latter perhaps representing a grisly mockery of her pretensions to another class. A veiled slave-girl suffered the loss of her clothes and also of her ears. The veil was not omitted by harlots as a means to greater seductiveness, although it may have had that effect. It was rather forbidden to them because it marked its wearer as a person of rank. We do not know what sort of veil was worn in Assyria.

It is not known to what extent Assyrian women actually did enter into the social life of the day. Babylonian law suggests that they had a role in that it recognizes serious charges which might be brought against an ale-wife who failed to report criminals or who diluted her wines. There are other indications of Babylonian women participating in daily activities outside the home. Assyrian women seem to have been somewhat more restricted. The demands of daily life and the financial costs of supporting a person who cannot leave the house are likely to have prevented all but the wealthy from completely secluding their women. The craftsman and the farmer probably included the women of his household in the work-force.

The Assyrian laws do not include a discussion of women in religious life. We are therefore very much in the dark about their role in this area. The laws do include a section indicating that a woman who utters blasphemy is responsible for her own sin.[16] There seem also to be indications of a period of sacred prostitution for women prior to marriage, such as was reported of Babylon by Herodotus and Strabo.[17] It is generally assumed that Assyrian women played roles similar to those of Babylonian women, bringing offerings to the temples of the various deities of the pantheon, serving as priestesses, and sometimes becoming sacred prostitutes.

If we compare the general status of women in Assyrian and Babylonian culture, we find the two to be similar. The Assyrian laws continue the leadership of the family by the patriarch and reveal the role of women as property as well as companions and

---

[16] 2; *Assyrian Laws*, p. 381.
[17] *Assyrian Laws*, p. 18; Herodotus, *Histories*, i.199; Strabo, *Geography*, xvi.1.20.

clan members. The Assyrian laws are visibly harsher than the Babylonian and grant to the husband wider powers of retribution and punishment. As we turn from these cultures to the Old Testament a significant difference will appear. Old Testament law is theologically based. This in turn affects the understanding of personal relations and circumscribes individual rights.

2
Women in Israelite culture

A. MANKIND

As we begin our examination of the Old Testament, it is important
to consider the basic framework within which it understands human life as well as its approach to the relationship of men and
women. The opening chapters of Genesis provide us with fun-
damental information about this subject. I shall deal with them
only briefly in this chapter. We will look at them in greater detail
in chapter 8 when we look at Paul's use of them in his teaching.

1. Humanity and its task in Genesis 1 and 2
The world is God's and all that is in it belongs to him. Genesis 1
stresses God's shaping of his creation and his creation of mankind
for a particular role in it. When the rest of the creation is complete,
God declares, 'Let us make man in our image, in our likeness, and
let them rule . . . over all the earth, and over all the creatures . . .'
(Gn. 1:26). Mankind, male and female together, is created to be
the image of God and to rule the earth under him.

The next chapter adds additional information to this general
description of mankind's relation to the earth. Genesis 2 describes
God's formation of a garden, in which he will meet with Adam
and which Adam is to tend and defend (Gn. 2:15; *cf.* 3:24). The
whole earth is given to mankind to rule over (Gn. 1:26–30); the
garden is the place of fellowship, the place where mankind will
meet with God, the sanctuary (Gn. 3:8).

Genesis 2 has another contribution to make to our knowledge
of mankind and of creation. The man who was made to rule
creation and to have fellowship with God in the garden was not
made to live and work without human companionship. We are

told that it was 'not good for the man to be alone' (2:18). We have already learned from Genesis 1 that both men and women image God and rule the creation under him. Here in Genesis 2 we are given further specifics about the formation of the woman. To end the loneliness of the man and to join him in ruling the earth to the glory of God, God shaped a woman from the flesh of Adam. God's calling to the race came to the two of them, 'Increase in number; fill the earth and subdue it' (1:28). The loving companionship of the two would issue, in due course, in the birth of children and mankind would become a community serving God through their love and service of him and of one another.

Human dignity stems from the fact that mankind is God's image. The meaning and dignity of daily life also grow from this root. Even in the fallen world this continues to be the case. As a man ploughs a field, plays with his children, builds a house, or works in his office, he contributes to the task given to the race, to the mastering of the earth. If, as he does these things, he destroys the earth or hurts his neighbours, he does not faithfully reflect God's concern and respect for the creation. His life thus distorts the image of God. As women share in the work of ruling the earth in a godly manner, either alongside the men or in the home, they are involved in the fulfilment of the calling of the race. Their labour, like the man's, will either glorify God by faithfully mirroring his relationship to creation and to people, or it will be a distortion of the truth and destructive both to the earth and to the race.

A basic Old Testament view of men and women, therefore, understands both to be the image of God and to be called to show forth that image in their daily lives.

2. The calling of Israel

The nation of Israel was called to be a demonstration of the saving work of God. In their daily life, in their relations to one another, and in their relations to the nations around, Israel was to show the fruits of godliness and the power of God. Within this frame each Israelite had a place. The laws of the nation guided the people in their relations. Each person, living out his or her daily life, made a contribution to the statement of the nation concerning faith in God. The detailed concern of the whole of the Old Testament for the treatment of one Israelite by another reflects this. Within the nation a special concern was to be shown to the weak and powerless by those in positions of strength and power. The stranger, the orphan, the widow were singled out for special care. Passage after passage reminds Israel that she has known weakness and suffering and God's deliverance from them. She is called to show a similar mercy, to image God, in her relations to such people. The sad testimony of the prophets is to Israel's failure to reflect the love, justice and mercy of her Lord.

In this chapter we shall study the relation of the sexes in Israel's law and life. The Old Testament offers us a variety of sources of information about the relation of the sexes. Whereas we know Assyria and Babylon primarily through their respective law codes and somewhat through personal letters, the Old Testament offers us narrative portions, poetry, prophetic literature and proverbs to add to the knowledge which we gain from the legal codes.

A further issue must be taken into account as we look at the Old Testament. The historical periods under discussion cover a period of more than a millennium and their cultural settings range from nomadic life with Abraham to the wealthy urban monarchy of Solomon and even to the dire poverty of the city of Jerusalem at the return of the exiled Jews from Babylon. Care must be taken in comparing different portions of the text. In addition to these areas of diversity we should be aware that the actual practice of the nation fell short of the prescriptions of the law. The prophets and the poor consistently complain of the failures of those in positions of strength and, as we shall see, the law incorporated numerous provisions to safeguard those who might be abused.

What then were the roles of men and women as they imaged God within the nation of Israel?

B. FAMILY STRUCTURES AND MARRIAGE LAWS

1. Her father's house

The Israelite family pattern was patriarchal and centred around the tribe or clan. The nation itself was related by blood ties as its members were all 'children of Abraham'. The tribes traced their relationships back through their patriarchal fathers and within the tribes individuals identified themselves by their 'father's house', which expression can be functionally equivalent to 'family'. Thus, in 1 Samuel 9:20–21, Samuel says the desirable things of Israel are available to Saul and to his father's house, and Saul responds by noting that his tribe is the smallest of Israel and his family the least of all the families of Benjamin. 'Family', for Saul, meant his 'father's house' rather than simply his wife and children. The essential flexibility of the idea of 'family' can be seen from the fact that the entire nation may be a family, as in Amos 3:2 ('You only have I intimately known of all the families of the earth'), or the term can be as narrow as the house of Noah, which included but his wife, his sons and their wives (Gn. 7:1, 13).

The 'family' concept had other dimensions of flexibility. Patriarchal authority is reflected in the equivalence of 'family' with 'father's house'. The authority implicit in the term 'father' was very great. Within the family the husband and father was the undisputed head. So much was this the case that a 'husband' was the *ba'al* (ruler or one having dominion) of his wife; similarly, to *ba'al* (become ruler over) a woman is to marry her (Dt. 21:13; 24:1; Is. 54:5; Mal. 2:11; *cf.* Is. 26:13). The relation of son and father also involved authority and leadership; thus Naaman's slaves call him 'father' (2 Ki. 5:13) and the disciple of a prophet is his 'son' (2 Ki. 2:12).

Men and women alike grew up in a nation which thought of itself as an extended family, with profound commitments to the 'father's house', which terminology might point to immediate family, the clan or tribe, or even to the nation as a whole. The laws of Israel both presume and inculcate such commitment and corporate identity. The consistent identification of individuals by ancestry and by family units reflects the depth to which such thinking had penetrated. A person did not think of him or herself as an individual, but as so-and-so, of the tribe of so-and-so. Existence was corporate existence.

2. Arranged marriage

Given such a framework, it should not be surprising to find that within Israel the father was generally the one who arranged marriages for both sons and daughters. It is therefore Abraham rather than Isaac who sends for the latter's bride (Gn. 24) and to Abraham rather than to Isaac that Bethuel shows kindness by consenting to send his daughter (Gn. 24:49). It is, correspondingly, the father's decision whether his daughter will be given to a particular man (Ex. 22:17). The father's exercise of his prerogatives, however, was not done without consultation. Both Bethuel and Laban, his son, give consent to the marriage of Rebekah (Gn. 24:50–51) and Rebekah's mother and brother are apparently not out of line in suggesting that she should be consulted about when to leave with Abraham's servant (Gn. 24:55–58). In a similar vein, Samson asked his mother and father to get him his bride and the two of them objected to his choice of a Philistine girl (Jdg. 14:1–4).

3. Failure of male headship

It is impossible, in the light of the textual evidence, to avoid the conclusion that Israelite family life preserved the leadership and authority of the husband at virtually every turn. It should also be noted that that authority was subject to serious misuse, as, for instance, when Abraham lied about his relation to Sarah out of fear for his own life (Gn. 20).

Judah (Gn. 38) provides another example of moral failure by a patriarch. When his oldest son, Er, died childless, Judah commanded his next son, Onan, to marry the widow, Tamar. Custom provided that the first son of the new (levirate) marriage would be considered a son of the dead Er and 'continue his father's name', inheriting the double portion of the first-born son. In the absence of an heir to Er, Onan as the oldest surviving son would have inherited the double portion. It is therefore not hard to imagine the selfish motive which led Onan to practise *coitus interruptus* with Tamar and to 'spill his seed on the ground'. For his refusal to sire children by Tamar, Onan died by the hand of God.

With the death of Onan, the levirate obligation fell upon Shelah, Judah's next son, who was as yet too young to marry. Judah feared giving Shelah to the woman who had outlived his two sons. He accordingly left her as a widow in her father's house, even after Shelah had grown up. Tamar evidently grasped what was happening and took advantage of an opportunity presented by the death of Judah's wife. Guessing his lustful desire for a woman, she dressed herself as a harlot and, completely veiled, presented herself to him while he was travelling. He chose to have intercourse with her and she became pregnant. Thus she, by trickery, made him fulfil the levirate obligation which he had neglected when he did not give her the third son, Shelah.

When Judah heard of Tamar's pregnancy he assumed her guilty of adultery and announced the usual death sentence as her penalty, only to be forced to retract it when she vindicated herself by proving the child's paternity. The patriarch's lust was turned by his resourceful daughter-in-law into a device to force him to do his duty. Pedersen has pointed out that Tamar has been honoured by Jewish women as a persistent and devoted wife who 'raised up seed' to her husband rather than dishonoured as a slut.[1] We cannot help but see Judah as a failure who stands condemned for his refusal to exercise his patriarchal leadership in a right way. Tamar, on the other hand, is seen as a clever wife who risked death to achieve her goal. Judah, the patriarch, showed himself selfish and sinful. His failure did not destroy his role or his responsibility to be patriarch, but does show how perversely power can be abused.

4. Concern for the oppressed

The laws and practices of Israel show a deep awareness of the dangers of the abuse of power. As a nation she had known oppression and suffering in Egypt. The exodus was the act of the God of Abraham, Isaac and Jacob, who announced to Moses, 'I have indeed seen the misery of my people in Egypt. I have heard them crying out because of their slave drivers, and I am concerned about their suffering. So I have come down to rescue them. . .' (Ex. 3:7–8). The memory of this deliverance was kept alive in the daily prayers, weekly sabbaths, annual feasts and jubilee cycles of the nation. The laws of Israel called upon her to be in her life the image of her God and to be holy because he was holy (Lv. 19:2). In practical terms, this meant, 'When an alien lives with you in your land, do not ill-treat him . . . Love him as yourself, for you were aliens in Egypt . . . I am the LORD your God, who brought you out of Egypt' (Lv. 19:33–36).

It was not only the alien who needed protection. The hungry were given the grain at the margins of the field and the grain which fell upon the ground (Lv. 19:9–10). These 'gleanings' provided them with food. The widow and the orphan were to be objects of particular concern, since they were particularly vulnerable to abuse (*e.g.* Ex. 22:22–24). Women taken captive in war were likewise provided for (Dt. 21:10–14). Proverbs speaks of the blessings of riches, and also of the judgment of God upon those rich who do not remember the poor among their brethren (Pr. 22:22–23).

In virtually every case in which strength or power is granted, corresponding warnings about its abuse are also given. A major note in the prophetic condemnation of the faithlessness of Israel

[1] J. Pedersen, *Israel, Its Life and Culture* (Oxford, 1949), p. 79.

has to do with her failure to show mercy and concern to those in need or open to abuse.

The position of the husband and father was a position of responsibility and authority which was open to much abuse. Israel's laws provide for the happiness of the wife and for the protection of wives and children from selfish abuse by husbands and fathers. The relative independence of the Assyrian or Babylonian man with respect to his family was not paralleled in Israel.

5. Inheritance

The legal code of the Old Testament does not treat the rights of married, divorced and widowed women in the same detail as the Assyrian and Babylonian codes. This may to some extent reflect the simpler, less urban setting in which the law was established. It certainly created the necessity of specialists and judges to interpolate in order to deal with cases not laid down by precept.

The inheritance laws of Israel are similar to those of the nations already considered in that they pass property through the male line. Much attention is given to the maintaining of the 'name' of a man through his heirs (*e.g.* the levirate laws). The daughters of a house were married outside it and 'built up the house' of their new husbands. Accordingly they did not normally inherit the property of their fathers; instead they received their portion as dowries and gifts. Job presents something of an exception in that his daughters were given an inheritance (Jb. 42:15). It would seem that a man might make an unusual disposition of his property if he so chose.

The case of the daughters of Zelophehad (Nu. 27:1–11) provides information about a modification of the usual rule of male inheritance. They complained that they were the sole heirs of their father and that his name should not be done away. Moses ruled that, in the absence of sons, the daughters should next inherit, followed by the man's brothers and then others as usual (27:8–11). This ruling has particular value in that it shows that the women were not by-passed in inheritance because they were considered stupid or incompetent. Male heirs usually carried on the family property and name. In their absence, however, the property went to the daughters, who were to marry a person of their choice from within their own tribe to prevent the inheritance being lost to the tribe (Nu. 36:1–9).

The Mosaic law does not make provision for the independent

inheritance of widows. The care of the widow goes instead to the inheritor of the estate. Thus, in the book of Ruth, the widow Naomi became the responsibility of her sons upon the death of her husband. Upon the death of the sons, both Ruth and Naomi were without anyone to support them and in a country away from their patriarchal inheritance. Upon their return, there was as yet none who had taken up the inheritance of the dead Elimelech and his sons. Naomi, the widow of Elimelech, was in charge of the property and offered it to Boaz as a kinsman with a right to inherit and with a levirate obligation to raise up seed to the family of the dead men. Boaz provided for Naomi in his payment for the land and for Ruth by marrying her (Ru. 4:1–12).

In a case in which a man left young heirs or very little property which no heir would assume, the widow was responsible to raise the heir or, in the latter case, simply left with what she had (as was Naomi's case). The repeated Old Testament injunctions to remember and not to abuse the widow and the orphan bear eloquent, if condemnatory, evidence to the number who emulated Judah (Gn. 38:14) and the kinsman to whom Boaz spoke (Ru. 4:1–6) by refusing to provide for their kinsman in need.

6. Divorce and sexual offence

The Old Testament says little about criteria for divorce. Deuteronomy 24, a passage discussing remarriage, mentions divorce incidentally. It presumes that a man may divorce his wife if he finds 'something indecent' ('*rwt dbr*) in her (24:1). The precise meaning of 'something indecent' has been the subject of much debate. Possible meanings range from a moral offence to anything which displeases her husband. We shall discuss this passage further in connection with Jesus' debate with the Pharisees as recorded in Matthew 19:3–12.[2] Apart from these ambiguous words, the Old Testament does not speak about grounds for divorce. Nowhere does it mention women divorcing their husbands.

Deuteronomy 22:13–29 notes two instances in which a man may never divorce his wife: if he falsely accuses her of unchastity before marriage, and if he has seduced her. A parallel discussion of seduction, found in Exodus 22:16–17, provides insight into a central difference between the Old Testament view of sexuality and those of the Assyrians and the Babylonians.

[2] Chapter 4, pp. 95 ff.

Exodus 22:16–17 reads:

> If a man seduces a virgin who is not pledged to be married and sleeps with her, he must pay the bride-price, and she shall be his wife. If her father absolutely refuses to give her to him, he must still pay the bride-price for virgins.

In this text, as in the corresponding section of the Assyrian laws, the seducer must compensate the father for the loss of the 'payment for a virgin', which can no longer be expected in the light of the girl's loss of virginity, and must follow through by marrying her. The father's option to refuse her to him is also parallel. The Assyrian law includes a provision by which the seducer's wife is taken and prostituted in retaliation for the abuse of a virgin. As we noted above in the discussion of that law, it is the violation of a family/clan member and the damage to property which the Assyrian law deals with through the retributory violation of the wife and the payment for the virgin. In Israelite culture the sexual relation itself was sacred and restricted to certain contexts. Retribution by the sexual violation of the man's wife would be an affront to God and adultery. It could not be sanctioned by the law.

The sanctity of sexual relationships is further seen in the attitude of the biblical law to prostitution. Both the Babylonian and the Assyrian codes made specific provision for the regulation of prostitutes. They had no objection to sexual relations with such women, seeing them as in no way threatening the families of the land. Biblical law has often been seen as cast from the same mould. The case is argued as follows: in the Old Testament, technically speaking, adultery can be committed only by or with married women. An unfaithful husband who goes to a prostitute does not come within the purview of the criminal law. From this it is deduced that men might use women as they pleased so long as they did not violate marital or paternal rights.

Under closer examination, however, biblical evidence does not support the deduction. The law makes it clear that a married woman may sleep with none but her husband (Dt. 22:22). The same restriction applied to a betrothed woman whose marriage had not yet been consummated (Dt. 22:23–24). It was a capital offence to have sexual intercourse with an engaged or married woman. Further, it was a criminal offence to have sexual intercourse with an unengaged girl (Ex. 22:16–17) and fathers were forbidden to prostitute their daughters (Lv. 19:29; 21:9).[3] Further still, in contradiction to the practices of other nations which seem to have institutionalized sacred prostitution, Israelite law flatly prohibits it as an abomination (Dt. 23:17–18). It would seem that there were no Israelite women legally accessible to the would-be user of a prostitute.

It is sometimes suggested that women from other nations might be used with impunity. Investigation shows that there are in fact no laws which prohibit harlotry with foreign women. It should, however, be noted that laws dealing with foreigners would not be the way in which matter of this sort would have been handled. The Mosaic law enacted regulations applicable within Israel. It systematically eliminated all Israelite women from roles as prostitutes. Foreigners within Israel were not subject to a special set of laws, but were treated as the home-born (Ex. 12:49) and thus came under the protection and the jurisdiction of the civil aspects of the Israelite law. Deuteronomy 31:10–12 directs that the Levites read the law every seventh year to the assembled men, women, children, *and to the aliens* living within the towns. Foreign women within Israel were thus not to be made prostitutes; this too would fill the land with harlotry and bring the judgment of God. Thus the law closed off the legitimacy of either native or foreign women as prostitutes. Sadly, Israel's history testifies that both native and foreign women did in fact work as prostitutes within Israel. We conclude, then, that while the law does not speak directly to the promiscuous man, neither does it leave him any legitimate partners.

A further word is in order concerning the definition of adultery and the punishment of women offenders. We noted in our previous discussion that other cultures considered adultery as a clan or property offence. As will be discussed below, the Old Testament saw it as more than simply a violation of property rights. It must be noted, however, that the passages of the civil code which discuss the matter are thinking in terms of crime against the rights of a father or husband, punishment, damages and responsibility rather than other more purely moral dimensions. It is in terms of

---

[3] It is sometimes suggested that the forbidden prostitution here is cultic in nature, *i.e.* a father may not dedicate his daughter to be a sacred prostitute in the service of the Lord. While this was no doubt especially relevant for the priests of Lv. 21:9, it hardly seems likely that this law is narrow enough to permit a father to make his daughter a secular prostitute.

the former that adultery is defined and the death penalty is assigned to guilty partners of either sex. We must look in places other than passages dealing with adultery to understand the Israelite attitude toward harlotry or prostitution.

The Mosaic law speaks consistently and repeatedly against harlotry, closely associating it with wrong worship. This is done from two perspectives. Firstly, Canaanite and other Semitic peoples included in their worship sacred feasts which were held in the presence of their idol and coupled with sexual communion with the deity through intercourse with sacred prostitutes or with persons who devoted themselves to the deity. The God of Israel was never sacredly present in an idol and never communed with through sacred intercourse. He forbade such worship within Israel (Dt. 23:17–18) and forbade his people to enter into the worship of other gods (Ex. 20:3–6). It is in the light of such Semitic practices that we understand the 'harlotry' of Israel with the Moabites in Numbers 25:1–15, where we are told that the men of Israel gave themselves to immorality with the daughters of Moab, who invited them to the sacrifices of their gods, where the people ate and bowed down before their gods.

A second perspective from which harlotry and wrong worship are to be understood has to do with the role of the Lord as the husband of Israel. Throughout the Old Testament the marital relation is seen as illustrating and reflecting the relation of God and his people. It is this image, which may never come to expression in sacred prostitution, which results in Israel's being called either an adulteress or a harlot when she turns to other gods. Thus in Ezekiel 16 she is the unfaithful bride, while in chapter 23 the idolatrous Northern and Southern Kingdoms become daughters who act as prostitutes from childhood. Adultery and prostitution cry out against the covenant of God. Although the law does not prescribe penalties for the man who enters into extra-marital relations, its view of them is writ large in its protection of the marital relation, prohibition of prostitution, and its hatred of both harlots (Pr. 7) and those who use them (Je. 5:7). The narrative portions of the historical books and the prophets make it clear that Israel was no more obedient with respect to harlots than she was with respect to foreign deities (1 Ki. 3; Is. 23:16).

We conclude that in Israel marriage was respected and protected by laws which paralleled those of the nations around her with respect to the punishing of the violation of the rights of fathers and husbands. A significant difference occurs as a result of the facts that Israel's God cannot be worshipped by sacred intercourse and that the marriage relation is sacred, being viewed as patterned after and reflecting the relation of God and his people. Therefore prostitution, both sacred and profane, has no place among God's people and the *talio* principle cannot be applied to sexual assault.

C. WOMEN IN SOCIAL LIFE

1. The centrality of marriage

Marriage and the production of a family, in particular the production of male heirs to carry on the name and the family inheritance, were of major importance to Israelites of both sexes. If a person should remain single, it was viewed as a disaster. Men who could not gain wives and women who were given no husbands considered themselves deeply deprived. It is, therefore, not surprising that we find very few unmarried persons in the Old Testament. Nor should it be a surprise that as we examine the role of women in Israelite society, we shall be looking primarily at those things which married women did.

2. The importance of having children

For most Israelite women the great events of their lives were birth, marriage, giving birth, and death. A woman who had given birth, especially to a son who could carry on the family name and inheritance, had a special place of honour. Without children she lamented her fate, and was sometimes scorned. The social activity of which women were most proud and for which they were sometimes most valued was the bearing of children. So much did both men and women value the production of offspring that both Abraham's and Jacob's wives offered their husbands their servant girls when they themselves had not borne children (Gn. 16; 30). In Rachel's case, the birth of the son by the servant is a matter of great joy and Rachel counts herself virtually the mother of the child: 'God has vindicated me; he has listened to my plea and given me a son' (Gn. 30:6). Matters did not work out as well for Sarah. Her servant, Hagar, began to despise her mistress when she learned that she was with child (Gn. 16:5). Samuel's mother, Hannah, suffered a similar fate, being despised by Peninnah, the other wife of Elkanah, for her barrenness (1 Sa. 1:1–7).

3. Other activities of women

The bearing and raising of children, although central in the lives of Israelite women and a much longed-for achievement, was not all that was permitted them. Sarah and other wives of the patriarchal period were the wives of nomads and ran whatever size of household their husbands had, evidently managing the domestic servants (Gn. 16:6). As life took on an agricultural tone the women became involved in field work, although we may suspect that this was not the chosen activity of a wife but more a matter of necessity, as in the case of impoverished Ruth who gleaned in the fields of Boaz (Ru. 2).

As Israel became a nation with cities and urban dwellers with wealth, possibilities of cloistered women and also of women with responsibilities in large households began to emerge. The Song of Solomon knows a cloistered woman to whose walled garden her lover comes.[4] Their relation clearly reflects a deep personal relationship of love.

Proverbs 31 presents a very different view of a woman who loves a man. She is not an actual person but an ideal figure. The idealization makes her all the more interesting. What is an ideal wife for the writer? It is not a woman who can do nothing but sit in the harem and await her lover! The ideal woman is capable of prodigious achievements. She is tremendously valuable to her husband (31:10). He perceives her (correctly) as very capable and has confidence in her, which confidence proves well founded as she makes a fine profit from her business ventures (31:11). In the running of her prosperous household she is involved in the manufacture of clothing for her family and servants at both the level of purchase and of sewing (31:13–14, 19, 21–22). Her long hours (31:15, 18) and careful supervision of the servants bring blessing and honour to her husband and to herself (31:23–31).[5]

It is worth noting that this woman goes well beyond the confines of her private dwelling. In verse 14 she is likened to a merchant ship bringing cargo from far off, while in verses 16 and 17 she is involved in real estate and agriculture. Her activity in purchasing a field and in planting it (herself!) is noteworthy, as land was of tremendous importance to the Israelite, being an inheritance from

[4] The imagery of the poem indicates that the woman herself is the walled garden. The poetic figure, however, presumes that women might literally have such private quarters.

[5] This woman would be described in certain segments of Judaism as being her husband's 'glory'; cf. the discussion of 1 Cor. 11:7, p. 174, below.

God as well as a means of livelihood. It is striking that nowhere in the poem is she described as spending time with her husband, who delights in her as more admirable than all others (31:28–29). It is perhaps not surprising that the poem does not dwell on this issue, as it is her resourceful industry rather than her affection which is being lifted up. This portrait makes an admirable balance when laid alongside the Song of Solomon.

4. Women as subordinate authorities

One thing which does not appear in the text of Proverbs is the legal relation of the woman to her husband. The husband, or father of a girl still living in her father's house, had a legal right to revoke legal commitments or vows which she might make (Nu. 30:3–16). This right was not coupled with any concept of women's stupidity or inability to make decisions. It was, rather, connected with the man's legal responsibility in the household. Some authors have suggested that the Old Testament viewed women as children in that the father possessed the same right of revocation with respect to his children. The error of this is clear when the legislation of Numbers 30 with respect to widows and divorced women is considered. When no longer under the authority of a husband, a woman was able to make vows and commitments which were legally binding (Nu. 30:9). In other words the husband's legal role rather than the woman's inferiority or inability forms the basis of his right to revoke her vow. Parallels to this sort of authority structure are found in many present-day business situations in which delegated authority is subject to review.

Many modern students of the Old Testament are seriously offended by its patriarchal structuring of the family and clan. Some feel that the appointment of men to the role of representative chief of families and clans assumes that women are inferior beings. P. K. Jewett and V. Mollenkott, for instance, think this is a crucial issue which must not be ignored. Both clearly feel that 'if a woman must of necessity be subordinate, she must of necessity be inferior'.[6] Such reasoning is easy to trace in rabbinical thought and in the thought of the Christian church. It is not, however, biblical. The appointment of the Levite house of Aaron to serve as priests

---

[6] P. K. Jewett, *Man as Male and Female* (hereafter *Male and Female*) (Grand Rapids, 1975), pp. 8, 71ff.

of God and as Israel's representatives before him meant that all other Israelites were of necessity subordinate to them. Did it mean that other Israelites were of necessity inferior to them? Korah and others drew this conclusion and opposed the Aaronic priesthood on precisely such grounds, arguing that all the congregation was holy and that Moses and Aaron were wrongly exalting themselves above it (Nu. 16:3). Their error was rejected by God. Moses' reply to them made it clear that Aaron was not high priest because he was somehow superior, but by divine appointment: 'It is against the LORD that you and all your followers have banded together. Who is Aaron that you should grumble against him?' (Nu. 16:11).

The husband's role in the home is also presented in the Old Testament as a matter of divine appointment rather than as a consequence of either sociological or psychological assumptions. The idea that women are somehow inferior simply does not appear. Indeed, the Old Testament offers a number of examples of women who were far wiser than their husbands. Abigail shows herself wiser than her husband Nabal (whose name means 'fool') and more concerned for the honour of God than David (1 Sa. 25). Zipporah, Moses' wife, showed her responsiveness to the Lord by circumcising their children when Moses had failed to do so (Ex. 4:24–26). Despite their failure and the wise actions of their wives, Moses and Nabal retained the responsibilities and authority which were theirs as husbands. A similar point can be made regarding Aaron's moral failure in the making of the golden calf (Ex. 32) and the sins of his sons Nadab and Abihu (Lv. 10:1–5). The calling of the sons of Aaron to serve as priests was *not* based on their personal superiority.

Wives and daughters were subordinate authorities in the Old Testament. In so far as the church has assumed that this implies that they are somehow intrinsically inferior to men, the church has been in error. In so far as contemporary critics impute such a view to Scripture, they too are in error.

5. Veiling customs

As we come to the end of our consideration of the role of Old Testament women in social life, a word about veiling customs is perhaps in order. We have seen that the Assyrian laws lay considerable stress upon the necessity of veiling women of rank and prohibit the veiling of harlots and slave-girls. The veil was thus a sign of dual import. It marked its wearer as related to a man and did presume his responsibility for and authority over her. It was, however, perceived as a mark of the dignity and rank of its wearer rather than as a sign of her 'inferior' status. The Old Testament contains no legislation concerning veils. It does, however, provide some incidental information about them. Genesis 12 presumes that when Sarah appears in Egypt she will be seen to be a beautiful woman. The Islamic total veiling customs were obviously not practised by Abram! The same observation appears to be appropriate in the case of Rebekah, whom Abraham's servant perceived to be a beautiful woman when he saw her at the well (Gn. 24:16). We learn that Jacob preferred Rachel to her sister Leah because of her beauty and form (Gn. 29:17–18) and must presume that she too went without an Islamic veil. When Hannah, the mother of Samuel, prayed at Shiloh, Eli was able to see her lips moving in prayer (1 Sa. 1:12–13). This would have been impossible if she were fully veiled.

The fact that these women evidently went without a veil does not, however, mean that it was unknown. When she learned from Abraham's servant that the man approaching her was her prospective husband, Rebekah veiled herself (Gn. 24:65). It would appear that her bridal status demanded a modesty with Isaac which was not necessary at the well or with the servant on the journey. Jacob's failure to know the difference between Rachel and Leah on his wedding night (Gn. 29:21–30) has sometimes been ascribed either to his never having seen her face before or to a custom of veiling brides. The text, however, shows that it was precisely for Rachel's good looks that Jacob loved her (29:17). While it is possible that his failure to recognize Leah was the result of a veil which she wore throughout the wedding night, it does not seem as likely as another explanation suggested by the discussion of the banquet of verse 22. Could it be that after the banquet Jacob was unable to distinguish between the woman whom he loved and her sister because of the amount which he had drunk at the festivities?

Isaiah too knew of veiled women, although it was not in a marital custom. His attack upon the proud and wealthy women of Jerusalem calls for the stripping away of their veils (Is. 3:16–24). From the context, however, it is clear that women at least sometimes went without veils, for some of the adornments to be stripped away would not be seen under a veil. The veils which he mentions may well be ornamental.

When the actual evidence of the Old Testament is taken into

account, it must be concluded that there is none to demonstrate that the Israelites practised veiling after the model of Islamic practice, nor after Assyrian. As we shall see below, the same cannot be said of later Rabbinic Judaism.

6. Women as judges and prophetesses

The offices of the judges and prophets in Israel stand just on the civil side of the line which divided the civil from the cultic (religious) activities, although, as with all authority within the state, their authority was ultimately divine in origin. The judges were raised up by God to govern and to deliver the people. The role of the prophets was more verbal than that of the judges in that they communicated words from the Lord. The roles of both prophet and judge were frequently played by a single individual. Among the judges of Israel, Deborah stands out, being a woman (Jdg. 4–5). Her introduction in the book of Judges is singularly impressive:

> Deborah, a prophetess, the wife of Lappidoth, was leading Israel at that time. She held court under the Palm of Deborah . . . and the Israelites came to her to have their disputes decided. She sent for Barak son of Abinoam . . . and said to him, 'The LORD, the God of Israel, commands you. . . .' (Jdg. 4:4–6).

Deborah holds several roles at once. She is a prophetess and manifestly speaks for God, passing on his commands to others. She is also a judge to whom Israelites willingly submit, many evidently travelling some distance to reach her. She is also a wife. The three roles do not seem to have appeared incongruous to the author of Judges. Deborah's authority extended not only to the cases brought her as judge, but was readily accepted by the fearful Barak, who wished not only her command but also her physical presence.

It has sometimes been suggested that Deborah's calling as judge and prophetess constituted a shaming of Israel. The evidence for such a view is simply lacking in the text. Barak is shamed by the fact that he, the warrior who would not go forth at God's command, will not have glory for his victory but that it will go to a non-combatant woman, Jael. There is no shame implied in the fact that he received direction from Deborah; the shame derives from his unwillingness to obey.

Miriam, the sister of Moses, never served to judge the nation but did function as a prophetess. We are given little indication of her work beyond her song at the crossing of the sea and her joining with Aaron in jealousy (Ex. 15; Nu. 12). Huldah (2 Ki. 22:14–20) is a prophetess whose role is somewhat more clear. Upon the finding of the law by Hilkiah, King Josiah sent five dignitaries to Huldah the prophetess the wife of Shallum to inquire as to what the Lord would do about the nation's disastrous disobedience to the law (2 Ki. 22:11–13). Huldah's words of response were from God. It appears that the author of 2 Kings accepted without qualm the role of a woman as prophetess and wife and, in that capacity, spokesman for God to the king.

The Old Testament does not offer many examples of women holding civil office. When it does, however, it shows no prejudice against them on account of their sex, as such. It appears to be accepted that God raised up Miriam, Deborah and Huldah as prophetesses and that Deborah was raised up as a judge. At least in the cases of Deborah and Huldah we know that these women were married. Without evidence to the contrary we must assume that the civil and religious functions of these women did not overturn their domestic legal status (although we may assume that Deborah spent less time than others in domestic chores and that our maxim 'A woman's place is in the home' is misguided!). Examples of women who were false prophets (Ne. 6:14) further support the conclusion that women were accepted as prophetesses in that the complaint of Nehemiah is not against their sex, but against their effort to undo him.

Athaliah, the usurper queen, is the only example of a female monarch in Israel (2 Ki. 11:3). Her presence has been used to demonstrate *both* the evils of women as queens and the right of women to the office. It would seem wrong to use the little which is said of her to support either case. We do not find a condemnation of her for holding office, although a woman. We do, however, find that she should not have come to power.

Deborah and Athaliah are examples of women with responsibilities in national government. Did women play a role in local government? To answer this question we must consider the role of the elders in Israel's government.

As we have noted, the tribes of Israel were patriarchally governed by older men (elders). The role of the elders, however, passed through a variety of stages during the nation's history. During the nomadic period, patriarchal government was the only form. When Moses became leader of the tribes, the structures necessarily changed. As God's spokesman, Moses was the central authority figure. The patriarchs (elders) of the tribes took on a decidedly secondary role. During the wilderness wanderings the elders and the appointed judges shared the Spirit given to Moses (Nu. 11:16–25). During the period of the conquest of the land and of the judges, we meet elders of cities and of districts (Jdg. 11:3–11; Ru. 4; 1 Sa. 11:5–11; 16:4; 30:26–31). It is not clear how these elders were selected. They did, however, exercise civil functions. Government by male elders was common in the surrounding nations as well (Nu. 22:4, 7; Jos. 9:11; Jdg. 9:2). During the period of the monarchy, especially at its inception, the elders were very powerful. Both David and Absalom sought them for political support (2 Sa. 17:4, 15; 19:11). As the monarchy grew stronger, the role of the elders appears to have diminished.

The question which presents itself to us in this study is whether the absence of female elders is to be viewed as principial and continuingly normative (prescriptive), or as historical and not required (descriptive). The origin of the elders lies alongside that of the tribal patriarch in a blend of family and civil authority. They continue to be tribal officials under Moses, but begin to change with the settling of the people into the farming and urban economy of Palestine. The elders of the cities are no longer clearly family-connected and appear to be more like civil authorities. Neither the origin of these elders, nor the changes in their roles are prescribed by God. They simply appear and they change. Our knowledge of the eldership is largely descriptive. Are women barred from such offices? The Old Testament nowhere addresses this issue. The elders, as we have noted, are presumed rather than prescribed.

Despite the silence concerning women elders we are able to approach the subject indirectly. Deborah, as judge over Israel, appears to have dealt with cases brought to her from various parts of the nation. Such cases would have fallen initially under the jurisdiction of the elders. From a formal point of view, therefore, Deborah was functioning as the final court of appeals in the civil system. The office of the judge was not elective, but one to which God raised individuals by his gifts and calling. The national prominence of Samuel and Samson appears to have resulted naturally in their beginning to function as judges in the land (1 Sa. 7:15; Jdg. 15:20). Samuel's sons came to office by their father's appointment (1 Sa. 8:1). It is not clear how Deborah obtained her office.

The mention of her office of judge alongside the fact that she was a prophetess suggests that her functioning as a prophetess may have raised her to national prominence as the public roles of Samuel and Samson raised them. From such a prominent charismatic role it would be a natural step to functioning as a judge. However unusual it may or may not have been for women to serve in major civil roles, the example of Deborah shows that it was not principially impossible. The fact that the people willingly brought cases to her for adjudication indicates a public acceptance of Deborah. From the example of Deborah I conclude that the Old Testament recognizes a place for women in roles of civil authority.

Social customs of the day probably militated against women holding such posts in most circumstances. Approached from this angle, the lack of any criticism of Queen Athaliah for ruling as a female monarch makes good sense and supports the conclusion that women might, in practice as well as in principle, serve in civil capacities. I personally think it unlikely that many women actually served it such capacities. Twentieth-century Western culture has held a higher general view of women than did ancient Near Eastern culture. Despite this, it is only in the last two or three decades that we have seen women gain a position from which they could be counted as viable candidates for public office except in the most extraordinary circumstances. In the light of this fact, I suspect few women served in public office in Israel. The fact that they could, however, opens wide the door for discussion of the appropriateness of women doing so in our day.

Esther is another example of a Jewish woman in an important public role. She was the wife of a pagan king, however, and does not really set a precedent which helps our understanding of women in public life in Israel. From another perspective, however, she is important. Her love of her people and her willingness to risk her life for their sake have made her a heroine everywhere her story has been read. Her wisdom and daring further underscore the fact that women were not looked down upon in the Old Testament, but had instead an honoured place. Miriam, Deborah, Abigail, Huldah, Rahab, Ruth, Naomi, all these and others stand out as examples of wise and capable women who were lifted up for honour and imitation by the Old Testament. Women were not usually in the public eye; they were, however, used mightily of God in the deliverance of his people and, whenever they do appear in public roles, are readily accepted in them.

D. WOMEN IN RELIGIOUS LIFE

The Lord called all Israel to hear, to learn and to obey the law. Moses commanded the reading of the law to the entire population, 'Assemble the people – men, women and children, and the aliens living in your towns – so that they can listen and learn to fear the LORD your God and follow carefully all the words of this law' (Dt. 31:12). Women had a natural place within the assembly of God's people which heard and was expected to respond obediently to the commands of the law. As morally responsible persons they received God's promises and came under his judgments as well (Dt. 31:12–13; 13:6–11; 17:2, 5; 29:18).

1. Private worship

The participation of women went beyond the hearing and obeying of the law generally. They were free to approach God in prayer (Hannah, 1 Sa. 1:10; Rebekah, Gn. 25:22; Sarah, Gn. 30:6, 22). They are not presented as somehow unacceptable to God or unworthy of his direct attention. Thus he responds to their prayers (Gn. 25:23; 30:6, 22) and appears to them (Gn. 16:7–14; Jdg. 13:3, 9). Women were able to participate in sacrifices and offerings. Men, as heads of households, brought many of the sacrifices but the families shared in the eating of them (1 Sa. 1:4–5). In the case of Hannah it would appear that she was the bringer of the sacrifice in the year that she brought Samuel to Eli (1 Sa. 1:24). In cases of purification, the women were not represented by their husbands and brought their own sacrifices to the priests (Lv. 12:6; 15:29).

The three great set feasts of the year were mandatory for the men of Israel, who represented their families at them. The women were not required to go.

With respect to vows, the women came under the legal and religious aegis of their husbands. Their vows might be revoked by their husbands or fathers but would stand if not specifically revoked (Nu. 30:3–16). The Nazirite vows, involving a high degree of devotedness, were open to both men and women (Nu. 6:2–20). These vows required purity which was similar to that of a priest during his service in the temple in the presence of God.

2. Public worship

Women not only participated in the individual and family worship of God, but appear to have had certain roles in the public worship.

The bronze basin used in Moses' tabernacle was made from the mirrors of the women 'who served at the entrance to the Tent of Meeting' (Ex. 38:8), although we do not know what their service was. Whatever the service of the women at the door of the tent of meeting, we have numerous records of women who participated in the worship of God by singing. Miriam and the women of Israel are reported to have sung and danced at the great victory over Pharaoh (Ex. 15:20–21). Women evidently had a place among the choirs of the temple as well (1 Ch. 25:5; 2 Ch. 35:25; Ezr. 2:65).

3. Priestly service

The priesthood can be traced through several stages in the Old Testament. In patriarchal times the head of the household or tribe offered the sacrifice. Thus, for instance, Noah offered sacrifice for his family, sons included (Gn. 8:20), and Abraham built altars for his family commemorating major events in their relation with God (Gn. 12:7; 13:18, *etc.*). The same pattern is observable among the other patriarchs and in Job. It would appear that the patriarchal leadership role extended not only over the personal and domestic affairs of his family, but also over the religious matters as well. He served as representative before God in public worship. It should be noted, however, that this public role does not negate what we have previously noted about women's direct approach to God in other situations.

Significant changes came about with the Mosaic legislation. The Lord had set apart for himself every first-born male in Israel. The sons of Levi were chosen to replace the others in the service of God in the tabernacle and temple (Nu. 3:12–13). Of the males of the tribe, only those without blemish (physical deformity) might serve. The priesthood itself was also restricted under Moses. Males of the levitical house of Aaron were singled out to serve as priests (Ex. 28:1–3). Their service was closely regulated and strict rules set out to ensure their physical wholeness (unblemished state) and to maintain their continuing ceremonial cleanliness (Lv. 21ff.).

As we consider the role of women in Israel, we must note that their exclusion from the priesthood is not sexist in the twentieth-century sense of the term. Only whole Aaronic males were chosen to serve as priests. All blemished Aaronic males, all other males and all females were excluded. The Mosaic provision stands in a historical continuum and continues the practice of having representative males serve to officiate in public worship functions. This restriction of the priesthood to men stands as something distinctive to Israel. Her neighbours had numerous women priests although it is not clear what their actual roles in worship were. We conclude that the appointment of representative male leaders in priestly office is a consistent pattern in the worship of Israel throughout her generations.

E. CONCLUSIONS

Our survey of the role of women in Babylon, Assyria and Israel shows the radical differences between ancient Near Eastern and twentieth-century life-styles. To the eye of a twentieth-century examiner the most visible difference is the male-dominated structure of the family, which has been partially discarded in the West during this century. The most visible difference, however, is not the most profound. Recent attention to the respective roles of men and women causes us to focus upon the dominant male role in the ancient Near East. As we noted above, however, the hub from which the differences between ancient Near Eastern law and modern views radiate is the contrast between tribal or clan concepts and modern concepts which consider the individual in abstraction from the social unit. We noted that marriage laws, criminal codes and inheritance regulations all take their form in the light of an assumed sense of corporate life. The head of the family unit, whether it was a single family or an extended family, was the senior man or patriarch. His was an executive role which included both rights and obligations. Thus, for example, he gave his daughter in marriage . . . and he supported the widow.

In all three of the cultures which we examined there was no suggestion that women were in fact inferior beings. In the absence of a husband, each culture assumed that widows were capable of raising children and of managing estates. The woman's subordinate legal status within the family was not, at least formally, based upon assumptions of intrinsic inferiority, although we may suspect that many ventured their own reasons for the legal differences between the sexes.

A comparison of the three cultures with respect to marriage and sexual laws, women's role in social life and women in religion reveals significant parallels and certain significant differences. With respect to practices regarding betrothal, marriage gifts and violation of sexual standards there are major areas of similarity.

Patriarchally arranged marriages for both sons and daughters was practised by all three. An exchange of gifts between parties provided the woman's father with compensation for her loss, while a commensurate dowry provided the bride with social security in case of widowhood or divorce and provided the husband with the use of funds to replace those which he had given his father-in-law. If he divorced his wife, the husband had to return the dowry funds to her.

Divorce was the prerogative of the husband in all three cultures. Only in Babylon could a woman initiate divorce proceedings, and then only at considerable risk. Adultery (illicit sexual relations by or with a married woman) was treated by all three nations as a capital offence. Offences against unmarried women led to damages being assessed on behalf of the offended family/tribe and a liability being laid upon the man for the upkeep of the woman.

A profound difference in attitude toward sexual relations as such was seen to exist between Assyria and Babylon on one hand and Israel on the other. In the former nations sexual offence was considered only as it related to family rights. Israel's view was shaped by her understanding of marriage as a reflection of the relation of God to his people and of God as one who cannot be worshipped with the use of idols. This view of God and of the marriage relation effectively made sexual expression a sacred activity. Communion with a deity through sacred prostitution became an abomination to Israel and the distortion of the marriage relation a sacrilege rather than simply a property/clan offence. In practical terms the difference meant that Israel abhorred prostitution, sacred or secular, while the other nations made legal provision for it. It had further implications in the penal sanctions. Assyrian law extended the principle of the *talio* (an eye for an eye) to the prostitution of a man's wife in retaliation for illicit use of a girl. Israel was permitted neither this nor the brutal Assyrian disfiguration of the offender. The harsh Assyrian law tended to make the offended husband or patriarch the arbiter and executor of justice within his own home. He was thus empowered to exact a punishment on his wife 'as he will' in various cases. Among the Israelites the patriarchal authority was circumscribed by the law.

In the social realm we found women in all three cultures largely occupied with the provision of children and heirs and with the keeping of the home. While this role was no doubt preferred by and for women, it was not the only one available, nor did it necessarily exclude involvement in commercial affairs. Each culture knew women who engaged in a variety of civil and commercial activities. Single adult women who inherited and widows might act independently of men while married women and minors acted under the legal authority of their husbands or fathers. The woman of Proverbs 31 (admittedly seen through the eyes of a man) does not seem to chafe at the fact that her husband is legally responsible for her actions; she interacts commercially with men with great freedom.

Personal religious life is not much discussed in the civil codes of polytheistic Assyria and Babylon. The biblical records of monotheistic, theocratic Israel do include discussion of women in personal relation to God. We noted their freedom of access to him and his appearances to them. Their personal relationships with God do not seem to have been mediated by their husbands or fathers.

With respect to public acts of worship we noted that Assyria and Babylon had priestesses, although their role in relation to priests is unknown. The worship of both societies also included sacred prostitution as a means of communion with deity. In patriarchal Israel the obligations and responsibilities of the head of the family/clan evidently included the leadership in worship and specifically priestly duties. Under the Mosaic administration the priestly function was still further restricted to the unblemished males of the Levites and of the sons of Aaron. Other men and women were precluded from the leadership in public religious exercise. Cultic prostitution after the model of the surrounding nations was adamantly rejected in Israel.

Our examination of the ancient Near East and of the biblical records in particular has shown a thoroughly patriarchal structure throughout. Male authority in marriage, legal responsibility in civil matters and leadership in priestly functions are uniformly witnessed to in Israel. We will close this section with a few comments drawing together what we have observed of the relation of men and women in the Old Testament. We may discern in the Old Testament a distinction between the civil realm, on one hand, and the family/marital and priestly on the other. In the family/marital situation the man exercised over-all responsibility and attendant authority whenever the husband and wife were in view. This did not eliminate areas of initiative and/or responsibility for women, who were subordinate authorities. Children of both sexes were called to honour both parents. In the absence of a man, however, we found that the wife became the head of the home (although we may presume that widows generally remarried quickly if possible).

In the religious sphere the same principle can be observed. Wherever public religious exercise was in view, whether in the patriarchal tribe or in the Mosaic administration, men were called upon to function in priestly roles, offering sacrifices, *etc*. In the case of the priesthood of the sons of Aaron, there could never be a situation such as that of the widow, in which there was no man to lead; there was accordingly no possibility whatsoever of a woman being a priest. Women's participation in public worship included both song and dance. In private religious exercise, where a public relation to a man was not in view, women spoke for themselves.

The social realm is strikingly different from the other two. In this realm women had much greater freedom. They could enter into trade with men as peers and direct them as servants. They could function as commercial peers of men with respect, for instance, to the buying and selling of fields (Pr. 31; Naomi, Ru. 4). This freedom was not perceived as competitive with or exclusive of the husband's role. A woman without a husband acted as a peer of her male commercial peers and acted without male review of her decisions (thus Naomi, Ru. 4; *cf.* Nu. 30:9). A woman who was married or a minor acted as a peer with her male commercial peers, but her actions were subject to the review of her husband or father (thus the woman of Pr. 31; *cf.* Nu. 30:3–16).

Women were not known to have served as elders of tribes, villages or cities in Israel and did not generally serve as regents. They were, however, called on occasion to serve as prophetesses and Deborah served in the high official capacity of judge. These roles were outside the family structure as the women were in no way their husband's legal agents when they spoke for the Lord or rendered judgment by the law.

We may summarize by saying that a principle of appointive male leadership in marriage and in public religious exercise can be discerned in the Old Testament. In civil life women met men as peers, although the marital relationship continued to apply for married women. It is worth noting, as we leave this period and turn to consider Judaism and Graeco-Roman culture in the time of Christ, that the evidence in hand does not teach women's intrinsic inferiority but rather a situational subordination. As we shall see, matters changed between the Old Testament period and the time of Christ.

3
Women in New Testament times

A. JUDAISM

The Old Testament canon closes after the Babylonian exile with the Jewish people living once again in the promised land, but in circumstances of poverty and weakness as compared to their former status. The New Testament presents its readers with quite a different view. It shows a nation of millions living in relative wealth under Rome, a state unknown to the Old Testament. In addition, the New Testament knows and recognizes as authorities groups such as the Pharisees and the Sadducees who have no role at all in the ancient state of Israel.

It is not only the externals which have undergone changes. The Jewish people had to make decisions about their relation to Greek and Roman overlords and, probably with less formal reflection, to the cultural patterns of those who ruled over them. The problem of adaptation became yet more complex after the destruction of the Jewish state in AD 70. From that time the faith of Israel had to adjust to the loss of the temple, of sacrifice and of a national existence.

The impact of the events of AD 70 is important for our study because the most extensive material concerning that early period is contained in the Mishnah and the Talmud, which were compiled between two and six centuries after Christ. It is difficult to discern which traditions in these works do in fact date from the time of Jesus. Some progress can be made in this area because Mishnaic and Talmudic attitudes can be cross-checked by comparison with earlier materials which are datable, such as the Apocryphal books, the writings of Philo and Josephus, and the New Testament. Patterns which are common to the inter-testamental Apocryphal books, the New Testament and writings contemporary with it, and the later Talmud may be safely assumed to have been generally present among Jesus' contemporaries. Care must be taken with materials which cannot be so traced.

1. Basic attitudes toward women

Whereas the Old Testament does not give us any specific texts which offer a basic evaluation of women-as-such, beyond the comments of the opening chapters of Genesis, inter-testamental Judaism (Judaism from the period between the close of the Old Testament and the start of the New Testament) and post-New Testament Judaism do, and their comments are worth looking at before examining their views of the roles of women in marriage, social life and religion. Throughout Jewish literature, from the Old Testament even to the present, there is high praise for the virtuous wife and condemnation of the wanton or faithless one. There is little of this sort of discussion, either in praise or scorn, for husbands, who have produced the literature.

a. Jesus ben Sirach

One of the earliest inter-testamental statements on women comes from the Apocryphal book of the Wisdom of Jesus ben Sirach, more commonly known as Ecclesiasticus (note: this is not the canonical book Ecclesiastes). The book is generally dated as having been written at about 190 BC. Ben Sirach writes,

> A woman's beauty delights the beholder,
>   a man likes nothing better.
> If her tongue is kind and gentle,
>   her husband has no equal among the sons of men.
> The man who takes a wife has the makings of a fortune,
>   a helper that suits him, and a pillar to lean on
> (Ecclus. 36:22–27, Jerusalem Bible).

It is clear that ben Sirach values a wife highly and that, in a sense, he says that 'The woman makes the man'. In chapter 26 he writes,

> Happy the husband of a really good wife;
>   the number of his days will be doubled.
> A perfect wife is the joy of her husband,
>   he will live out the years of his life in peace.

A good wife is the best of portions,
    reserved for those who fear the Lord
(Ecclus. 26:1–3, JB).

His estimate of a poor wife is correspondingly intense, but in the negative,

Any spite rather than the spite of woman! . . .
I would sooner keep house with a lion or a dragon
    than keep house with a spiteful wife . . .
No wickedness comes anywhere near the wickedness of a woman,
    may a sinner's lot be hers! . . .
Low spirits, gloomy face, stricken heart:
    such the achievements of a spiteful wife . . .
Sin began with a woman,
    and thanks to her we all must die.
Do not let water find a leak,
    do not allow a spiteful woman free rein for her tongue.
If she will not do as you tell her,
    get rid of her
(Ecclus. 25:13, 16, 19, 23–26, JB).

With regard to a certain kind of daughter, he writes,

Keep a headstrong daughter under firm control,
    or she will abuse any indulgence she receives.
Keep a strict watch on her shameless eye,
    do not be surprised if she disgraces you.
Like a thirsty traveller she will open her mouth
    and drink any water she comes across;
she will sit in front of every peg,
    and open her quiver to any arrow
(Ecclus. 26:10–12, JB).

Ben Sirach's view of bad women reveals his estimate of the true source of mankind's fall, Eve, and his view of the handling of difficult women, 'Get rid of them.' Modern feminists have rightly pointed out that there is a more than a bit of chauvinism here when his view is compared with the text of Genesis 3 in which God lays the blame and the curse at Adam's feet rather than Eve's.

In a later chapter we will contrast ben Sirach and the apostle Paul on this point.[1]

b. Philo and Josephus

The writings of Philo and Josephus, contemporaries of Paul, provide two samples of Jewish attitudes toward women in general at the time of Christ. Philo wrote from Alexandria and was deeply influenced by Greek thought; Josephus wrote with an eye to justifying Jewish ways to a Roman audience. We must, therefore, be cautious of taking them as typical of Judaism in Palestine. As we shall see, however, their views stand in line, more or less, with both ben Sirach and the subsequent 'rabbis' (Pharisaic scribes). The agreement of these other witnesses makes it more likely that the views of Philo and Josephus are not atypical. Philo expresses himself on the difference between men and women as follows: 'the attitude of man is informed by reason (*nous*), [that] of woman by sensuality (*aisthēsis*).'[2]

Josephus states his case yet more tersely: 'the woman is inferior (*cheirōn*) to the man in every way.'[3]

Philo's remark sounds surprisingly contemporary, especially if we use 'feelings' or 'insight' rather than 'sensuality' to render the Greek word *aisthēsis*. His observation can even be defended as representing general patterns which have obtained in the West for many years. Recent feminism and biological studies have, however, called into question the necessity of such patterns of behaviour and thought. It remains to be seen whether it is more our hormones or our training which have tended to make women, generally speaking, more sensitive to persons' feelings than men and men, generally speaking, more prone to defend their views rational(istic?)ly than women. Whatever our opinion of Philo's remark, it is clear that he intended to say that the female was the less rational sex, which fact was, from his perspective, a defect.

Josephus' remark is made in the midst of a discussion of marriage within Jewish law and evidently looks back to Genesis 3 or to his interpretation of the Old Testament generally. He explains the implications of his position in the following sentence: 'Let her

[1] Chapter 8, pp. 214ff.
[2] *De Opificio Mundi*, 165, as quoted by Oepke in G. Kittel (ed.), *Theological Dictionary of the New Testament* (hereafter *TDNT*) (Grand Rapids, 1965), 1, p. 782.
[3] *Contra Apionem*, ii. 201. Josephus' remark is often quoted. It is sometimes questioned whether the text which we have is in fact genuine at this point. We assume here that it is.

accordingly be obedient (*hupakouetō*), not for her humiliation, but that she may be directed; for authority has been given by God to man!' His logic seems clear enough. Women are inferior to men in every area. With respect to decisions, therefore, it is best that they submit to the better judgment of men. In Philo and in Josephus we have something which we did not find in the Old Testament or even in ben Sirach; we find an explicit teaching of intrinsic female inferiority.

c. The Talmud

The Talmud is yet more explicit in its teaching of women's inferiority. Its general attitude is reflected in its frequently classing women with children and (Gentile) slaves (mBer. 3.3; mR.Sh. 1.8; mSukk. 2.8; mB.M. 1.5).[4] To modern ears, the most offensive statement on the subject is probably that of Rabbi Judah ben Elai (c. AD 150) who

> used to say, 'A man is bound to say the following three blessings daily: "[Blessed art thou . . .] who hast not made me a heathen", ". . . who hast not made me a woman"; ". . . and who hast not made me a brutish man" ' (bMen. 43b).

To this citation the Talmud appends the following exchange of Rabbi Aha ben Jacob who

> overheard his son saying '[Blessed art thou. . .] who hast not made me a brutish man', whereupon he said to him, 'And [should you say] this too!' Said the other, 'Then what blessing should I say instead?' [He replied] '. . . who hast not made me a slave'. And is this not the same as a woman? – A slave is more contemptible (bMen. 43a).

The term 'brutish man' essentially means 'illiterate'. Rabbi Aha thus chided his son about claiming to be literate or educated. His son asked what else should be said than the traditional blessing,

---

[4] Citations from the Mishnah are taken from H. Danby, *The Mishnah* (Oxford, 1933) and are indicated by the prescript 'm'. Abbreviations of the tractates follow his list, p. 806. References to the Babylonian Talmud are taken from I. Epstein (ed.), *The Babylonian Talmud* (London, 1935) and indicated by the prescript 'b'. Those from the Jerusalem Talmud are translated by the author from M. Schwab, *Le Talmud de Jérusalem* (Paris, 1960) and indicated by the prescript 'j'. References to the Midrash Rabbah are taken from N. Freeman and M. Simon, *Midrash Rabbah* (London, 1939).

to which his father suggested that he substitute 'slave'. The Talmud, or perhaps the son, then asks whether a slave is not the same as a woman, referring to the fact that the rabbis considered the two categories to have similar obligations of obedience to the law because of their similar status of being under a man (bHag. 4a). The distinction offered, that a slave is more 'contemptible' than a woman, means either 'less valuable' or 'worthy of more contempt'. Neither meaning is of much comfort to many modern readers!

This generally low rabbinic view of women resulted in their being used frequently as examples of undesirable traits. Fear of sexual impropriety resulted in a policy of avoidance of women (mAb. 1.5; bErub. 53b). An estimate of a woman's ability to learn serious matters is to be seen in a passage relating an incident involving Rabbi Eliezer, in which a 'wise' woman asked him about the different sorts of deaths which met the Israelites who had worshipped the golden calf (Ex. 32). She felt that they had all shared in the same offence and should therefore have died in the same manner. He responded,

There is no wisdom in woman except with the distaff [spindle]. Thus also does Scripture say: *And all the women who were wise-hearted did spin with their hands* (bYom. 66b).

The text goes on to give hypothetical reasons for the different sorts of death recorded in Exodus 32. The Talmud takes pains to present the woman as a 'wise' woman, and then to expose her as being without understanding. Women were generally assumed by the rabbis to be persons incapable of learning about religious things. It is therefore not at all surprising that this 'wise' woman is shown as missing the point altogether. As we shall see when we discuss the role of women in religion within Judaism, some rabbis actually forbade instructing them in religious affairs. With this much general introduction to our topic, let us consider specifically the role assigned by Judaism to women within marriage.

2. Marriage and sexuality

a. Isolation of women

i. Seclusion

The Jewish community of the post-Old Testament era showed deep concern for sexual temptation. We have seen the concern of

Jesus ben Sirach with regard to a wayward daughter and the disgrace which she would bring to her father. The rabbinic texts do not spend much time discussing wayward men, although they, like Proverbs, warn against the prostitute's home. The approach most often taken by rabbinic Judaism to sexual temptation seems to have been the reduction to a minimum of any sort of contact between the sexes. This was accomplished in a variety of ways. In wealthier places, women were expected to remain indoors. Ben Sirach (c. 200 BC) urges fathers to 'guard' their daughters well (Ecclus. 42:11). The writer of 4 Maccabees (c. AD 35) places the following comment on the lips of a woman of great faith.

> I was a pure maiden and left not my father's house, and I kept guard over the rib which became woman's body. No seducer of the desert or ravisher of the field corrupted me, nor did the seducing serpent of deceit defile the purity of my maidenhood . . . (4 Macc. 18:7–8).[5]

For the writer of the book, an Alexandrian Jew, a virtuous urban woman stayed in her father's house. It is interesting to note as well that men are cast here as seducers, a role which they seldom play in Talmudic literature. In a similar vein, Philo expressed his opinion that 'all public life with its discussions and deeds . . . (is) proper for men. It is suitable for women to live indoors and to live in retirement' (*De Specialibus Legibus*, 169). The seclusion of women helped allay the fears of husbands and fathers. Ben Sirach reflects upon such anxieties (42:9–14), remarking 'the worry (a daughter) gives (her father) drives away his sleep' (verse 9). The Talmud echoes this, declaring 'The world cannot exist without males and females – happy is he whose children are males, and woe to him whose children are females' (bKidd. 82b).

ii. Not spoken to

Despite the urging of Philo and, perhaps, those wealthy enough to afford the practice, it was not practical for most Jews to keep women entirely indoors. Women were needed in the fields and in the shops. The New Testament describes Palestinian practice in exactly the period of which Philo and Josephus speak. It is clear

---

[5] Taken from the translation of C. Emmet, *The Third and Fourth Books of the Maccabees* (London, 1918).

from the New Testament witnesses that Palestinian women were not secluded.

In Talmudic times there seems to have been sentiment in favour of seclusion or cloistering of women, but also a recognition that it was not practical for all. It is therefore no surprise that we find regulations in the Talmud and in the Mishnah (some of which date from more than a century before Christ) dealing with relations with women *outside* the house. The Mishnah reports Rabbi Jose ben Johanan (*c.* 150 BC) as saying, '. . . talk not much with women', and adds,

> They said this of a man's own wife: how much more of his fellow's wife! Hence the Sages have said: He that talks much with women brings evil upon himself and neglects the study of the Law and at the last will inherit Gehenna (mAb. 1.5).

Further remarks speak against speaking to or being alone with women, especially married ones (bKidd. 70a, b; 81a; mAb. 1.5; bErub. 53b; bBer. 43b; mKidd. 4.12). These attitudes naturally went alongside an attitude that it was improper for a woman to talk with a man. The Mishnah, for instance, discusses situations in which a woman may be divorced without a financial settlement. In that discussion it rules,

> These are they which are put away without their *Kethubah* [marriage settlement]: a wife that transgresses the Law of Moses and Jewish custom. . . . If she goes out with her hair unbound, or spins in the street, or speaks with any man (mKet. 7.6).

It appears from the face of the text that the Mishnah was so deeply set against verbal exchange by or with married women that it authorized divorce without settlement for even talking with a man. It may not be quite so strong, in that it may intend to speak of talking with '(just) any' man. The Talmud interprets the 'talking' mentioned in the Mishnah as conversation with a young man or suggestive conversation (bKet. 72b). Whatever the exact meaning of the reference, it is clear that conversation between the sexes was not to be lightly entered into.[6] The Mishnah cited above

---

[6] This point is relevant to the conversation of Jesus with the Samaritan woman recorded in Jn. 4:5–30. It will be discussed below in chapter 4, pp. 84f.

(mKet. 7.6) brings to our attention another step taken by the Jews to ensure the separation of the sexes: veiling.

b. Veiling practices

Veiling practices within Judaism are of particular importance as they relate directly to the New Testament practice as reflected in Paul's discussion in 1 Corinthians 11:2–16. The goals of this chapter preclude devoting a large amount of space to the study of coiffure and veiling among the Jews and in Graeco-Roman culture. The appendix at the back of this book provides a study of this topic at moderate length. Its conclusions are relevant to this chapter and to the discussion of 1 Corinthians 11 in chapter 7 below.

The investigation of Jewish veiling practices in the time of Christ is made difficult by the lack of specific graphic information such as sculpture or art, by the lack of precision in the terminology used to refer to veiling, and by later Islamic practices. The evidence available to us concerning Jewish practice stems largely from Talmudic and other late sources. The question we must ask is whether these may legitimately be presumed to represent Palestinian practice in the time of Christ. A majority of students of the field have assumed so.

A close look at the evidence, however, suggests that they may be mistaken.

Observations and conclusion from the Appendix

The following observations, based upon materials presented in the appendix to this book, summarize my conclusions concerning coiffure and veiling in the first century of this era.

1. Evidence taken from first-century and rabbinic sources must be carefully weighed before being accepted as reflective of general Palestinian practice in the first century. A study of evidence for the seclusion of women shows that, in an effort to promote their cause, first-century writers sometimes presented practices of the wealthy or pious ideals such as the seclusion of women as though they were the common practice. The Talmudic authors likewise sought to promote their ideals. This sometimes led them to overstate their case or to read the pious practices of the day anachronistically back into the past. It is therefore possible that veiling evidence from the Talmud or even first-century writers may overstate its case by making a pious view appear to be a general practice.

2. Graeco-Roman practice of the day, as evidenced by art and literature, did not include mandatory veiling of any sort. Facial veiling was unknown and whether or not women pulled their shawls (*palla*, Latin; *himation*, Greek) over their heads was a matter of indifference.

3. Graeco-Roman custom *was* concerned with the coiffure of women. Loose and hanging hair was a sign of mourning. A woman's hair was generally dressed with great care. It was frequently braided and decorated, sometimes with very costly ornaments. The dressed hair was sign of rank and dignity.

4. The Old Testament includes no requirement of veiling for women, although it presumes that their hair will be put up (Nu. 5:18). The inferential evidence from the Old Testament precludes full facial veiling but is not incompatible with veiling by drawing a shawl over the head. Evidence from a monument of Sennacherib (705–681 BC) witnesses such a veil, although its purpose is unclear.

5. Loosed hair was a sign of separation among the Hebrews. Mourning, leprosy, Nazirite vows, accusation of adultery, and repentance all called for such a coiffure.

6. Josephus, a contemporary of Paul, testifies explicitly to the practice of drawing the *himation* over the head as a veil.

7. The evidence of the late second-century Mishnah is difficult to assess. Its use of the Hebrew word *pr'*, which meant loosing hair or uncovering the head in the Old Testament, is ambiguous and may include unveiling it as well. Such a broadening of the meaning of the term is easily understood, as any covering must be removed if hair is to be loosed.

8. The evidence of the Talmud indicates that by somewhere between the third and the sixth century it had become the practice of Jewish piety for women to go outside with a shawl drawn over their heads. Full facial veiling was not the practice of Talmudic Jews.

9. The Talmud uses the Hebrew word *pr'* to refer both to removing a covering and to loosing hair.

10. By the time of the Pesikta Rabbati, after the Islamic conquest, the Jews of Palestine understood veiling according to the Islamic practice of full facial veiling and projected this practice backwards as they read the older history and as they made illustrations from it.

From the ten observations above, the following five conclusions

68

relevant to the question of Jewish veiling practices in the time of Jesus may be drawn.

1. The Old Testament assumes that a woman's hair will be put up; it nowhere requires or even illustrates the veiling of women as a general custom. This applies to full facial veiling and to veiling with a shawl over the head. The latter custom may, however, have existed.

2. There is almost no likelihood that the Jews of the time of Christ practised the full facial veiling of women after the pattern of Islam.

3. It is possible that it was the practice of Jewish piety in the first century for women to wear a shawl over the head when out of doors.

4. In less wealthy areas and in areas of weaker tradition, more lax piety, or of either Greek or Roman influence, it is likely that veiling by a shawl would have been a matter of either indifference or neglect.

5. Among Jews, Greeks and Romans alike loosed hair was a sign of distress and not a hairdo for adult women. Women of all three societies put their hair up and decorated it in various, sometimes expensive, ways. Their hair, so done, was sign of their dignity and honour.[7]

c. Marital relationships

As we have seen, Judaism was concerned about the relationships of single persons and concerned to minimize contact between persons of opposite sex. Its commitment was overwhelmingly in the direction of the marital state. The blessings of marriage were appreciated and the command to reproduce and to fill the earth was taken very seriously. It was said, 'Any man who has no wife lives without joy, without blessing, and without goodness . . . without Torah and without a [protecting] wall . . . [and] without peace' (bYeb. 62b). Of the man who would not marry and sire children, it was said, 'He who does not engage in the propagation of the race is as though he sheds blood [i.e. lives are lost]' (bYeb. 63b). It was expected that all persons would marry if possible.

Despite the positive attitude toward marriage, there were varied

[7] The evidence above has been gathered without reference to New Testament texts. This has been done because they will be dealt with later and could be held to represent Christian traditions. It is my opinion, however, that they support the conclusions drawn here.

attitudes toward wives. Rabbi Hiyya brought his tormenting wife gifts, remarking, 'It is enough for us . . . that they rear up our children and deliver us from sin [by being our sexual partners]' (bYeb. 63a, b). A different opinion is attributed to Rabbi Akiba, whose wife is said to have permitted him years of absence for study. When she came to him after twenty-four (!) years away, he directed his disciples, 'Make way for her . . . for my learning and yours are hers [because she let me be away for study]' (bNed. 50a).

Within Jewish marriages there was no question of authority. The husband was in charge. A woman was under her father's authority until the age of twelve and a half, at which time she came of age and could decide for herself whom she would marry (bKidd. 79a). Generally, however, she was given in marriage prior to that date, in which case she had no say in the matter. While she was a minor, her father was regarded as having control of her and therefore as having the right to impose vows upon her. After her marriage, these rights were considered to have passed to her husband (mNed. 10–11). There is some question, however, about the actual implementation of some of the rules of this sort set forth in the Mishnah and Talmud. Despite this, it is clear that the husband was the final authority in the home, being the one to whom both wife and children owed obedience and who should be obeyed by children when parents differed (bKidd. 31a; mKer. 6.9).

A woman's role was primarily in the home, although the Talmud knows numerous other activities for women. It nowhere provides an index of her duties, but does mention some (in a list of usual duties which she ought not to do during menstruation for fear of sexually arousing or ceremonially polluting her husband). They are 'mixing of [the wine and water in] the cup, and the making of the bed, and the washing of his face, his hands, and his feet' (bKet. 4b). These duties are, with the exception of washing him, not foreign to household duties assumed by many contemporary women. Jewish women are also found doing farm work (mEduy. 1.12) and running shops (mKet. 9.4). It is presumed that a wife will do these things under the authority of her husband unless she is a widow (mKet. 9.4).

3. Women in public life

The Talmud has very little to say of women in public life. It was generally assumed that they would stay at home or work under their husband's authority unless widowed. Both Deborah and Huldah presented notable problems for the rabbis. Deborah comes up for mention only four times in the Talmud. On the two occasions in which she received more than a passing mention, she is depreciated for boasting (bPes. 66b) and for haughtiness (bMeg. 14b). Huldah's role as prophetess is a problem, as she lived while there were male prophets alive. How could Josiah have sent for a word from God through Huldah instead of through Jeremiah? Answers suggested range from the suggestion that she was a relative of Jeremiah's and that he did not mind, to the suggestion that he had gone to retrieve the ten lost tribes and was not around (bMeg. 14b). The second mention of Huldah is found in an interesting anecdote which more or less sums up the rabbis' attitude toward women in public roles:

> Rabbi Nahman said: Haughtiness does not befit women. There were two haughty women, and their names are hateful, one being called a hornet [literal meaning of Deborah] and the other a weasel [literal meaning of Huldah]. Of the hornet it is written, *And she sent and called Barak*, instead of going to him. Of the weasel it is written, *Say to the man*, instead of 'Say to the king [Josiah]' (bMeg. 14b).

Rabbi Nahman objected to these two prophetesses taking roles of authority as they spoke in the Lord's name. Women directing men were out of place for him.

4. Women in religious life

a. Individual worship

The place of women in the religious life of Judaism must be considered under three separate headings: individual worship, public worship, and teaching or learning functions. With respect to the first, the rabbis considered that the commands of the law were generally applicable to women, with the exception of all positive precepts for which there was definite time assigned (bBer. 20b). The exception stemmed from their monthly menstrual period, during which they were ceremonially unclean. With the exception of such positive commands (and three others), it was expected that women would live obedient pious lives.

b. Public worship

Matters were somewhat different with respect to matters of public worship. When the temple of Herod was yet standing, the women were restricted to the court of Gentiles and the court of women (Josephus, *Antiquities*, xv. 418). During their menstrual and post-natal times of ceremonial uncleanness they were not allowed to enter the temple area at all (mKel. 1.6). This same restriction applied to any man having a bleeding or flowing wound (mKel. 1.6). Traditions are divided as to whether women were allowed to participate in sacrifice by laying their hands upon the heads of animals or by waving the cut parts of them (T Men. 10.13, 17; mMen. 9.8; bHag. 16b).

Women had only a bit more freedom in the synagogue than in the temple. Synagogues were the local places of prayer and worship for Jewish communities. In them prayers and benedictions were offered and the Scripture read and expounded. In order to pronounce benedictions and recite certain prayers, indeed, in order to have a formal synagogue, a quorum of ten free adult men were required (mMeg. 4.3). The presence of women, slaves or minors was of no significance for the quorum. This rule explains why Paul could not go to a synagogue at Philippi but rather went to the 'place of prayer' by the river, where he met with the *women* who gathered there (Acts 16:13).

Regular attendance at the synagogue was not compulsory for women, although they were allowed to come to any services and expected to come to some (bHag. 3a). From Philo and from archaeological remains, it would appear that the women were frequently, if not generally, seated in separate sections or even in a balcony (Philo, *De Vita Contemplativa*, 69). Their part in the service was strictly receptive. Even the oral reading of the Scripture was not for women, although they were 'qualified': 'Our Rabbis taught: All are qualified to be among the seven who read, even a minor and a woman, only the Sages said that a woman should not read in the Torah out of respect for the congregation' (bMeg. 23a). A later version of this saying indicates that women should not be allowed to do so (T Meg. 4.11).

c. Teaching and learning

The passive role of women in worship is related to the rabbinic estimate of their ability to learn and of the propriety of teaching them. Women were permitted to attend synagogue because Deuteronomy 31:10–13 specifically required that they and children be included. The rabbis' view of a woman's role at the service is reflected in Rabbi Eliezer ben Azariah's comment on the respective purposes of men and women in Deuteronomy 31:10–13: 'the men came to learn, the women came to hear' (bHag. 3a). The women were to hear the Scripture and the exposition, but were not expected to learn or to gain deep understanding.

The extent to which this was taken seriously can be gauged from other remarks. In a passage cited above (p. 63), we noted that Rabbi Eliezer pointedly demeaned a 'wise' woman who asked a question about the interpretation of a passage by declining to answer her and by declaring that 'there is no wisdom in woman except with the distaff [spindle]' (bYom. 66a). The version of the story presented in the Jerusalem Talmud contains the following addition,

> His son Horquenos said to him, 'Because of your response to this woman about a biblical exposition, you make me lose three hundred *cour* of honorarium [which she gave me for priestly service].' 'It is better that the words of the Law should be burned', responded his father, 'than that they should be given to a woman [much less be given to her for money's sake].' When the woman had left, the disciple said, 'Master, now that you have turned away this woman's question, what would you answer us about the issue?' (jSot. 3.4).

The vehemence of Rabbi Eliezer's response to his son and the fact that his disciples had no better understanding of the problem than the woman underscore the fact that he refused to answer her because he felt it was wrong to teach women rather than because her question was silly or obvious.

The Babylonian Talmud omits the disciples' question and leaves the impression that the 'wise woman' may have shown her ignorance by the obvious question which she posed. In the earlier Jerusalem Talmud, she is not described as 'wise', but rather as 'important' and the disciples' question is reported. The Babylonian Talmud hints, therefore, that Rabbi Eliezer did not answer because women are stupid and capable only of working wool. The Jerusalem version intends to convey that women, however important they may be or whatever they may pay, should not be taught about Scripture.

The Mishnah preserves another saying of Rabbi Eliezer on the subject of women and of their learning about the Scripture. In a discussion of the bitter-water rite we read,

> Ben Azzai says: A man ought to give his daughter a knowledge of the Law so that if she must drink [the bitter water] she will know that the merit [that she has acquired] will hold her punishment in suspense. Rabbi Eliezer says: If a man gives his daughter a knowledge of the Law, it is as though he taught her lechery (mSot. 4.3).

We already know that Rabbi Eliezer felt women should not be taught the law. Here we learn that he fears that the comforting knowledge of meritorious works relieving judgment would make women all the bolder in their sin rather than comfort them in the face of it. Presumably he did not think it would have the same effect upon the men whom he taught.

As might be expected, synagogue instruction was designed for and taught only to men (Josephus, *Antiquities*, xvi. 164). The rabbis opposed women as teachers in schools and even in homes except as teachers of their own children. In a context which speaks of fear of sexual impropriety, the Mishnah rules, 'An unmarried man may not be a teacher of children, nor may a woman be a teacher of children' (mKidd. 4.13).

Looking back over the discussion of the role of women in religious life, it can be seen that their position was not a particularly good one. Although they might attend worship and might individually pray to and obey God, women were shut off from almost all other aspects of religious life. This picture of women in the Talmudic era is relevant also for the time of Christ, if we are to judge by the words of Philo and of Hillel, who is reported to have said, 'many women, much superstition'.

5. Conclusions

Our discussion of the role of women in Judaism has presented a situation in which the subordinate role of women within patriarchal and Israelite society has hardened to a considerable degree and in which women have been relegated to a position of inferiority. The rabbis continued many old traditions and produced new ones which they thought would guard their people from sin. Increasingly this meant a separation of the sexes. Perhaps it was this distance which led to suspicion and ignorance, and the ignorance to contempt. As has frequently been noticed, the rabbis spoke most often of women in a depreciating manner. A woman's praise was found in her service in the home; criticism of her centred around her sexuality and her ignorance. The rabbinic hope for women and assessment of them is well expressed in Genesis Rabbah, which says,

> [God] considered well from what part he would create her. Said He: 'I will not create her from [Adam's] head, lest she be swell-headed; nor from the eye, lest she be a coquette; nor from the ear, lest she be an eavesdropper; nor from the mouth, lest she be a gossip; nor from the heart, lest she be prone to jealousy; nor from the hand, lest she be light-fingered; nor from the foot, lest she be a gadabout; but from the modest part of man, for even when he stands naked, that part is covered.' And as He created each limb He ordered her, 'Be a modest woman.' Yet in spite of all this, *But ye have set at nought all my counsel, and would none of my reproof* (Prov. 1.25). I did not create her from the head, but she is swell-headed . . ; nor from the eye, yet she is a coquette . . ; nor from the ear, yet she is an eavesdropper . . ; nor from the heart, yet she is prone to jealousy . . ; nor from the hand, yet she is light-fingered . . ; nor from the foot, yet she is a gadabout . . .' (Genesis Rabbah 18.2).

Against such background the Jewish men were taught to pray, 'Blessed art thou who hast not made me a woman!' Modern women might or might not be willing to offer the response which was taught to Jewish women, 'Blessed art thou who hast created me!'

B. THE GRAECO-ROMAN WORLD

The three centuries prior to the New Testament era were a time of increasing cultural exchange in the Mediterranean world. The conquests of Alexander the Great (d. 330 BC) linked the eastern regions from Greece to India to Egypt and introduced a simplified Greek (*Koinē*) as the common language. The rise of Rome led to a new set of relationships in the middle of the second century BC. By the time of Christ, Greece and Rome had had more than two centuries of cultural exchange and had, in many respects, become indistinguishable except in local differences. The major cities of the Mediterranean world shared a common culture.

If we try to examine in detail the role of the average woman in this culture, however, we become aware of two significant facts: our evidence is derived from the more wealthy classes, and there is not much of it. The poorer people left no literature and had no rabbis to record values and details of life. There must therefore be a certain tentativeness to the conclusions reached in this area.

The cultural exchanges of the period had another consequence which makes our task difficult: the rapid rate of change created a situation of virtual chaos with respect to customs. We can discern general trends among the wealthy and within the legal situation, but we are at a loss to demonstrate how these relate to most specific locations. With these reservations, let us review the place of women within Graeco-Roman civilization.

1. Ancient Greece
Before the period of assimilation, the Greeks and the Romans could be distinguished with respect to their attitudes toward women and sexuality. The Greeks thought very little of women and treated them largely as chattels. Women had no place in public life. The purpose of a wife was the production of legitimate offspring; other women or men served for pleasure. Sexual expression in Greece was not restricted as it was among the Jews, for instance. A man's wife was, of course, for him only, but extramarital activity on his part was fully expected and institutionally provided for through both male and female prostitutes.

2. Ancient Rome
Ancient Rome was no less male-oriented than ancient Greece, but had a different, more restrained attitude toward sexuality. Women were firmly subject to the authority of their father (*patris potestas*) and passed from that to the authority of their husbands. Within the family, however, they enjoyed a strong role. They were considered mistresses of the household and had inheritance rights which produced many wealthy widows. Marriages were indissoluble from the woman's side and difficult for men to dissolve. This resulted in a more secure role for the woman. Although men enjoyed extramarital relations which were forbidden their wives, homosexuality was not accepted as it was in Greece. An ideal of loyalty to one's spouse (not necessarily sexual loyalty for men)

was generally held, reflecting a better quality of personal relation between husbands and wives than was seen in Greece or in the Orient. Wealthy Roman women were educated to some degree, a very different situation from that of most Greek and Oriental women. It would be fair to conclude that wealthy ancient Roman women, while subject to their husbands, whose rights over them and their daughters extended even to execution, enjoyed the most favourable and respected position of all Mediterranean women. It seems likely that women of the lower classes enjoyed fewer of these benefits.[8]

3. New Testament times

As the New Testament period approached, the dominant Roman culture saw a progressive improvement in the lot of its women. They had always circulated freely with the men, but now some even began to hold positions in public life. They enjoyed independent legal rights and commanded their own property. The improvement in social status came at a time when other areas of culture were in great flux. Roman society had become much more loose regarding sexual *mores* and divorce became much easier as a result of new forms of marriage which either party might dissolve. Political marriages helped to contribute to the deteriorating situation, as they lasted so briefly.

The effect of the improved lot of wealthy and noble women may not have been very great among the poorer classes. In such classes women were generally more integrally involved in the daily lives of their husbands, but had less access to education and fewer opportunities for independent lives. We have some indication of the possibilities open to women of the middle classes from the activities of Lydia, the owner of a dye-stuffs firm at Philippi (Acts 16), and Priscilla (Prisca), who shared with her husband in the tent trade (Acts 18). Lydia was a Greek Jewess and Prisca Roman.

The amelioration of the lot of wealthy Roman women can be paralleled among the wealthy women of Greece. It is likely, however, that the women of lower rank in Greece and in Asia Minor were not as much benefited as their Roman counterparts, for the basic Greek attitude toward women was poorer. The major cities

[8] A more lengthy discussion of the role of Roman women is available in the lucid work of J. P. V. D. Balsdon, *Roman Women, their history and habits* (London, 1962). For a discussion of Greek women, see the article of Oepke, *gunē*, in *TDNT*, 1, pp. 776–779. His bibliography is somewhat dated but still excellent.

to which Paul travelled were of sufficient size and commercial activity that the new status of Roman women was likely to have affected them.

C. CONCLUSIONS

Our survey of cultures relevant to New Testament times is now complete. As twentieth-century persons we can appreciate the great difference between the ways in which the cultures of both the Old Testament and the New Testament eras understood their women and the way in which our culture does. Our examination of marital relations showed that, without exception, the cultures examined assumed male leadership and legal responsibility. The exercise of that role, however, differed greatly from place to place and from era to era. The Assyrian husband and the ancient Roman husband held virtually unrestricted right with respect to their wives. The Babylonian, Israelite and Talmudic husband was limited by law or by custom in the exercise of his authority. From the evidence which we possess it would seem that women were often considered to be inferior, not only with respect to legal rights, but also as human beings. In some cases this came to explicit expression; in others it is more inferential.

Women held differing roles in the social lives of the cultures which were looked at. They participated in commercial life everywhere, although they often played subservient roles. Only in Roman culture were they given public office, and then very seldom. Within Judaism and also within Greek culture they were considered unfit for public life.

The role of women in the religious life of Babylon and Assyria is known to us only through the cultic priestesses and the cultic prostitutes. These women were evidently subordinate to the priests, but they did participate in worship. Of the role of the average Babylonian or Assyrian woman in the worship of her day, we know nothing. Israelite women enjoyed a personal relation with the Lord and were required to attend certain of the public ceremonies, but did not lead in public religious exercise or function as priestesses. Within Judaism, as contrasted with Old Testament practice, we found that women were much more excluded from worship and religion, being considered unfit to learn or inappropriate to teach. Graeco-Roman worship at the time of Christ was very diverse. Women functioned as worshippers and sometimes as priests or priestesses in various cults, while others excluded them.

Of the societies which we studied, only the Jewish ones were integrated around the worship of a single deity. This gave these cultures a religious framework within which life as a whole was understood. The religious commitments of Jews brought the marriage relation, and its sexual aspects in particular, into a sacred realm. As a result the Jews stand alone in opposing prostitution as an acceptable practice (although this does not mean that it was not practised). Among each of the other cultures sexual fidelity was demanded of wives but was not expected of husbands. Sexual regulation was more a matter of personal property rights and the guarding of the family through the production of legitimate offspring than a matter of religious or even moral import. In Roman culture of the Christian era the double standard broke down somewhat, but not in the direction of expecting fidelity of the husband! Increasingly the wealthy Romans and those Greeks influenced by them accepted looser marital ties and an increased amount of promiscuity by women as well as men.

It is against the transitional cultural situation of the Roman era that we must evaluate the New Testament teaching about the role of women. Some grasp of the increasingly chaotic social structures of Roman society and the increasingly conservative tendencies developing in Judaism is necessary to see Paul and Jesus in their proper perspective. Their teachings are not in line with the Judaism of their day. Nor are they an adaptation of the Greek and Roman practices. Their views are closer to those of the Old Testament, and yet they are both shaped by something quite new. The distinctive element in their views came from the new thing which they proclaimed, the arrival of the kingdom of God with power.

4

Women in the ministry and teaching of Jesus

A. THE KINGDOM HAS COME . . . AND WILL COME

At almost every point, the life, teaching and ministry of Jesus called upon people to think new thoughts in new ways. The angel's announcement of his birth drew from a bewildered but willing Mary the exclamation, 'How will this be?' (Lk. 1:34). Similar words are recorded on the lips of Nicodemus, a ruler of the Jews, whom Jesus told that the kingdom had come and called upon to rethink his understanding of the kingdom of God and of Jesus himself (Jn. 3:9). Not only his words, but also Jesus' behaviour frequently raised questions or called upon people to revise their ways of thinking. Simon, a Pharisee who did not understand forgiveness, love and gratitude, learned about them when he questioned whether Jesus, as a well-known rabbi, should allow a woman who was a known 'sinner' to wash his feet with her tears, dry them with her hair and rub on an expensive ointment, all the while kissing Jesus' feet (Lk. 7:36–50). At another point Jesus forced a ruler of a synagogue to reconsider what it meant to 'work' on the sabbath day when he showed his compassion for a crippled woman by healing her (Lk. 13:10–17).

It is not only the persons of the first century who can have such an experience with Christ. If our understanding of Jesus has not grown beyond a (correct) childhood understanding of 'gentle Jesus meek and mild' who welcomed and blessed the little children (Mk. 10:13–16), we shall find it hard to relate to the angry man who scourged the money-changers in the temple of God and threw their goods all over the floor as he overturned their tables (Jn. 2:14–16). A similar problem awaits us if we are used to thinking of Jesus as simply a product of his day or to assuming that, were we to study them, his views would (of course) be in line with what we consider the best and most enlightened thought of our day.

As we consider the teaching of the gospels with respect to the place of women in the ministry and teaching of Jesus, we must beware of laying hold of only those bits which are comfortable for us and also of trying to mould him to conform to our preferred versions of male or female chauvinism. We must instead come prepared to hear his teaching and to have our own thoughts reshaped by him.

Those who faced Jesus in his lifetime were often trying to fit him within their expectations of him and of what a prophet or Messiah ought to be like. He was well aware of the discrepancy between his actual ministry and their expectations of a military Messiah, and frequently used that difference as a way of teaching. Matthew's gospel shows us a good deal about the unwillingness of Jesus' generation to hear the news which he brought them. In chapter 11, the generation which refused both John the Baptist's austerity and Jesus' willing entrance into everyday life is likened by Jesus to peevish children who wish to 'call their own tune' and who complain, 'we played the flute for you, and you did not dance; we sang a dirge, and you did not mourn' (Mt. 11:16–19). Jesus' contemporaries expected the messengers of the kingdom of God to behave in a particular way and could understand neither John's austere call for repentance nor Jesus' demonstration of concern for and rejoicing over the repentance of tax collectors and 'sinners' (Mt. 11:18–19). They awaited instead the heralds of a kingdom which would come visibly, totally, and with the judgment of God upon 'sinners'. The kingdom which Jesus announced was indeed a kingdom of salvation, but its arrival was in different stages from those expected.

The parables of the kingdom (Mt. 13), which follow Jesus' discussion of his generation's response to himself and to John, carefully taught those with 'ears to hear' that the kingdom has indeed come and is working in an unexpected way among men, but that its fullest realization and the cosmic judgment of God will be later.

Whereas his contemporaries expected, as did John, that the kingdom's arrival would mean the burning of the chaff (Mt. 3:11–12), Jesus taught that the kingdom's arrival was not the time of harvest, but of the sowing of seed which would bring varying results (Mt. 13:3–9, 18–23). The kingdom's work, he taught, would be as quiet and unobtrusive as yeast in meal, but would permeate the whole lump (Mt. 13:33). The judgment, he assured them, would come and the king would separate the tares from the wheat, but only at the end of the age (Mt. 13:24–30, 36–43).

Failure to grasp the manner in which the kingdom was manifest in Jesus' life and work caused many to judge that the kingdom had not come as he claimed and to dismiss him. As we examine Jesus' ministry and teaching (and that of the apostles) with respect to women, we must be sensitive to the already-here-but-not-yet-fully-realized nature of the kingdom. In the area of marriage, for instance, Jesus taught that the arrival of the kingdom with power (Mt. 12:28–29) produced two contrasting results. Moses' concession of divorce because of the hardness of Israel's heart is overthrown among the sons of the kingdom, who are called to realize anew, by the power of God, the Creator's original design for permanent marriages (Mt. 19:3–9,26). The restoration of marriage to the pattern of 'the beginning' was, however, not all that Jesus had to say about the impact of the arriving kingdom upon that relation. Some would, for the sake of that kingdom, make themselves eunuchs (Mt. 19:10–12). This calling, also demanding God's strength, was new with the arrival of the kingdom and looks forward to the status of all believers in the time of the full realization of the kingdom at the resurrection, when they will no longer marry or be given in marriage (Mt. 22:23–33).

From what has been said it is evident that, for Jesus, the kingdom has indeed come, but has not come in its final state. Further, its arrival has led to a situation in which some will permanently marry and others will permanently remain single. It would be possible to seize one or another of these valid strands and to seek to make all believers conform, either by marrying or by remaining celibate. Neither approach would faithfully reflect Jesus' teaching; to maintain either *by itself* we should have to suppress evidence of the other. In doing so we should be joining those who tried to press Jesus into the mould of their own expectations. As will become clear in the remaining chapters, some recent answers to the question of the roles of women among the people of Jesus Christ have focused on only one aspect of the situation and have sought to deny others in order to achieve harmony. We must seek to take in all of the evidence and not to let our fervent grasp of one aspect separate us from others. To be specific, the teaching of

Jesus and of his apostles represents a break from that of Judaism in their day. It established new roles for women in the life and the worship of the people of God, roles which are closer to the Old Testament than to Judaism. It also renews certain older, creational relations. It would be destructive to focus on either the new or the renewed to the exclusion of the other. The following chapters will repeatedly raise the key theme of the arrival of the kingdom of God, stressing that it has come with the arrival of Jesus Christ, and that it will come in its fullness at his return. Its present manifestation is therefore, in a certain sense, partial. A critical task of the student of the New Testament, therefore, is to ask what the present meaning of the kingdom is in various aspects of life. In this book I am trying to outline the present implications of the kingdom which Jesus brought for the relationship of women and men.

This chapter is divided into two parts, examining the role of women in the personal ministry and in the teaching of Jesus respectively. In them the startling contrast between Jesus' views and the social *mores* of his day will become clear. The next chapter compares Jesus' views with those of the apostolic church. Both chapters are concerned to do more than simply catalogue differences and similarities. They are intended to present the rationale of the biblical teaching as well. If we can grasp this we shall understand not only the 'what' of biblical teaching, but also something of the 'why'. This information should better enable us to apply its teaching to our own lives.

B. WOMEN IN THE PERSONAL MINISTRY OF JESUS

1. Women as people

a. 'Whosoever' does the will of my Father

'Pointing to his disciples, he said, "Here are my mother and my brothers. For whoever does the will of my Father in heaven is my brother and sister and mother" ' (Mt. 12:49–50). It may be said that the most striking thing about the role of women in the life and teaching of Jesus is the simple fact that they are there. Although the gospel texts contain no special sayings repudiating the views of the day about women, their uniform testimony to the presence of women among the followers of Jesus and to his serious teaching of them constitutes a break with tradition which has been described as being 'without precedent in [then] contemporary Judaism'.[1]

As herald and bringer of the kingdom of God, Jesus preached his message to the whole of society. He nowhere shares the disdainful and condescending attitudes of so many of his contemporaries toward those in need. He saw lepers and young rulers, Pharisees and tax collectors, prostitutes and little girls, mothers-in-law and single women as equally in need of his message and he delivered it without prejudice or fawning deference. It may be said that the foundation-stone of Jesus' attitude toward women was his vision of them as *persons* to whom and for whom he had come. He did not perceive them primarily in terms of their sex, age or marital status; he seems to have considered them in terms of their relation (or lack of one) to God. It is this axis which explains how Jesus was unaffected by the prejudices of his day toward the poor, the lepers, the Samaritans, the prostitutes, the tax collectors, and women in general. The place, therefore, to begin our study of Jesus' relation to women is with his own declaration about his relation to mankind and about the basis upon which persons may be related to him.

Matthew 12:49–50 (*'whoever'* does the will of my Father, quoted above) sets Jesus apart from the teachers of his day. Matthew quotes this saying at the end of his discussion of Jesus, John and the kingdom and just before the parables of the kingdom. Jesus' family had come looking for him. Now that he had begun his public ministry, his kinship relations were seen in a new light; blood ties no longer took the same sort of precedence in his relation to people, a point also made in his response to Mary at Cana (Jn. 2:4).

The evangelists' descriptions of his response to his family tell us something of major importance about Jesus' teaching. Jesus stretches his hand out in the direction of his *disciples* (Mt. 12:49–50) or the *crowd* (Mk. 3:32–35) and says that whoever does the will of his father is his mother, sister and brother. Women were in the crowd and apparently identified as 'disciples' in a general sense. They, as the men, could be his 'family'. From this text we learn that Jesus, unlike the rabbis, taught women, willingly receiving them among his followers. They were persons for whom he had a message and were treated as such. The gospels provide us with

[1]W. Forster, *Palestinian Judaism in New Testament Times* (London, 1964), p. 124.

84

a number of examples of Jesus' respect for and teaching of women. These stand in marked contrast to the sort of interaction which we would expect of someone like Rabbi Eliezer.[2]

b. A woman with whom Jesus wanted to talk

Jesus' encounter with the Samaritan woman (Jn. 4:5–30) is a good example of his willingness to dismiss conventions of men which stood in opposition to his purpose. From the perspective of the rabbis of the day, the woman had, as it were, three points against her. Jesus, the Jewish rabbi, should not have talked to her because she was a Samaritan, a woman, and immoral. Alone with her at the well, Jesus initiated a conversation with the purpose of bringing her the good news of the kingdom. She was surprised by his request for water and responded, 'How is it that you, a Jew, ask a drink from me, a Samaritan woman?' (4:9). The later rabbis held that Samaritan women were to be considered always menstruous (and therefore ceremonially unclean). This tradition was perhaps not yet customary, but her response shows that the animosity upon which it was based was clearly present. Such attitudes meant no more to Jesus than the Pharisaic avoidance of tax collectors, which he also ignored. His disciples were not as free as their master and, upon their return from town, were surprised to find him alone and talking with a woman (4:27).

Jesus' conversation with the woman shows his concern to communicate about himself and about the kingdom. She emerges as a sharp person who is responsive. A discussion of water which leads to eternal life (which she did not fully grasp) was followed by a direct discussion about her immoral changing of husbands. Conceding Jesus' 'prophetic' insight into her life, she tried to change the subject to focus upon the controversy between the Jews and the Samaritans over the correct place of worship. Jesus answered her question about worship, but led on to a discussion of true worship and to an identification of himself as more than a prophet, as the Messiah whom she expected.

The subject-matter of Jesus' conversation with the woman was theologically profound. There is no suggestion that her sex affected the manner of Jesus' dealing with her. It is interesting to note the contrast between the response of this Samaritan woman to the message of Jesus and the response of Nicodemus, the ruler of the

[2]Cf. chapter 3, pp. 63, 72f.

Jews, in the preceding chapter (Jn. 3:1-21). The wise ruler came under cover of night and shook his head in consternation, asking how such things could be. His expectations of the Messiah and the kingdom did not match what Jesus taught. This nameless Samaritan woman heard not only about the kingdom but even the uncovering of her own sin, and yet responded in faith. She, unlike Nicodemus, made no effort to keep her relation to him secret, but announced to all that he knew all that she had done (4:29).

c. A clever, persistent woman

Jesus' encounter with a Canaanite woman provides another look at his willingness to deal with women and his respect for them. Matthew's account (15:22–28) is as follows,

> A Canaanite woman. . .came to him, crying out, 'Lord, Son of David, have mercy on me! My daughter is suffering terribly from demon-possession.' Jesus did not answer a word. So his disciples came to him and urged him, 'Send her away, for she keeps crying out after us.' He answered, 'I was sent only to the lost sheep of Israel.' The woman came and knelt before him. 'Lord, help me!' she said. He replied, 'It is not right to take the children's bread and toss it to their dogs.' 'Yes, Lord,' she said, 'but even the dogs eat the crumbs that fall from the master's table.' Then Jesus answered, 'Woman, you have great faith! Your request is granted.'

Matthew presents this incident just after an exchange with the Pharisees about what makes a person 'clean' or 'unclean'. Jesus rejected the Pharisees' external ideas of defilement (washing of the hands) and emphasized the importance of what is in the heart. Matthew makes it plain that the disciples failed to grasp clearly what Jesus was saying. This exchange with the Canaanite woman makes Jesus' point clearly. The Canaanites were considered 'unclean'. The disciples want her sent away, but Jesus responds to her persistence. In the exchange, she shows a keen wit and a willingness to accept what the Lord says. She is an example of 'that which proceeds from the heart' making a person 'clean'. From the perspective of our study of Jesus' response to women, we must note that he shows respect for the faith of this woman and for her argument. He took women seriously.

d. Two women who act upon their trust

Rabbinic literature uses women negatively more often than positively. In it they may exemplify patience or support for their husbands, but more often they are a temptation to men or to be avoided. Women are almost never used to exemplify trust in God or theological insight. The gospels stand in marked contrast. The texts which we have looked at already make this clear. A look at two other women shows that Jesus considered women could exercise and exemplify such virtues.

Luke 7:36–50 reports an incident at the home of Simon the Pharisee in which a repentant woman who had been a 'sinner' entered the dinner-chamber and anointed Jesus' feet. Simon would never have permitted such a person to touch him. Jesus used her as an example of faith and love:

> 'Do you see this woman? I came into your house, [Simon]. You did not give me any water for my feet, but she wet my feet with her tears and wiped them with her hair. You did not give me a kiss, but this woman, from the time I entered, has not stopped kissing my feet. You did not put oil on my head, but she has poured perfume on my feet. Therefore, I tell you, her many sins have been forgiven – for she loved much. But he who has been forgiven little loves little.' Then Jesus said to her, 'Your sins are forgiven.' The other guests began to say among themselves, 'Who is this who even forgives sins?' Jesus said to the woman, 'Your faith has saved you; go in peace' (Lk. 7:44–50).

The devotion and faith of the sinful woman put the Pharisee, Simon, to shame and show his lack of trust in and love for Jesus. Simon has not performed even basic acts of hospitality for his honoured guest. The faith of the sinful woman led her to acts of public love and gratitude. It is she, not the Pharisee, who exemplifies godly faith in action. Once again we have an example of Jesus dealing with persons as individuals and without reference to their sex.

A woman who has suffered for years with an issue of blood provides another example of a woman acting upon her trust in Jesus (Mk. 5:25–34). We are told by Mark that she had suffered much from doctors, but had only become worse with time. As Jesus walked through a crowd she touched his cloak and was healed. Jesus, aware of her touch and of the healing which she received through it, stopped and, much to the consternation of his disciples, asked who had touched him as he worked his way through the crowd. The fearful woman fell at his feet and told of her healing. Jesus said to her, 'Daughter, your faith has healed you. Go in peace and be freed from your suffering' (Mk. 5:34). In this vignette we see a woman who exemplifies faith of a great sort. She was convinced that even a touch would heal her; her implicit trust is reminiscent of that of the centurion who was sure that Christ's command alone, without his presence, would be enough to heal his servant (Lk. 7:2–10).

A further point is worth making in connection with this woman of faith. A person with a running wound or vaginal bleeding is ceremonially unclean. In touching this woman, Jesus himself became ceremonially 'unclean' (although, as Lord, Creator and Healer, the category becomes inapplicable to him). The same result would come from his contact with Jairus' daughter, to whom he was going. Throughout his ministry Jesus demonstrated his willingness to deal with such people and, in the parable of the 'good Samaritan' (Lk. 10:25–37), reprimanded the leaders of the day for their placing concern for personal 'cleanness' above concern for others. Jesus met people as individuals and responded to them according to their need, whether they were lepers, Samaritans, tax collectors, or women with bleeding.

e. A daughter of Abraham

Luke reports Jesus' healing of a crippled woman in a synagogue on a sabbath day (Lk. 13:10–17). She had been in bondage to her ailment for eighteen years. Luke reports, 'Jesus . . . said to her, "Woman, you are set free from your infirmity." Then he put his hands on her, and immediately she straightened up and praised God' (13:12–13). The woman's response shows a right appreciation of God's work. The leaders of the synagogue were not as perceptive. They did not understand the sabbath as a day in which God gives rest to his people and reprimanded Jesus and the crowd for 'working' on the sabbath. Jesus pointed out their willingness to unbind their animals on the sabbath so that they might drink and then said, 'Should not this woman, a daughter of Abraham, whom Satan has kept bound for eighteen long years, be set free on the Sabbath day from what bound her?' (13:16). The title 'son of Abraham' was one of great pride for Jewish people, but very seldom was a woman called a daughter of Abraham. In John 8:31–47 Jesus denied the claim to Abraham as father to unbelieving Jews. They, he said, were children of their father, the devil. Here he frees a woman, whose faith makes her a child of Abraham, from bondage imposed by Satan. As we have seen before, Jesus measured people by faith, not by sex.

2. Women in the parables

We have noted Jesus' attitude toward women, and his willingness to use them as examples of faith and love as he encountered them in life situations. The parables and teaching material of Jesus further illustrate his acceptance of them as a valuable part of humanity.

In the parables, as elsewhere, he does not make a point of announcing his break with rabbinic customs; he simply accepts women as whole and worth-while persons. The parables portray women in natural activities which illustrate various points which Jesus wished to make. Thus, a woman kneading yeast into flour illustrates the hidden but pervasive work of the kingdom (Mt. 13:33). A woman looking for a lost coin (from her dowry?) illustrates the concern of God for lost sinners (Lk. 15:8–10). Prepared and unprepared bridesmaids are examples of readiness for the Lord's return (Mt. 25:1–13). A persistent woman confronting a lazy judge teaches about the need for faithful prayer and not losing heart (Lk. 18:1–8). And a poor widow who gives the little that she has shows that devotion is not measured by the magnitude of our gifts but the commitment of our hearts (Mk. 12:38–44).

3. Women and learning

The examples which we have seen thus far are drawn from situations which did not necessarily involve formal teaching. Other passages show Jesus' attitude toward women receiving such instruction. In Luke 10:38–42 we are given a glimpse of Jesus as he teaches his disciples in the home of Lazarus and his sisters. We have seen the view of Rabbi Eliezer, who would burn the Torah before instructing women in its truths.[3] Note the contrast of Jesus' view:

a woman named Martha opened her home to him [Jesus]. She had a sister called Mary, who sat at the Lord's feet listening to

---

[3] Cf. chapter 3, pp. 72f.

what he said. But Martha was distracted by all the preparations that had to be made. She came to him and asked, 'Lord, don't you care that my sister has left me to do the work by myself? Tell her to help me!' 'Martha, Martha,' the Lord answered, 'you are worried and upset about many things, but only one thing is needed. Mary has chosen what is better, and it will not be taken away from her.'

In Jesus' opinion, Mary had made the right choice in listening to him. Other things could wait; she should learn from the Lord while he was there. Jesus was clearly not of the rabbis' opinion that women should hear but could not learn or that their only wisdom was with the spindle.[4]

We find a similar respect and concern for women and their knowledge in other passages. In John 11:1–44, for instance, we find Jesus carefully extending the faith of the two sisters, Mary and Martha, in connection with the death of Lazarus. Martha, who was too busy to listen, is carefully brought by the Lord to a confession of Jesus as Messiah and as the source of resurrection from the dead (verses 20–27). Her growth is his goal, even in the midst of her tears of mourning for her brother. Mary, who had listened at Jesus' feet, is given no instruction but only asked where the body was laid (verse 34). Jesus' handling of the two women shows a sensitivity to their individual needs and reveals a conviction that women's needs matter.

The passages which we have looked at thus far show clearly the basic attitude of Jesus toward women. He did not share the rabbinic attitude of Rabbi Eliezer, nor even the prejudices of the scribes of his day. His message was for sinful people of all sorts. Those who responded and did the will of his father, men and women alike, became his 'family'. In his ministry he considered women important hearers of his word.

4. Women participating in the ministry of Jesus

Our study of Judaism at the time of Christ showed that the rabbis considered that a woman's part in religion was restricted to personal piety and periodic attendance at worship. The rabbis, generally speaking, did not consider it appropriate that women should be taught about the law. Nor did they consider women capable of

[4] Cf. chapter 3, p. 63.

learning about it. The Old Testament does not discuss women as students of the law, but does presume that they will attend religious assemblies and be taught by the Levites. We saw that the rabbis were especially concerned for temptations to immorality which might result from personal contact between the sexes and therefore legislated to prevent even verbal communication as far as possible.

The ministry of Jesus sets aside such rabbinic views and practices at many points. Jesus, as we have seen, considered his teaching to be for women as well as men and pointedly sought to teach women. Further, he ignored customary separations in situations in which his ministry would be hampered by them. With the possible exception of Mary and Martha, all of the women whom we have discussed thus far have been in casual or occasional contact with Jesus. Were there women who were not only recipients of Jesus' ministry but also participated in it? We have good evidence of men (the twelve disciples) who shared in it; are there women?

Luke's gospel has frequently been noted as being particularly concerned with women. The observation is a good one. One of the pieces of information unique to the Lucan narrative is the description of Jesus' travelling companions, found at the beginning of the eighth chapter:

> After this, Jesus travelled about from one town and village to another, proclaiming the good news of the kingdom of God. The Twelve were with him, and also some women who had been cured of evil spirits and diseases: Mary (called Magdalene) from whom seven demons had come out; Joanna the wife of Chuza, the manager of Herod's household; Susanna; and many others. These women were helping to support them out of their own means (Lk. 8:1–3).

From these brief remarks of Luke we gain a tantalizing insight into the entourage which followed Christ. Luke is not relating information about the crowd which gathered to hear Jesus, nor is he simply listing persons who encountered him. This appears to be a part of his close circle. Elsewhere, we learn of persons who follow Jesus and turn away after hearing hard sayings (Jn. 6:66) and of a group of seventy who were sent out two by two on a mission (Lk. 10:1–20), but those followers are never named. Here we have a group of women who are linked with the twelve disciples as Jesus' companions.

The presence of these women is a matter which should not be overlooked, nor must it be overplayed. It has occasionally been suggested that these women served as concubines or as female apostles. Such speculation must be recognized as such. Luke's text does not leave the role of these women in doubt. They were women who had benefited from the ministry of Jesus and who contributed to the support of that ministry. It is absurd to pretend that the text offers any warrant for seeing them as concubines; and it stretches the text unwarrantably to suggest that they should be considered female apostles. The text itself sets them parallel to the twelve as travelling companions rather than as apostles. There is no suggestion anywhere else that Jesus employed women in such a role. The only positive information which we have from Luke about their contribution to the ministry has to do with financial affairs. We will learn more when we look at Mark's comments.

The presence of these women must have been a matter of considerable comment as Jesus travelled. It was not uncommon that a rabbi should have a band of followers; it was most unusual that the followers should include women. There was no doubt speculation about their role and perhaps misunderstanding. This is especially likely in the light of rabbinic sensitivity to contact between the sexes. Luke does not tell us whether the women usually travelled with the Lord. It would be interesting to know.

The accounts of the crucifixion and resurrection give us more information about these women. Matthew and Mark comment on the presence of Mary Magdalene and Mary the mother of James the younger and Joseph, standing at a distance watching the crucifixion. Also mentioned are Salome and the mother of the sons of Zebedee (unless they are the same person) (Mt. 27:55–56; Mk. 15:40). Mark, in his description of the women, adds, 'In Galilee these women had followed him [Jesus] and cared for his needs. Many other women who had come up with him to Jerusalem were also there' (Mk. 15:41). This tells us more about their active role in Jesus' ministry. In many ways it parallels the role of the disciples, who listened and ministered to Jesus' needs. Apparently the women were especially active when Jesus ministered in the North, near their homes. They had come down for Passover with the party which accompanied Jesus.

We learn of their continuing care in the account of the removal of Jesus' body after the crucifixion. Mary Magdalene and Mary the mother of Joseph watched him being placed in the tomb and returned after the sabbath to anoint his body, thereby becoming the first witnesses to the resurrection (Mt. 27:61; 28:1–7; Mk. 15:40 – 16:7). Neither the women nor the disciples were really ready for the resurrection. The women had to be convinced by the angel. John's account notes that Jesus appeared to Mary directly (Jn. 20:10–18). Recent authors have called attention to the ironic fact that Jewish law prohibits women from acting as witnesses and yet it was women who were made the first witnesses to the resurrection. Their witness impressed the disciples very little. Luke reports that the disciples 'did not believe the women, because their words seemed to them like nonsense' (Lk. 24:11).

These same women, who were present on the travels of Jesus and at his death, were also present among the disciples in the period between then and Pentecost and, as we shall see when we look at the apostolic church, were presumably among those upon whom the Holy Spirit came at Pentecost (Acts 1:12–14; 2:1–4, 14–47).

From these relatively few comments about the presence of women who participated in the ministry of Jesus, we can draw certain conclusions. The most obvious is that Jesus was accompanied in his travels by women as well as by men. The inner circle of his companions seems to have been fairly stable and included the women whom Luke and Mark identify as having travelled with him. From Mark we learned that they took care of him, from Luke that those with money evidently contributed to the financial support of his work.

There is no evidence that these women had any 'official' functions as 'apostles' [persons sent out] or alongside the twelve who would *later* become apostles. It should be noted, however, that Jesus did not delegate very much authority to followers of either sex. We read of the twelve receiving special authority and once of a group of seventy being temporarily commissioned. Otherwise we hear nothing of delegated authority. It is therefore impossible to draw conclusions from the activities of these women which offer insight into the role of women in authoritative roles in the church. What is clear, however, is the accepted presence of this group of women within the close circle of those who travelled with and presumably learned regularly from Jesus. Their presence is a radical break with Jewish practice. It is also a fitting conclusion to this examination of the role of women in the ministry of Jesus. In our study we have found that Jesus stands independent of his culture in his relation to women. Apart from the disciples, whom he called for a special purpose, Jesus seems to have made no distinctions between classes of persons in his bringing of the good news of the arrival of the kingdom. Women stand alongside men in the universal invitation to enter the kingdom through Christ: 'whoever does the will of my Father in heaven is my brother and sister and mother' (Mt. 12:50). It is this, of course, which is echoed by Paul in his great proclamation of who may enter the church:

> There is neither Jew nor Greek, slave nor free, male nor female, for you are all one in Christ Jesus. If you belong to Christ, then you are Abraham's seed, and heirs according to the promise (Gal. 3:28–29).

C. WOMEN IN THE TEACHING OF JESUS

Contemporary Christians approach the question of the 'role of women' with a particular set of issues in view. We are generally concerned about authority relationships, and about those within the home and the church in particular. The teaching of Jesus is singularly unhelpful in these areas. He does not discuss marital authority; nor does he lay out a hierarchy for the church. It remained for the apostles to discuss these matters within the context of the emerging church, after the resurrection and ascension of its Lord. The teaching of Jesus is not, however, irrelevant to the topic. His words, as we shall see, form an indispensable foundation to the apostolic teaching and set out a framework within which the apostles worked. The gospel narratives inform us of the Lord's teaching about the man-woman relationship in four crucial areas: marriage, divorce, celibacy and lust. In each of them Jesus stands in marked contrast to the thought of his day.

1. Jesus' attitude toward marriage

Christian marriage ceremonies have traditionally stressed that Jesus showed his blessing of marriage by his attendance at a wedding at Cana in Galilee (Jn. 2:1–10). In this the ceremony is no doubt correct. Some Christians, however, have wondered whether Jesus really would have commended marriage. Two texts in particular have caused this problem (which bothers the conscience of some). Luke 20:27–38 appears to contrast 'sons of this age', who marry and give in marriage, with 'sons of the resurrection', who do not. Matthew 19:11–12 indicates that some will make themselves eunuchs for the sake of the kingdom, while others will be unable to accept such a teaching. Do these texts show that Jesus was really against marriage?

Luke 20:27–38 records an exchange between Jesus and a group of Sadducees concerning the resurrection of the dead (Mt. 22:23–33 and Mk. 12:18–27 are parallel). The Sadducees sought to show the idea of a resurrection to be absurd by presenting the hypothetical case of a woman who was seven times widowed. 'Whose wife', they asked, 'will she be at the resurrection?' Luke records Jesus' answer as follows:

> The people of this age marry and are given in marriage. But those who are considered worthy of taking part in that age and in the resurrection from the dead will neither marry nor be given in marriage, and they can no longer die; for they are like the angels. They are God's children, since they are children of the resurrection (Lk. 20:30–36).

In this text Jesus is not presenting the 'sons of this age' as a group which is exclusive of the 'children of the resurrection'. The point under debate was not the appropriateness of marriage in the present, but the status of such marriages in the resurrection. Jesus' point is therefore that while those who are presently alive (sons of this age) do participate in marriage, the same persons, in the resurrection, will no longer do so. The parallel passages in Matthew and Mark make this clear. They read, 'At the resurrection people will neither marry nor be given in marriage; they will be like the angels' (Mt. 22:30). Jesus presumes that marriage is appropriate in the present, but that it will cease in the resurrection.

Jesus' contrast of the present with the future has further significance for our study than putting to rest tender consciences. It reveals something of Jesus' eschatology, especially when added to other passages which we have studied. Jesus did not consider the kingdom to have come in its final form in his own ministry. It was he who announced that the kingdom had drawn near (Mt. 4:17), and had indeed come upon his hearers in his word (Mt. 12:28). According to him, people were actually entering the kingdom during his life (Jn. 3:8; Mt. 11:11–13). We learned from the parables that Jesus saw the great judgment as yet future. The Jews anticipated that it would come with the arrival of the kingdom. Obviously, Jesus' teaching required a reshuffling of ideas about the kingdom, but that was not all. Nicodemus was taught that only those born anew, of the Spirit, could perceive the kingdom (Jn. 3:3). Those who were not born anew, Jesus said, perceived the effect of the Spirit's work in the lives of those who were, but could not tell the source of that effect any more than they could tell the source of the wind which rustles the trees (Jn. 3:7–8). Some of the life changes of which Jesus spoke are laid out in the sermon on the mount and the beatitudes (Mt. 5–7). When we take these teachings about a changed manner of life and lay them alongside the teachings about a yet-future judgment and about a change in marriage relationships at the resurrection, we begin to see the framework of Jesus' teaching about the kingdom. Its present manifestation is not to be seen in the judgment or in the reshaping of the physical creation. Those remain in the future (Mt. 24–25; Rom. 8). The kingdom manifests itself in the present in the changed lives of its members. We gain further insight into the meaning of the present form of the kingdom for the relation of man and woman from Mt. 19:3–12, a crucial passage for any study of Jesus' view of these matters.

2. Marriage, divorce and celibacy: with God all things are possible

a. Matthew 19:3–12 in context

Matthew 19:3–12 presents an encounter between Jesus and some Pharisees over the issue of divorce. The passage has been the centre of much theological debate and has frequently been considered apart from its context. Such a procedure is a mistake. The chapter as a whole discusses the single-minded dedication called for by the kingdom. This is discussed by means of three episodes. The first is the controversy with the Pharisees over divorce. Jesus' stringent teaching in this area astonishes even his disciples (verses 3–12). The second incident employs the faith of children to illustrate the single- (not simple-) minded trust of faith (verses 13–15). The third incident reveals that a rich young ruler is prepared to render obedience to the ten commandments, but is not utterly committed to the kingdom (verses 16–26). The common thread of the sections is total devotion to the kingdom. Verses 25–30 conclude both the episode with ruler and the chapter. In them the disciples are told that the sort of service called for by the kingdom is possible only through God and that those who serve will not be without reward. The chapter must, then, be considered as a whole and may be seen as teaching about the implications of the kingdom's arrival for these areas in the lives of Jesus' followers. Matthew's account of the first episode is as follows:

> Some Pharisees came to him to test him. They asked, 'Is it lawful for a man to divorce his wife for any and every reason?' 'Haven't you read,' he replied, 'that at the beginning the Creator *"made them male and female"*, and said, *"For this reason a man will leave his father and mother and be united to his wife, and the two will become one flesh"*? So they are no longer two, but one. Therefore what God has joined together, let man not separate.' 'Why then,' they asked, 'did Moses command that a man give his wife a certificate of divorce and send her away?' Jesus replied, 'Moses permitted you to divorce your wives because your hearts were hard. But it was not this way from the beginning. I tell you that anyone who divorces his wife, except for marital unfaithfulness, and marries another woman commits adultery.' The disciples said to him, 'If this is the situation between a husband and wife, it is better not to marry.' Jesus replied, 'Not everyone can accept this teaching, but only those to whom it has been given. For some are eunuchs because they were born that way; others were made that way by men; and other have made themselves eunuchs (renounced marriage) because of the kingdom of heaven. The one who can accept this should accept it' (Mt. 19:3–12).

b. The historical context

Two observations setting Matthew 19 in historical perspective are in order before pursuing its content. The first has to do with then-current events as reflected in the Marcan parallel to Matthew 19, which includes a further comment about divorce. Mark reports, 'Anyone who divorces his wife and marries another woman commits adultery against her. And if she puts away her husband and marries another man, she commits adultery' (Mk. 10:11–12).[5] It

---

[5] Three textual variants of verse 12 are found in the Greek text. They do not seriously affect our conclusions at this point. We have adopted the reading of the Western and Caesarean text, indicating that a woman 'put away her husband'. For a clear discussion and references

was not Jewish custom for women to divorce men. Herodias, the wife of Herod Antipas, had written a letter of separation from her previous husband and left him for Antipas. John the Baptist denounced the new marriage as adulterous. The Pharisees' question and Jesus' reply may both be consciously addressed to that situation as well as to the matter at hand. Jesus boldly supports John and condemns Herodias and Antipas, exactly the sort of response which the Pharisees wanted as it could be used to arouse the authorities against him. He goes on, however, to a deeper level, discussing divorce from a perspective which never entered the Pharisaic debates.

A second historical observation relates to Jesus' assertion that either the man or the woman may commit adultery against the other. As we have seen in the preceding chapter, Jewish law recognized adultery as an offence against a husband which could be committed only by or with a married woman. Jesus says that a man who divorces his wife and marries another commits adultery against his wife (Mt. 19:9). This moves beyond the formal legal categories to the moral issue (a procedure which was followed in the sermon on the mount, Mt. 5). This step is radical in its historical context, placing husband and wife on the same level, but, as we shall see below, springs naturally from Jesus' view of marriage and divorce.

c. The debate about divorce

The Pharisees sought to force Jesus to enter a long-standing debate within Jewish circles. All parties agreed that divorce was legitimate; the two basic schools of Pharisaic thought, those of Shammai and Hillel, were divided as to the meaning of Moses' teaching that a man should give his wife a bill of divorce if 'she becomes displeasing in his eyes because he finds "something indecent" about her' (Dt. 24:1). The school of Rabbi Hillel, generally more tolerant, held that a man might divorce his wife if she spoiled his food.[6] Some later rabbis went so far as to permit divorce if a man found a woman whom he preferred more.[7]

The school of Shammai took a much stricter stand. They under-

---

to the literature cf. W. Lane, *The Gospel According to Mark* (hereafter, *Mark*) (New International Commentary, Grand Rapids, 1974), p. 352.

[6] bGitt. 90a; Siphre Dt. 24:1; mGitt. 9.10; jGitt. 9; jSot. 1.1.

[7] Rabbi Akiba, c. AD 135, is most commonly cited; cf. bGitt. 90a.

stood Moses to permit divorce only for a 'shameful thing' or 'indecency' (Hebrew *'rwh dbr*). Scholars have debated the precise meaning of Moses' phrase and Shammai's use of it. Because Jesus' answer must be judged in the context of the Hillel-Shammai debate, we will consider the meaning of Deuteronomy 24:1 in the Old Testament and in rabbinic thought.[8]

i. What did Deuteronomy 24:1 mean in its Old Testament context?
The exact meaning of 'an indecent thing' in the Mosaic text cannot be defined. Certain boundary lines can, however, be discerned. The term 'indecency' (*'rwh*) has as its root an idea of nakedness or bareness and comes, in biblical language, to include a variety of things. The verbal form is used to describe having sexual relations with a person; thus 'to uncover the nakedness' of a person is to have sexual relations with that person (Lv. 18:6; 20:18–19). The same expression can describe an action which puts a person to public shame by exposing him or her in a naked state. In such cases it means 'shamefully expose' (La. 1:8). Slightly more figurative uses of the verb describe 'laying bare' or 'exposing' foundations by destroying the buildings above them (Ps. 137:7). The adjectival form of the word picks up the idea of shamefulness or indecency.

The expression of Deuteronomy 24:1, 'an indecent thing' (*'rwh dbr*), occurs at only one other place in the Scriptures, Deuteronomy 23:9–14. This passage discusses uncleanness in the camp. It directs that men who have had nocturnal emissions and are therefore unclean should stay outside the camp until sundown and that the Israelites cover their own excrement. The reason for these requirements is given in verse 14: 'For the LORD your God moves about in your camp to protect you. . . . Your camp must be holy, so that he will not see among you "anything indecent" and turn away from you.' It is not clear whether the unclean man is included as something indecent or whether the term is restricted to unburied excrement. In either case we have here a meaning of 'indecent

---

[8] For the rabbinic discussion, *cf.* mGitt 9.10; bGitt. 90a; jSot. 1.1. For discussions of the Jewish materials, *cf.* Strack-Billerbeck, *Kommentar zum Neuen Testament aus Talmud und Midrasch* (Munich, 1923–1961), 1, pp. 312–320, esp. pp. 312–315 and J. Bonsirven, *Le divorce dans le Nouveau Testament* (Tournai, 1948), pp. 7–24. W. Lane's treatment of the Marcan parallel passage is particularly clear (*Mark*, pp. 351–358). R. H. Charles' work, *The Teaching of the New Testament on Divorce* (London, 1921) is a useful older work. J. Murray's volume on *Divorce* (Philadelphia, 1961) provides lengthy discussions of the relevant biblical texts and of the implications of Jesus' words for contemporary practice.

thing' which refers to shameful exposure of something without connotations of sexual immorality.

As we approach Deuteronomy 24:1, we have a range of meaning for 'indecent thing' which includes shameful acts, shameful exposure and illegitimate sexual relations. We may dismiss the latter from consideration because a married woman who was found guilty of illicit sexual relations was an adulteress and was not divorced but rather stoned (Lv. 20:10). This leaves us with a meaning for the expression which indicates a shameful deed of some undefined sort. The ambiguity which we face also faced the rabbis and paved the way for their debates.

It is in order to ask why the text of Deuteronomy is so vague about this crucial issue of divorce. A look at the context helps. The goal of the passage is *not* to define the grounds for divorce. Deuteronomy 24:1–4 is a prohibition of a man marrying for a second time a woman whom he has divorced and who has married another since. Verse 1 does not focus upon the grounds for the divorce as such, but rather discusses the first divorce only to set the stage for the following discussion. The second husband is said to divorce her simply because he 'dislikes' (or 'hates', *sn*) her (verse 3). The point of the recital is the fourth verse, which prohibits her returning to the first husband. The vagueness about 'valid' grounds for divorce stems from the incidental function of both the 'indecent thing' of verse 1 and the 'hatred' or 'dislike' of verse 4.

ii. How did the rabbis interpret Deuteronomy 24?

The rabbis were concerned to regulate the life of the Jewish community. Divorce is an event of great importance in the life of any individual or society. This was especially the case in Jewish society which highly valued the family. It thus became important to spell out what constituted sufficient grounds for divorce. The Old Testament does more to regulate the financial consquences of divorce than to spell out conditions on which it may be granted. Deuteronomy 24 is the primary text concerning 'grounds' for divorce and therefore was subjected to searching exposition. The rabbis *had* to define its meaning. The two dominant Jewish interpretations were formulated in the century before Christ by Rabbis Hillel and Shammai.

The *school of Hillel* took as its starting-point the relative freedom of the man. The text of Deuteronomy 24 envisages a situation in which the wife 'no longer finds favour in his sight' or 'becomes displeasing to him'. The second divorce comes merely because the husband 'hates' or 'dislikes' her. The Hillelites therefore held that anything which led to such a situation was sufficient grounds for divorce. They ultimately accepted Deuteronomy 24:1 as authorizing divorce either for a shameful thing or for any 'thing' which led to the husband's displeasure.

The *school of Shammai*, on the other hand, stood by a closer exegesis of the text and insisted that it allowed divorce only for 'a shameful thing' or 'an indecency'. It is difficult to tell what Shammai meant by the phrase. Many scholars have translated it as 'unchastity'. By 'unchastity' some scholars meant 'illicit sexual relations'; others meant 'unbecoming behaviour'. The Talmudic rabbis seem to have a similar uncertainty. In some texts 'an indecency' is left to stand in its ambiguity. Elsewhere the rabbis add further explanations such as spinning in the street, going out 'uncovered', or not wearing enough clothes (jSot. 1.1). These actions were regarded as flagrant violations of marital propriety and as potentially seductive. The fact that other punishments were prescribed by the Old Testament for illicit intercourse (execution) and for suspicion of adultery (bitter-water rite) makes it unlikely that by 'indecency' Shammai meant only proven adultery or even suspicion of it. *Had he meant such acts, we would expect other texts than Deuteronomy 24:1 to enter the discussion.* It is most likely that he meant other actions which would be gross offences against marital propriety, or perhaps those which suggested the possibility of sexual impropriety.

If this was Shammai's view, we can understand the specific examples added by the Talmudic rabbis. The lists of 'indecent acts' which they offered were intended to define the boundaries of 'indecency' in terms of their own day. Their lists are thus in keeping with the spirit of Shammai's regulation, even though the specific kinds of behaviour listed might not be the ones which he had in view.

iii. How did Jesus interpret Deuteronomy 24?

The Pharisees who asked Jesus about divorce came to 'test' or 'tempt' him (Mt. 19:3). The testing probably related to the situation of Herodias rather than simply to the rabbinic debate. As we have noted, Jesus' answer to them does indeed inform them about Herodias, but it also carries the debate to an altogether new level.

Both sides of the rabbinic debate agreed that Deuteronomy 24:1 authorized divorce. They differed only as to which situations provided grounds. Jesus' answer removes the discussion from the level of the destruction of marriage to that of its creational design. Genesis 2, in Jesus' opinion, shows the Creator's intent that marriage should produce a new and indivisible unity, 'one flesh'. The Genesis pattern, he says, is the norm and man should not separate what God has joined (Mt. 19:6). His opponents sought to meet his argument by citing Deuteronomy 24, which they supposed to show that the 'one flesh' of marriage was divisible for various reasons. 'Why then,' they asked, 'did Moses command that a man give his wife a certificate of divorce. . .?' (verse 7). Jesus responded by interpreting Moses in a fashion which overturned *both* sides of the rabbinic debate: Moses did not command divorce, he permitted it because of the hardness of your hearts (verse 8). This carries the debate to a yet deeper level, for it implies that the act of divorce is not only against the creational design, but an act of a hard-hearted, rebellious person: sin. The next verse confirms this, 'I tell you that anyone who divorces his wife, except for marital unfaithfulness (*porneia*), and marries another woman commits adultery' (verse 9). Thus, whereas the Pharisees had taken Moses' concession of divorce as God's design, Jesus took it as a regulatory measure to deal with the result of sin.[9]

Our examination of the actual text of Deuteronomy 24:1–4 has shown that Jesus is correct in holding that Moses did not command divorce or lay down conditions under which it was legitimate. Moses suffered divorce and regulated remarriage. The rabbinical debate over legitimate grounds was, in fact, entirely beside the point. Their difficulty in ascertaining the meaning of 'indecency' resulted from an effort to make the text speak where it was not intended to. Jesus' view relieves the Christian of the interpretative labours of the rabbis. It does not, however, leave us with no difficulties.

iv. What grounds did Jesus allow for divorce?
Matthew twice quotes Jesus as indicating that divorce is valid only for 'marital unfaithfulness' (*porneia*, 5:32; 19:9), Much ink has been spilled over the meaning of Jesus' exception and the relation of

[9] In our later discussion of Paul's teaching, we will have occasion to note that Jesus' attitude toward the Mosaic regulation of divorce is paralleled by that of his apostle toward slavery. In both cases an aberration from the creational design is regulated without being endorsed.

Matthew's account in chapter 19 to the parallel accounts in Mark and Luke, which do not include the exceptive clause.[10] It would be inappropriate to review the entire debate at this point, but it is important to give some attention to the meaning of *porneia* and to the relation of Matthew to Mark and Luke.

According to the lexicon, *porneia* means 'prostitution', 'unchastity', 'fornication', or other kinds of unlawful intercourse. Derivative applications are to be found in which the term may mean other kinds of unfaithfulness, metaphorically discussed as sexual unfaithfulness. For Jews, the term brought to mind religious unfaithfulness, in particular idolatry. The term is aptly rendered 'marital unfaithfulness' when applied to married persons. Recent studies have found that it was also used to refer to marriage within forbidden degrees of blood relationship (Lv. 18).[11] Which of these meanings is appropriate to 'except for *porneia*' in Matthew 5:32 and 19:9?

We are helped by consideration of the response of the disciples and by the historical situation at the time of Christ. The disciples were shocked at the strictness of Jesus' view. It seemed radical enough that they concluded 'If this is the situation between a man and his wife, it is better not to marry' (Mt. 19:10). An adequate explanation of 'marital unfaithfulness' must account for the disciples' surprise.

Roman rule had created a historical situation in which the Jews no longer had the right to execute criminals. The Sanhedrin would try prisoners by Jewish law and could ask the Roman procurator to authorize a death sentence, but this was practical only in the most extreme situations (*e.g.* the execution of Jesus). Adultery was far too common a crime for the Sanhedrin to hear each case and refer it to the procurator. Jewish practice therefore substituted divorce for execution. In Talmudic times an adulterous woman was denied the right to remarry, being as though dead (executed). The schools of Hillel and Shammai did not, therefore, debate whether divorce might be the result of conviction of adultery. A similar situation obtained with respect to marriage within forbidden degrees of kinship. In this case, too, it was expected, and

[10] The works cited in footnote 8, p. 98 provide the reader with an introduction to further literature on the subject. Two other valuable resources are P. Bonnard, *L'Evangile selon Saint Matthieu* (Neuchatel, 1970) and H. Baltensweiler's standard work, 'Die Ehebruchsklauseln bei Matthaus zu Matth. 5: 32; 19:9', in *Theologisches Zeitschrift*, 15 (1959), pp. 340–356.

[11] H. Baltensweiler, 'Die Ehebruchsklauseln.'

indeed required that the marriage be severed. The question which was put to Jesus about divorce 'for any and every reason' probably had in view only the rabbinic debate and assumed that he would respond either by affirming Hillel's view, 'for any and every reason', or by affirming Shammai's, restricting it to 'indecent things', *i.e.* gross offences against marital obligation (perhaps even to those which suggest the possibility of sexual impropriety). If we take *porneia* at its common face value, as illicit intercourse, Jesus' response rejects both rabbinic views! In essence he says, 'Within the framework of your debate, *all* of the reasons for divorce are wrong. Whoever divorces his wife on the ground 'permitted' in Deuteronomy 24:1–4 commits adultery when he remarries. Only *porneia* is a valid reason.'

It is difficult to know whether *porneia* should be restricted in meaning to include only forbidden degrees of relation or whether the broader sense of marital unfaithfulness should be adopted. The broader meaning has the distinct advantage of being the more natural and common meaning of the word.[12] In the absence of other considerations it would be the assumed meaning. In the absence of such considerations, we will adopt the broader, more natural meaning.

We can now see why the disciples were so surprised at Jesus' teaching. He was far stricter than the rabbis. He disallowed divorce for all of the reasons which had been adduced in connection with Deuteronomy 24:1 and permitted it only on grounds which were unknown in the Old Testament. He permitted it only for sexual violations of the marriage bond, violations which, under the Old Testament, would have meant a death sentence. According to Jesus only illicit sexual relations (*porneia*: adultery, homosexuality, bestiality) provide reason to terminate a marriage.[13]

v. Why don't Mark and Luke include 'except for porneia'?
The accounts of Mark and Luke provide no exception for divorce on the grounds of unfaithfulness (*porneia*) and have often, on that

---

[12] Our discussion does not follow those of many modern exegetes who tend to prefer either the narrower meaning or to find the exceptive clause a Matthean addition which blunts Jesus' intention by adopting Shammai's view. But, had Matthew wanted to uphold Shammai's view, he would have chosen *aschēmon pragma* (shameful thing).

[13] J. Murray's discussion of the major issues involved here is very useful and lucid (*Divorce*, pp. 3–54). The church has often debated the right of remarriage for a person who legitimately procures a divorce. Murray argues convincingly that it is presumed (pp. 33–43). I would add to his discussion the observation that, under Old Testament law, each of the offences included under *porneia* presumed the right of remarriage.

account, been held to represent the 'true' and uncompromising stance of Jesus. Such a view, setting Matthew against the other synoptists, is quite unnecessary. The agreement of the three should be carefully noted. Jesus' teaching, as we have seen, does away *entirely* with the Mosaic divorce provision (Dt. 24:1). *All three synoptists* faithfully report this fact. Matthew and Mark provide an explanation of his reasoning (Luke does not). They concur in showing the 'one flesh' concept of Genesis 2 to be at the heart of Jesus' view of marriage. How then is Matthew's exception to be explained?

Students of the gospels have noted that Matthew shows a particular concern to speak to Jewish readers, while Mark and Luke addressed themselves to Gentiles. Matthew's record of Jesus' discussion includes a piece of information which is of particular importance to Jewish readers. Although Mosaic divorce provisions were dismissed, marital unfaithfulness still constituted a rupture of the 'one flesh' relation; in the absence of stoning, the termination of the relationship might appropriately be effected by divorce. This information is suited to Jesus' original audience and to Matthew's. It is of less importance to the Gentiles to whom Mark and Luke wrote. To them only Jesus' main point was advanced: divorce is not an 'option'. We conclude that the synoptists are not to be set against one another. They have faithfully recorded the teaching of Jesus, but in differing detail. However much we may wish Mark and Luke had added the exceptive clause (to satisfy our desire for 'harmony'), its omission does not contradict Matthew's inclusion of it.[14]

vi. Conclusions

Our lengthy reflection on the content of Jesus' reply to the Pharisees' question concerning grounds for divorce has led us to the conclusion that he rejected both the view of Hillel and that of Shammai and taught that the Mosaic 'permission' was to be seen as incidental to the regulation of remarriage and that divorce was a violation of the divine design. Only sexual infidelity severs a marriage relation. The disciples correctly perceived that Jesus made no provision for the sort of divorce commended by ben Sirach in Ecclesiasticus 25:26: 'If she will not do as you tell her, get rid of her!' If righteousness demanded a permanent commitment

---

[14] Assumptions concerning Marcan priority do not affect this conclusion.

of the sort called for by Jesus, they concluded, it would be better not to marry. We shall now turn our attention to Jesus' response to their conclusion: 'Not everyone can accept this teaching, but only those to whom it has been given' (Mt. 19:11).

d. Who will receive Jesus' teaching?

To which 'teaching' does Jesus refer? Scholars have divided for various reasons, some preferring verse 9, others verse 10 or verse 12. The context favours Jesus' words about divorce in verse 9 as the referent as it continues the discussion about divorce to which the disciples had alluded. Verse 10, the disciples' suggestion that it is better not to marry, is unlikely to be the referent as Jesus was not advocating celibacy, but rather faithful marriage. As we shall see below, the disciples had correctly seen the difficulty of acting righteously, but misunderstood how it was to be achieved. New strength rather than no marriage was the answer. Verse 11 can be applied to the saying about celibacy in verse 12, but doing so breaks the flow of the conversation and makes the end of verse 12 redundant. We shall therefore consider verse 11 to refer to Jesus' teaching on divorce in verse 9. He was saying, 'Not everyone will receive my teaching about divorce. Only those to whom it is given will do so.'

Jesus knew that his teaching on divorce would not and indeed could not be received by many but would be received by others. What divided the two groups? Both the context and content of Jesus' statement point to the answer. Moses addressed the hard-hearted, allowing their divorces. We may presume that the hard-hearted will still not seek God's creational design for marriage and will not receive Jesus' teaching.

Jesus' remark is not exhausted, however, by this contextual observation about who will not receive his teaching. He not only said that not all would receive his teaching; he said that only 'those to whom it is given' would do so. This expression is significant. According to Matthew, 'it is given' to some and not to others to receive the kingdom message.[15] Thus, when Jesus announced the kingdom in parables he said, 'He who has ears to hear, let him hear' (Mt. 13:9,43). To the disciples 'it [was] given to know the secrets of the kingdom of heaven' (Mt. 13:11). As a result, while

---

[15] Matthew knows of other things 'given' by divine choice, cf. Mt. 6:11; 7:7,11; 9:8; 10:19; 12:39; 13:12; 16:4; 20:23; 21:43; 25:29; 28:18.

others' hearts were 'dull' or calloused, the disciples were 'blessed'; their eyes saw and their ears heard (Mt. 13:15–16). Those who receive Jesus' teaching are those 'to whom it is given', those who receive the message of the kingdom, the sons of God (Lk. 20:36; *cf.* Mt. 22:30) or those 'born again' by the Spirit (Jn. 3:3,5–8). Only those with such a gift from God will be able to receive Jesus' teaching about the nature of marriage; without God, it is impossible (*cf.* Mt. 19:26). Others will remain hard-hearted. Jesus' saying is for believers.

e. Should believers become eunuchs for the sake of the kingdom?
The disciples concluded that the permanent marriage demanded by Jesus forced those who sought the kingdom's righteousness to remain single. They were correct in the conclusion that some would be 'eunuchs' for the sake of the kingdom, but wrong as to the motive. Jesus takes them beyond their negative motivation, teaching in verse 12 that, while some are eunuchs by birth or by the actions of men, others are single (make themselves eunuchs) for the sake of the kingdom. Not fear of having to cope with the problems of marriage, nor of its permanence, but devotion to the kingdom will lead some persons to this conclusion.

It should be noted that this conclusion is indeed radical within Judaism of Christ's day. The very term 'eunuch' was deeply pejorative. Such persons were barred from Jewish worship. Jesus himself no doubt drew more than one derogatory comment by his single status and was himself the prime example of a eunuch for the sake of the kingdom.

It is worth noting that the teaching about becoming eunuchs for the sake of the kingdom is not as extensively applied as that about divorce. Verse 11 contrasts the hard-hearted and 'those to whom it is given' with respect to their accepting Jesus' view of the true nature of marriage and divorce. All his followers were expected to view marriage as permanent. The teaching of verse 12 makes a different contrast. 'Some' of those who follow him will make themselves eunuchs for the sake of the kingdom; those who can accept this teaching should. Not all Jesus' followers were expected to be eunuchs; indeed, many were already married.

f. He asks the impossible!

Our look at Jesus' exchange with the Pharisees over the Mosaic divorce law has shown that he called his disciples to two very different courses of action, both radically opposed to those of the culture surrounding them. The two courses advocated by Jesus have in common a total commitment to God's way as right and good, a commitment which calls for self-denial. It is important not to miss the fact that devotion to God's way may, in Jesus' teaching, lead to either of two different courses of action. Both marriage and celibacy are appropriate. Permanent marriage is founded upon a commitment to the Creator's design. Celibacy is founded upon a commitment to the kingdom which has come and is coming. The present realization of the kingdom recognizes *two* overlapping patterns for the people of God. One is creational, the other 're-creational'. One will fade with the resurrection, when the other will be universalized (Mt. 22:30). Those who marry live out the creational design. They do not divorce except for unfaithfulness; even an appeal to the resurrection singleness is not a valid reason for divorce.[16]

The sort of devotion for which Jesus calls seems beyond the realistic to those who measure things by the state of the fallen world, as even the disciples did. Twentieth-century attitudes toward marriage and divorce are very far indeed from those of Jesus. The balance of Matthew 19, however, makes it clear that the sort of devotion for which Jesus calls is possible, but only with God's help. Verses 13-15 illustrate kingdom faith with the faith of little children. The little ones have full trust in the Lord and are not distracted by 'realism', as are adults, who measure the possible by the average or even the best of the fallen world. The children's single-minded (not simple-minded) faith is, of course, true realism. The rich young man of verses 16–22 is another who renders formal, but not whole-hearted, obedience to God. His 'realistic' concern for his wealth made him unwilling to risk all in total dedication.

The disciples were keen to perceive the totality of the kingdom's demands. Matthew surely intends their response to the rich young man's situation to apply to the debate over divorce as well: 'they were greatly astonished and asked, "Who then can be saved?" Jesus looked at them and said, "With man this is impossible, but

---

[16] This implication lies on the face of Jesus' teaching. It is drawn to the fore in 1 Cor. 7, where Paul confronts Corinthian ascetics.

with God all things are possible" ' (Mt. 19:25–26). The children accepted this; adults need to learn that 'the kingdom of heaven belongs to such as these' (verse 14). Kingdom obedience, be it with respect to marriage, divorce, celibacy or riches, is possible only with God; with men it is impossible.

3. Lust

In our discussion of rabbinic views regarding women, we noted that serious efforts were made to separate the sexes in order to avoid temptation. It is a common remark that the rabbis considered men tempted by women and by their presence and saw the removal of the temptation as the best recourse. Our study of women in the ministry of Jesus showed that he did not share the rabbinic position. Women were not cut off from his teaching or his presence. What accounts for this striking difference? We have noted that Jesus' view of women as humans for whom he had a message naturally accounts for his concern to teach them. Another element, however, must be introduced to account for his willingness to have the sexes intermingle. This element can be discerned in his teaching about lust.

As we have seen, the rabbis recognized the frailty and sinfulness of mankind and permitted divorce as a way of dealing with marriage failure. Jesus pointed instead to a gift from God which would allow men and women to live in marriage according to the Creator's design, or even as eunuchs for the sake of devotion to the kingdom (Mt. 19:11). Rabbinic thought saw the former as unrealistic and the latter as positively sinful, both from the point of view of temptation and of the obligation to reproduce (bYeb. 63a,b). Jesus viewed things from another perspective. In his teaching he stressed the arrival of the kingdom in power and that those who had entered the kingdom and had been born of the Spirit would behave in ways which would seem incomprehensible to those who did not know the work of the Spirit: 'The wind blows wherever it pleases. You hear its sound, but you cannot tell where it comes from or where it is going. So it is with everyone born of the Spirit' (Jn. 3:8; *cf*. Mt. 12:28; Jn. 3:3–7). Enabled by the Spirit, his disciples were called to a more profound commitment to God's law than the rabbis thought possible.

The difference between Jesus' profound or radical view of the law and that of the rabbis is the topic of Matthew 5–7, the sermon on the mount. In chapter 5 disciples are called to a righteousness which surpasses that of the scribes and Pharisees (Mt. 5:20). The examples offered make it clear that Jesus does not mean a more punctilious observation of the law, but a more profound commitment to its intent. He consistently criticizes their tendency to make the formal, legal requirement the limit of personal obligation. Thus not only murder, but also despite of the brethren is an offence (5:21–22); an eye for an eye limits legal retribution, but the extra mile shows true concern for another (5:38–42). Within this same pattern comes Jesus' teaching on adultery: 'You have heard that it was said, "Do not commit adultery." But I tell you that anyone who looks at a woman lustfully has already committed adultery with her in his heart' (5:27–28).[17] The central point being made is that the thoughts of a man's heart, as well as his deeds, are taken into account by God.

A very important subordinate point is to be observed as well. Jesus warns people to take account of their thought life, because it matters. He makes the assumption that they can and should curb their lustful thoughts. His approach to the subject focuses upon the thoughts of the man rather than the seductive presence of the woman.[18] In this he differs from rabbinic thought. It is not the presence of a woman, but the sinful thoughts of a man, which makes the situation dangerous. Jesus, therefore, called upon his disciples to discipline their thoughts rather than to avoid women. In this he was doing no more than to call upon them not to covet their neighbour's wives or daughters, but it entirely alters the situation of women in public gatherings. Jesus taught the relevance of obedience to the law for all persons. The ability to curb sinful thoughts is especially important to those who are to be faithful in marriage or to remain chaste in their singleness. 'Those to whom it is given' to receive Jesus' teaching need also to be given strength to obey, for 'with men it is impossible; with God all things are possible' (Mt. 19:11,26).

The Old Testament did not know the isolation of women or the fear of their seductivity which seems to have come over the rabbis.

---

[17] Jesus' mention of the eye leads him on to a discussion of the need to set anything aside for the sake of righteousness (verses 29–30). Origen, one of the great theologians of Alexandria, applied these literally and castrated himself. The occurrence of the same (hyperbolic) advice in a totally different context (Mt. 18:6–9) should warn us against Origen's deduction. These verses should be seen as related to the seriousness of the issue discussed in verses 27 and 28, but not as an explanation of the way to avoid adultery.

[18] This is not meant to say that a woman's dress and decorum are irrelevant or that they may not prove a stumbling-block, cf. 1 Tim. 2:9-10.

Jesus is much more radical in his day than he would have been in Old Testament times. It is his attitude, however, which made possible the free participation of women in the apostolic church, a participation which would have been unthinkable to Judaism. If we do not grasp Jesus' attitude toward lust, we cannot understand the relationship of men and women in his ministry and teaching or in that of the early church.

D. CONCLUSIONS

Our study of the role of women in the ministry and teaching of Jesus is now complete. The following points summarize the major conclusions to be drawn from it.

1. Jesus' practice and teaching may be said to differ, at certain points radically, from those of both the Old Testament and of rabbinic Judaism.

2. While Jesus' views on women and on the kingdom of God contrast sharply with the Judaism of his day, they are *not* best understood as a reaction to the theology and *mores* of Judaism. Jesus taught with personal authority and grounded his teaching in his understanding of the Old Testament and of the kingdom's mode of arrival.

3. Jesus preached that the kingdom of God was arriving in an unexpected form in his own ministry. He taught, contrary to Jewish expectations of an apocalyptic judgment, that the arrival of the kingdom would be in stages rather than all at once. In its initial stage it would exist alongside the kingdom of Satan and only at the end of the age would final judgment be rendered. Conformity to his thought demanded realignment of traditional ways of thought.

4. The presence of the kingdom is manifest in the power of God working in those who are 'born of the Spirit' and have 'entered the kingdom'. It affects their lives, calling them to particular patterns of life, the motivation of which will be difficult or impossible for those outside the kingdom to grasp.

5. With respect to the relation of men and women, the present results of the arrival of the kingdom with power may be seen both in permanent marriage and in celibacy.

6. The Mosaic 'permission' of divorce (Dt. 24:1-4) did not commend that course of action at all, but rather regulated a related

evil practice (remarriage to the first husband after marriage to a second).

7. The presence of the kingdom enables men to live once more according to the creational pattern of a permanent 'one flesh' relation.

8. According to Jesus, the marriage bond is broken only by sexual infidelity (*porneia*). Moses did not grant divorce for this offence; it was a capital crime. The Jews of Jesus' day could not execute; divorce was a substitute.

9. The presence of the kingdom will mean, for some, a celibate life (being eunuchs) this side of the grave. Not all will live this way.

10. After the resurrection, none will live in a marriage relation. The present dual expression, permanent marriage and celibacy, will give way to a complete absence of marriage relations.

11. Jesus considered the sin of lust to be individually controllable and thus that the presence of men and women together was not incompatible with purity before God. This opened the way for some of his distinctive (within the context of his day) practices.

12. In announcing the arrival of the kingdom to persons in need of God's deliverance from bondage, Jesus treated all kinds of persons alike as being in need. Lepers, priests, prostitutes, tax collectors, Sadducees, Samaritans, housewives and soldiers were thus all appropriate hearers of his 'good news'. His concern for many of these groups was an offence to then-contemporary Jewish (but not Old Testament) scruples.

13. Considered as persons, women have a natural place in Jesus' teaching. They illustrate both faith and unbelief. They receive his chiding and his blessing. Rabbinic teaching tended to use them as negative examples.

14. Women also have a legitimate place among the hearers of Jesus. In his view they can and should listen, do the will of God and become his 'family'. Rabbinic views tended to preclude women from biblical study. Women were not admitted to rabbinical schools.

15. Women were not only Jesus' hearers, they were also his followers. A group of them travelled with him and his disciples.

16. Women had a prominent role as witnesses to the crucifixion, burial and resurrection of the Lord.

17. The gospels do not discuss implications of Jesus' teaching and ministry for the relation of men and women within marriage.

Male 'headship' or 'authority' simply receives no mention, either for or against.

18. With the exception of the calling and appointment of twelve male apostles, the gospels do not comment on 'office' or 'authority' structures for the followers of Christ either before or after his death. We must look elsewhere in the New Testament for such information.

In the teaching of Jesus we can readily see aspects which set him off from the Judaism of his day. We can see other aspects which show lines of development which reach back to the Old Testament teaching, and still others which presume a new reality coming into being with his own ministry of the kingdom of God. How do these relate to the life and teaching of the church which his apostles raised up? To this issue we must now turn our attention.

ADDENDUM:
THE ROLE OF MARY, THE MOTHER OF JESUS

Mary, the wife of Joseph, the Nazarene carpenter, has been a model for Christian women throughout the history of the Christian church. Her central role in God's redemption of his people has, however, often been sadly distorted. It is worth while to devote a short space at this point to that which the Bible has to say about her.

Mary is introduced to us in the opening chapters of Luke and of Matthew. In them we learn that she is 'highly favoured' and that she, although virgin and engaged, has been chosen to bear a child who will be the son of the Most High and will save his people from their sins (Lk. 1:28, 31–32). Mary's response is little short of amazing. Faced with the prospect of being an unwed mother in a community which would view her as an adulteress, she responded in faith, humility and submissiveness: 'May it be to me as you have said' (Lk. 1:38). Her words are rightly seen as including a willing acceptance of a burden. Her lengthy song (Lk. 1:46–55) reveals a deep appreciation of the mercy and care of God for his people, especially for the poor and for the children of Abraham. Throughout the birth narratives Mary is consistently presented as a woman of quiet faith. She is never singled out as a person to be revered or imitated, except perhaps as a person of faith. The angel who announces that she has found favour with

God does not tell her why or how. Elizabeth, her cousin and the mother of John the Baptist, praises her as blessed because she has believed what the Lord has said to her (Lk. 1:45). This trusting image is furthered by Luke's remark that she stored up the events surrounding the birth in her heart and pondered them (Lk. 2:19). It was presumably through her that they became known to the gospel writers.

Mary plays a role in the bringing of Jesus to the temple for the offering for the first-born (Lk. 2:21–38). From this narrative we learn nothing about her save that Joseph was relatively poor, offering doves or pigeons (2:24; *cf.* Lv. 12:8 which instructs that those with meagre resources offer pigeons or doves instead of a lamb). The words of Simeon (Lk. 2:34–35) held sad news for her, but how she reacted is not told us.

Of Mary's actions as a mother we are given only a glimpse in the events of Jesus' visit to Jerusalem when he was twelve (Lk. 2:41–52). In the strained situation of their finally finding him in the temple she appears to have forgotten his mission and asks, 'Son, why have you treated us like this?' (verse 48). Jesus' reply, 'Why were you searching for me? Didn't you know I had to be in my father's house?' (verse 49), constitutes a mild rebuke, which Luke tells us they did not understand (verse 50). At the close of the incident Luke carefully reports that Jesus was obedient to his parents (lest Jesus' reply seem rebellious) and that Mary treasured these events in her heart as well (verse 51).

Mary appears twice in the narratives of the ministry of Jesus. In each case it is the evangelist's point to show that blood relationships do not apply in the usual way in the ministry of Jesus. Matthew 12:46–50 ('who is my mother and who are my siblings?') shows that Jesus 'family' relations are by faith rather than only by blood. He does not deny his relation to Mary, but, as he begins his public ministry, it is no longer primary.

Mary's other appearance is at the wedding at Cana in Galilee (Jn. 2:1–11). There she asks Jesus to work a miracle. His response ('Woman, what have I to do with you? My hour has not yet come') is easily misunderstood. 'Woman' is a rude, depersonalizing form of address in modern English, but was not at all so in that time. 'Dear woman' (NIV) or even 'mother' (NEB) are appropriate translations. 'What have I to do with you?' is a Hebrew and Greek idiom used to comment on interferences (2 Sa. 16:10; 19:22; Mk. 1:24; 5:7). Jesus is not denying his filial relation by his comment;

he is responding to the problem posed by her request that he help with the problem of insufficient wine. She evidently pressed him to act when he would not otherwise have done so. She thus 'interfered' with his plans. Mary's maternal role does not extend to the point of directing his exercise of his messianic calling. She and his siblings are to join the other 'disciples' in this area. Jesus' words to her would be well rendered: 'Dear woman, you are interfering. The time has not yet come for this sort of act.'

Mary appears again only at the passion narratives and the resurrection accounts. She is evidently among Jesus' followers and joins others in watching the crucifixion. Jesus shows special concern for her by asking John to care for her as though she were his mother (Jn. 19:26–27). Some have seen this passage as teaching that Mary should be considered 'mother' of all persons. It seems more likely that it is an example of the continuing filial concern of Jesus, who from the cross asked another to do what he no longer could. Mary continued with the disciples and was present at the ascension and Pentecost (Acts 1:14; 2:1).

The biblical evidence which we have surveyed draws a simple picture of Mary as a woman of faith and a follower of Jesus. Her grasp on his purpose seems sometimes to have been faulty, but nowhere is she presented as standing against him. Jesus himself showed a filial respect for her in his childhood, at the start of his ministry and in the hour of his death. It is important to note that she is nowhere held up as a special example for others or as a person whose assistance is to be sought to gain Christ's ear. Matthew 12:46–50 seem almost directly opposed to such a venture, placing her on a level with all others who do the will of God. Mary is an example of a godly woman who received the blessing of God and of his Son.

5
Women in the life of the apostolic church

The role of women in the teaching and community life of the church has been a subject of lively debate during the last few decades. The debate has raised a number of important questions. Central to these has been the question of the role of the Bible in structuring the faith and life of the church. Within some communions it has become clear that the Bible is viewed as the expression of the religious experience of previous generations, but not as divine revelation of a norm for faith in the present (*i.e.* the Bible testifies to the meaning of Christian faith and life as perceived by believers in other centuries; it does *not* legislate the meaning of either for the twentieth century). In such communions the explicit teaching of the New Testament has been explicitly set aside and, on occasion, ministers have been disciplined for insisting upon a view which both they and their opponents agree has been correctly held by the church for nearly two millennia to be the explicit teaching of Scripture. In such cases the change is not a matter of differing views of what the text of Scripture says, but rather differing views of how the church is to be related to what the text says.

In other communions the debate has taken other lines. Those who are concerned to be submissive to the text of Scripture have had to ask anew what the purpose and nature of the apostolic teaching really is. Is the New Testament a 'first application' of Christian truth which implicitly expects the church to go beyond it in later generations? Does it speak only to its own culture and time? Is the New Testament a definitive statement which allows no greater insight or alternative applications as the church reflects upon it? Is it a pattern for the church in every place and every age? Does it hold principles and give examples of their application? Are New Testament applications relative to the first century and not binding today? Should modern Christians seek out and apply the central apostolic principles rather than try to imitate apostolic practice? How do we recognize which principles are indeed central? Can the central principles conflict with other, less central ones? We shall have to interact with these questions as we study the role of women.

This book is written with a commitment to the Bible as the written Word of God and as its own interpreter. We shall therefore look to the text for the answers to our questions. The next few chapters will study the apostolic teaching and practice regarding the role of women in the church. We shall seek to determine what the apostolic teaching and practice actually were and also whether they were viewed as permanent legislation, as *pro tempore* (for their historical situation only), or in some other way.

This chapter will consider the evidence of the practice of the church. What did women do in the churches according to the testimony of the New Testament documents? The following chapters will consider certain crucial didactic (teaching) passages which speak to the role of women in the various spheres of life and about the relation of women and men. As before, I shall try to show the relevance of the texts to the question of the relation of men and women, and also to provide a feel for the situations to which they were first written. This is particularly important for an effective understanding of Paul's contribution, about which a wide variety of opinion exists.

A. WOMEN AS PEOPLE

We noted before that one of the most startling aspects of the role of women in the life and teaching of Jesus was the simple fact of their presence. A similar point needs to be made regarding the New Testament churches. Women are highly visible and active in the life of the church. A glance at the opening chapters of Acts helps to explain this phenomenon.

Luke opens Acts, the second volume of his account of Christianity, with the ascension of Christ. The little group which had watched its risen Lord ascend and which returned to Jerusalem to await the Holy Spirit is named (Acts 1:13-14). After the list of the apostles we are told of another group which joined together with them in prayer: 'the women and Mary the mother of Jesus, and his brothers'. Here in the very first accounts of the new community we find the women who had played a significant role in the community while Jesus was with them. They had previously been accepted into and now continued as part of the inner circle.

A short while later the group was assembled in one place and the wind of the Spirit came upon them; Pentecost had come (2:1–4). The list of participants is not given, although we are told that the tongues of fire settled on each of them and that all of them were filled and began to speak in tongues (verses 3–4). Peter's explanation of the event to the sceptical crowd in the temple seems to indicate that the women too spoke. Quoting Joel, he said, 'Your sons and your daughters will prophesy . . . on my servants, both men and women, I will pour out my Spirit in those days. . . .And everyone who calls on the name of the Lord will be saved' (2:17–18,21). From its very beginning women played a significant, vocal role in the church.

In his account of the expanding church, Luke took pains to make it clear that women were included. Acts 5 tells us that, despite official disapproval, the group of believers grew and 'more and more men and women believed in the Lord and were added to their number' (verse 14). When the gospel is taken by Philip to Samaria, the result is similar, 'When they believed Philip. . .they were baptized, both men and women' (8:12).

As Paul the former Pharisee set off on his missionary journeys, he understood that the gospel was for all persons, Jews and Gentiles, men and women. We read in Acts of women participating in church after church. Philippi (Acts 16:13–15), Thessalonica (17:4), Berea (17:12), Athens (17:34) and Corinth (18:2) all include women as noteworthy persons. The letters of Paul reflect the same state of affairs. Romans 16 lists many women who helped and worked with Paul. Other letters make provision for women within the organized functions of the church (*e.g.* 1 Tim. 5). The apostolic communities manifestly continued the practice of their Lord in the inclusion of women, but what was the role of the women within the communities?

B. WOMEN IN THE LIFE OF THE COMMUNITIES

On the day of Pentecost, Peter preached the gospel to the crowds which would hear him. Women were among their number. This growing assembly of believers 'devoted themselves to the apostles' teaching and to the fellowship' (Acts 2:42). From this we learn that the women of the church were taught. The church had left the pattern of the rabbis for the pattern of Jesus. A similar comment can be made about Paul's teaching of the women at Philippi (Acts 16:13) and can be inferred from the role of Prisca in the instruction of Apollos (Acts 18:26).

Not only was the gospel preached and taught to women, but women participated in the worship (vocally: 1 Cor. 11:5) and brought their offerings (Acts 5:7–10). In the case of Sapphira, we learn that her wilful joining in her husband's deception concerning the sale of their property resulted in a personal judgment upon her (Acts 5:9–10).

The church recognized the need of its poor, in particular its widows, and organized care for them (Acts 6:1; 1 Tim. 5:9). The women of the church, especially the widows, were active in the life of the body, communicating the love of Christ by deeds of mercy and hospitality (1 Tim. 5:10). We read of a disciple named Tabitha (Dorcas) who provided various services for the poor at Joppa and was raised from the dead by Peter (Acts 9:36–43).

Women were not only hosts to Paul (Acts 16:15; Rom. 16:2), but also hosted churches (Acts 12:12; 1 Cor. 16:19; Col. 4:15; Phm. 2). The ministry of Paul, in particular, was not without women as 'fellow-workers', persons worthy of note (*cf.* Rom. 16 where eight of the twenty–six persons mentioned are women and six of these receive specific comment). The women of the church were not only noted by Paul as an apostle. While still a Pharisee, Paul considered them members of a dangerous sect and had them thrown in prison as well as the men (Acts 8:3). The women of the early church certainly played a highly visible role.

It is important to proceed yet one more step before beginning to examine the teaching of the apostles concerning the role of women; we must ask whether the evidence of church practice suggests anything about the place of women in the more formally organized ministries of the early church.

C. WOMEN IN THE ORGANIZED MINISTRIES OF THE CHURCH

As we begin to investigate the more formal ministries of the early church from the evidence of its practice, it is important to note that the New Testament does not give us a directory for church order. It describes numerous activities and functions and indicates a certain number of formal offices. In many cases it is difficult to assess on what basis a given individual is performing a given task. Our present enquiry is further complicated by the fact that certain words such as *apostolos* (apostle/one sent out), *diakonos* (servant/ deacon/minister), *presbyteros* (presbyter/elder/old man) and *chēra* (widow) may be descriptive of a formal office, a function or a status. Only the context can decide in some cases. We may be glad that we do not finally have to work from the evidence of practice alone, but may appeal to specific teaching as well.

1. Women as fellow-workers

Outstanding among the women of the New Testament is Prisca (diminutive: Priscilla). She and her husband, Aquila, enter the biblical narrative in Acts 18:2 as acquaintances of Paul, having left Rome when Claudius ordered the Jews to go. They sailed with Paul from Corinth to Ephesus, where they set up in business (18:18–19). In Ephesus the two met and taught Apollos about the faith (18:24–26). Luke's narrative makes an interesting shift in the order of the names of the couple in the account. When they are first introduced, Aquila is first. This is common. From that point on, however, Priscilla is first. Luke does not explain the change, but commentators have, I suspect correctly, inferred that she was the more prominent.

When the couple reappear in the letter to the Romans, Prisca (Paul uses the more formal form, Luke the informal) is first and we learn that they have continued in the faith. Of them Paul says, 'Greet Prisca and Aquila, my fellow-workers in Christ Jesus. They risked their lives for me. Not only I but all the churches of the Gentiles are grateful to them. Greet also the church that meets at their house' (Rom. 16:3–5).

Neither Luke, in Acts, nor Paul informs us as to the exact nature of their risk for his sake, but Paul obviously thought it a great thing for the churches as well as for himself. The couple are once again hosting a church. Most interesting is Paul's reference to them as 'fellow-workers'. The term was used by Paul for a number of persons who worked with him (Rom. 16:9,21; 1 Cor. 3:9; 2 Cor. 1:24; 8:23; Phil. 2:25; 4:3; Col. 4:11; 1 Thes. 3:2; Phm. 1, 24). In some cases it identifies men such as Titus or Timothy, in others persons otherwise unknown. Once it links Paul with a whole church (2 Cor. 1:24). The common bond is that they have worked alongside Paul. In Philippians 4:3 we learn of Euodia and Syntyche, two women with a quarrel which needs to be resolved. Paul warmly identifies them as persons who have 'contended at my side in the cause of the gospel, whose names are in the book of life'. While any division within the body is important, most commentators consider it likely that these women were prominent in the church, especially as former companions of Paul, and that their quarrel was therefore particularly detrimental to the church.

The fact that Paul's ministry involved a significant number of women as 'fellow-workers' provides a sharp answer to questions about the propriety of women joining in missionary enterprises. A question which is not answered, however, is the role of the women in Paul's ministry. Did these women teach, preach, pastor, teach women? From Paul's words we simply cannot say; all we know is that they were close to him and a great help. We must look elsewhere for more detailed information.

Returning then to Priscilla, we may see her as a woman who was deeply involved in Paul's labour and of prominence in the church. Did she hold 'office' in the church? Of this nothing is said. Was she a teacher in the church? The only evidence which we have is that she taught Apollos together with her husband in her home (Acts 18:24-28). It would be a mistake to say that she was theologically ignorant! It would also be a mistake to suppose that Luke intended us to infer from his comment that she was acting as an elder or teacher in a formal sense. We must conclude from Prisca and the other women among the fellow-workers of Paul that women were involved in the missionary enterprise. We shall turn to other texts to enquire about their functions within the congregational structures of the New Testament church.

2. Women as prophets

Two passages specifically indicate that women functioned as prophets in the early church. Acts 21:9 mentions the four daughters of Philip the evangelist who were prophetesses. It appears from 1 Corinthians 11:5 that these daughters were not an exception.

Paul recognized that there were women in his congregations who prayed and prophesied. Women therefore had a place among those recognized as being gifted of the Spirit to address the congregation. In this respect they stand parallel to the prophetesses of the Old Testament. The presence of women as prophets does not help us with the contemporary debate over women officers as the prophets were not, by virtue of their office, elders or deacons. They exercised a particular verbal gift.

3. Enrolled widows

We have seen the activity of the early church in caring for the widows in Jerusalem (Acts 6:1) and Joppa (Acts 9:36–43). In 1 Timothy 5:3–16 we have a lengthy discussion of provision of support for widows who are in need. It has sometimes been thought that these women were enrolled as church employees. A close look at the text indicates that the roll is a welfare roll rather than an employment roll. Verses 9 and 10 do, however, give indication of the sort of life and deeds which were expected of the women of the church. It is certainly to be expected that women who demonstrated such loving service before being put on the welfare roll would continue to do so afterwards.

4. A woman apostle?

Romans 16 not only presents us with Prisca, but also with a variety of other men and women. In verse 7 Paul wrote, 'Greet Andronicus and Junias, my relatives (or fellow-countrymen) who have been in prison with me. They are outstanding among the apostles, and they were in Christ before I was.' In the midst of a long list of persons who have been workers alongside Paul we meet these two Jews who were believers before Paul himself and shared in his imprisonment. Their service makes them 'outstanding among the apostles'. Have we here an example of a woman being counted an apostle? In what sense?

Before pursuing the nature of their apostolate, it is necessary to note that the text is unclear whether *Junias* is a man or woman. The grammatical form does not permit certainty in either direction. Any conclusions drawn are therefore to be used cautiously.

Let us consider the implications of the text if Junias is a female. The grammatical form of Paul's reference (*epistēmoi en tois apostolois*) may mean either 'well known *by* the apostles' or 'well known *as* apostles'. It is unlike Paul to make something like acquaintance with the apostles a matter of praise. It is therefore more likely that he intended to say that they were outstanding as apostles. But what does that mean?

The term 'apostle' is used in several senses in the New Testament. It can be used to designate 'the twelve', as for instance when Matthias was chosen to replace Judas and was 'added to the eleven apostles' (Acts 1:26). Paul uses this sense with reference to himself, regarding himself as 'one born out of season' but still an apostle alongside the others (1 Cor. 15:7–9; 2 Cor. 12:11–12; Gal. 1:17,19). The term also has a more general usage which indicates one 'sent out' by a person or body as a representative. The specific nature of the task assigned the 'apostle/representative' would vary with each specific instance. Thus Paul and Barnabas, sent out by the church at Antioch in response to the call of the Spirit (Acts 13:2–3), are called 'apostles' by Luke (Acts 14:4,14). They are commissioned by the church in response to the gift and call of the Holy Spirit to act on its behalf in the spreading of the gospel. It seems (at least to me) that this is the most probable meaning of the apostolate of Junias (male or female) and Andronicus. It would be unthinkable that Paul would be identifying them as belonging to the twelve, or that, doing so, he would nestle them in the middle of a list of persons greeted. It would seem that the proper conclusion to draw from Paul's mention of Junias is that she (or he) was 'sent out' by a church with Andronicus and was outstanding in the appointed task. From the fact that these 'apostles' are grouped with a number of others who have worked with Paul we shall surely be close to the mark if we assume that these two were sent out by a church as missionaries and that their appointed service had, at least for a time, involved assisting Paul. Did this involve 'preaching' or 'teaching'? It would seem impossible that the communication of the gospel was not involved in their job although it is possible that women 'apostles' taught the women because in many settings men doing so would be highly suspect (*cf*. Tit. 2:3–5). What is not clear, however, is how their job relates to what we would today consider as the job of a 'preacher' or 'teacher' in the church. To speculate would be vain. To use Junias, who may be male or female, as an example of a 'woman preacher' or 'woman elder' would be irresponsible. Other, more clear texts must guide our decisions.

5. A woman deacon?
Phoebe (Rom. 16:1–2) is the most controversial female figure in Paul's letters. Of her he writes,

> I commend to you our sister Phoebe, a *diakonos* (servant/deacon) of the church in Cenchreae. I ask you to receive her in the Lord in a way worthy of the saints and to give her any help she may

need from you, for she has been a great help to many people, including me.

The debate over Phoebe revolves around her role as a *diakonos* of the Cenchreaean church. The term *diakonos* means 'servant' or 'one who ministers' to another. This is its meaning in the vast majority of its uses in the New Testament and in Paul's letters. Paul does, however, use the term to speak of church officers, 'deacons' (Phil. 1:1; 1 Tim. 3:8–13). When he does so use it, it is by the context that we must determine it. Is Paul commending Phoebe as a member of the church at Cenchreae who has served others, or as a deacon in that church? The word itself cannot decide the matter. Students of the New Testament must therefore turn to the context for help.

Paul does not commend people in his letters on a casual basis or for personal convenience. When he sends Timothy as his representative, he asks that he be received well (1 Cor. 16:10–11); likewise Titus and Onesimus, who is something of a special case (2 Cor. 8:16–24; Phm. 8–21). Phoebe, whom many believe to have been the bearer of Paul's letter, was introduced to the Romans in terms of her relation to her church and further commended on the basis of her past service to God's people. It is thus likely that she was in Rome in some sort of official capacity, as a *diakonos* of the church at Cenchreae. Whether it was as servant or serving officer, we cannot say.

In Romans 16:2 Paul says that Phoebe has been *prostatis* of many, even of himself. The term *prostatis* is sometimes seen as a key to understanding Phoebe's role. The masculine form of the word (*prostatēs*) means 'one who stands before' and thus frequently 'leader' or 'chief'. From this it is deduced that Phoebe was a leader in her church, a ruler, or even an elder. This interpretation fails to be convincing for lexical and for contextual reasons. Contextually, if we render *prostatis* by 'ruler' or 'leader' we make Paul to ask the Romans to help Phoebe because she has been a ruler or leader of many and even of himself. It is not likely that Paul was saying that Phoebe was his leader or ruler.

Lexical considerations make this outcome virtually impossible. The feminine form, which is used of Phoebe, means 'protectoress, patroness, helper'.[1] What Paul said, therefore, was that Phoebe

---

[1] W. Baur, W. Arndt and F.W. Gingrich, *A Greek-English Lexicon of the New Testament and Other Early Christian Literature* (Chicago, 4th edn. 1957), p. 726.

had been a helper of many, even of himself. In this light we conclude that Paul commended her to the Romans as a representative of the Cenchreaean church who had helped many, himself among them, and asked that she be assisted as necessary.

Was Phoebe a 'deacon' or a 'servant'? Paul's wording simply does not resolve the matter. If the name in the text were Timothy or Judas, ninety-nine per cent of the scholars would presume that *diakonos* meant 'deacon' and a few footnotes would remark that it could mean 'servant'. In the absence of other considerations all would probably do the same for Phoebe, but there *are* other considerations. On the basis of other passages in the Pauline letters many feel that Paul prohibits women from holding the office of deacon. If that is the case, *diakonos* may not be translated 'deacon' in Romans 16:1. We must therefore reserve our final decision concerning Phoebe until we have studied the relevant passages.

D. CONCLUSIONS

Our survey of the role of women in the practice of the New Testament church has shown that the apostolic churches followed the pattern established by their Lord by including women as integral members. Women attended worship, participated vocally, were taught, learned of the faith and shared it with others. They also played an active part in the daily life of the community, teaching one another and caring for the poor.

Whether or not they actually travelled with Paul (they are not mentioned among his travelling companions), they played a significant role as 'fellow-workers' alongside numerous men. The available texts do not make it clear what the labour of male or female fellow-workers was. Further light on this subject must wait until we study Paul's teaching. Our study has provided no clear information about women in the formal offices of the church. Nor have we examined any specific evidence about the marriage relationships of the believers. These two areas will receive special attention as we turn now to the role of women according to the teaching of the apostles.

6

Basic attitudes toward women and marriage in the apostolic teaching

Recent debate over the role of women in the life of the church has centred on the interpretation of the writings of the apostles, primarily of Paul. The last chapters of this study will look in detail at those passages in the epistles which relate to women in the body of Christ, in marriage, and in the formal 'offices' of the early church. As before, I shall make an effort to set each passage in context in order that its instruction not be distorted.

A. NO MALE AND FEMALE

You are all sons of God through faith in Christ Jesus, for all of you who were baptized into Christ have been clothed with Christ. There is neither Jew nor Greek, slave nor free, male nor female, for you are all one in Christ Jesus. If you belong to Christ, then you are Abraham's seed, and heirs according to the promise (Gal. 3:26–29).

These words of Paul represent a break of immeasurable proportion from his thought as Saul the rabbi. They have (correctly) been seen as heralding the reversal of the division of the race at Babel and the beginning of a new humanity. In recent years they have come to be seen as heralding a revolution in the relationship of the sexes as well. This 'Magna Carta of Humanity'[1] has been interpreted in diverse ways. It has been seen as setting aside all distinctions between the sexes, as pointing to the overthrow of subordination of either sex, and as irrelevant to the issue of subordination. We must seek to resolve this question.

[1] P. Jewett, *Male and Female*, p. 142.

1. Galatians 3:28 in context

Paul's letter to the Galatians revolves around the tension between Judaizing legalism (salvation based in part upon the works of men) and Pauline salvation by grace. A review of the argument of chapter 3 prior to verses 26–29 helps to provide a proper framework for its interpretation. The first part of the chapter develops the thesis that faith, not works, provides the basis of salvation and that those who approach God by faith, whether Jew or Gentile, will be blessed with 'faithful' Abraham (3:6–14, esp. 9, 11). It is Paul's explicit purpose to show that the fact that God saves by faith makes it possible not only 'that [Jews] might receive the promise of the Spirit by faith', but also 'that the blessing given to Abraham might come to the Gentiles through Christ Jesus' (verse 14).

The latter part of chapter 3 then carefully reviews the role of the law, arguing that the law was not intended as a way of salvation and that, coming after the promise of God to Abraham, it in no way voided that promise of salvation by faith without works. Chapter 4 discusses the implications of the new sonship which is enjoyed in Christ, apart from law.

The central issue at stake in Galatians 3 and 4 is the role of the law in relation to faith. A strong secondary theme is that Jew and Gentile both come to God on the basis of faith. It is within this frame that our text must be read. Verse 22 prepares the way by establishing that the law is not a special avenue of approach to God, open only to Jews, but a statement from which God *condemns both* Jews and Gentiles. Because *all* kinds of men are thus under judgment and can be saved only by faith, Paul insists, all men come before God on the equal footing, their race, state of bondage, and sex (Jew/Greek, slave/free, male/female) having no effect whatsoever on their right to stand before God. Thus, says Paul, 'You are all sons of God through faith in Christ Jesus. . . . There is neither Jew nor Greek, slave nor free, male nor female, for you are all one in Christ Jesus. If you belong to Christ, then you are Abraham's seed' (verses 26–29).

We conclude that, *within its context*, Galatians 3:28 addresses the question, 'Who may become a son of God, and on what basis?' It answers that any person, regardless of race, sex or civil status, may do so by faith in Christ. Here we have the apostolic equivalent of Jesus' welcoming of the outcasts and the Samaritans and Canaanite women. The gospel is for all persons.

2. Galatians 3:28 in relation to other Pauline texts

Many contemporary exegetes have wrestled with the fact that this text appears implicitly or explicitly at odds with other things which Paul said and taught. How, it is asked, can Paul say there is no slave and free and then proceed to give instructions to slaves and masters (Eph. 6:5–9)? How can he preach no more Jew or Gentile and then preach 'first for the Jew, then for the Gentile' (Rom. 1:16)? How can he announce 'no more male and female' and order women to be silent in the churches, not to teach, and to obey their husbands (1 Cor. 14:33–36; 1 Tim. 2:11–12; Eph. 5:22–24)? Answers to the problem fall into two basic categories: (1) Paul contradicts himself, or (2) the apparent contradiction is resolved by further study. Within these two categories there are a variety of options and space limitations prevent examining them all. I shall present what I consider to be a correct understanding of Paul's message. It will be developed further as we examine the other passages in question.

Our study of the context of Galatians 3:28 has shown that Paul was not reflecting upon relations *within* the body of Christ when he had the text penned. He was thinking about the basis of membership in the body of Christ. This means that it is an error to say that 'all one' in Christ means that there are no distinctions within the body. When we speak of allowing all men to join the army, we do not mean that there will be no distinction between the tank corps and the infantry, or between the captain and the major. If we call all persons to join our soccer team, it does not mean that all will be goalies or full-backs. While a military or sporting analogy has certain drawbacks when applied to the body of Christ, it is inescapable that Paul himself did not seem to feel any tension between his proclamation that all are one in Christ and his teaching that the one body of Christ has many different members or that his own authority was distinctive and all who would not acknowledge it should not be acknowledged (Gal. 3:28; 1 Cor. 12:12; 14:38).

It is worth while noticing, in this connection, that the apostle Peter seems to have shared Paul's view with respect to the sexes. In 1 Peter 3:1–7 Peter speaks of the unity of the male and female marriage partners as 'joint-heirs of the gracious gift of life'. In precisely this context he calls for a sex-role differentiation between the spouses. It would thus appear that Paul's willingness to see unity in Christ as not undercut by distinctions between believers is not unique to him, but more widely shared in the early Christian community. We conclude that there is no necessary conflict between Galatians 3:28 and other Pauline texts teaching distinctions between believers.

Having said this, it is vital to note that we have not yet resolved the more serious issue posed by the tension which we feel when we see the New Testament directing believers concerning slavery, kingship, marital authority, parental authority and other such distinctions. Does the New Testament regulation of these relationships constitute approval of them? Of only some? Of none? Deep within most believers is the conviction that slavery and racial distinctions are wrong within the fellowship of the body of Christ. This feeling is not dismissed by the observation that Galatians 3:28 does not address the matter directly. If slavery and racial distinctions are set aside, should sexual distinctions follow? I think not. I shall, however, defer a full defence of my conclusions until we have examined the relevant texts in more detail.[2]

B. APOSTOLIC ATTITUDES TOWARD MARRIAGE

In this section we shall look at marriage as an institution and at relations between the partners in particular. The letters of the New Testament reflect a high regard for marriage. In this, of course, they continue a pattern set in the Old Testament and in the ministry of Jesus. In this area the writings of Paul are worthy of special attention because of the complexity of his views on the subject.

The clearest and most explicit statement concerning marriage is found in Hebrews 13:4, 'Marriage should be honoured by all, and the marriage bed kept pure, for God will judge the adulterer and all the sexually immoral.' The same attitude of respect is evident throughout the letters. The theological understanding of marriage follows the Old Testament thought. Marriage is viewed as patterned after the relation of Adam and Eve in the garden and as reflective of the relation between God and his people (1 Cor. 11:11–12; 1 Tim. 2:13; 1 Cor. 6:15–17; Eph. 5:21–33). The sanctity of the marriage relation thus continued to be related to the sanctity of the relation between God and his people and the link between idolatry and sexual unfaithfulness continued to be strong (1 Cor. 10:6–8; 2 Cor. 11:2–3). The link is so strong in the mind of Paul

---

[2] See below, pp. 157ff.

that he talks about the Corinthian recourse to prostitutes in terms of their union with Christ. In 1 Corinthians 6:12–17 Paul points out that the believer who uses a prostitute is also a member of Christ and asks, 'Shall I then take the members of Christ and unite them with a prostitute?' (6:15). Turning the metaphor in a slightly different direction, he argues that bodily union with a prostitute is incompatible with spiritual union with Christ (6:16–17). In Ephesians 5 he once again draws the parallel between the marital union of husband and wife and the relation of Christ and his church (verses 31–32). These consistent parallels between marriage and God's relation to his people reflect a high view of marriage.

C. PAUL AND MARRIAGE: 1 CORINTHIANS 7

Despite Paul's high esteem for the symbolism of marriage, many have come to feel that he was, at heart, against marriage. The passage which has created this feeling is 1 Corinthians 7, in which Paul confronts a group of ascetics at Corinth. The nature of this study prevents a full examination of the chapter, but it is important to consider it briefly.[3]

1. The Corinthian situation

A few words about the Corinthian situation will help our understanding of the chapter. The Corinthian church had been started by Paul (Acts 18) and nurtured by Apollos (1 Cor. 3:5–9). It included both Jews and Greeks and was wrestling with questions of how to live the Christian life. In particular it seems to have struggled with two factors: the meaning of new life in Christ and its relation to the law of the Old Testament. Generously endowed with charismatic gifts (1:7; 12:1ff.), the church seems to have divided into factions, each one following a different course and thinking that it built upon the teaching of a well-known figure (1:10–17). Paul was not willing to have himself and his colleagues pitted against one another and therefore vigorously asserted both their unity and the importance of building theology firmly upon the teaching which he (Paul), as God's 'master builder', had laid down (3:1 – 4:7).

---

[3] For a more thorough treatment of the matters discussed in 1 Cor. 7 and of their relation to both Jesus' teaching and the Corinthian problem, cf. J. Hurley, *Man and Woman in 1 Corinthians: Some Exegetical Studies in Pauline Theology and Ethics* (unpublished PhD thesis submitted to Cambridge University, 1973), pp. 122–201. Available from the author.

The latter part of 1 Corinthians 4 discusses a central problem at Corinth. The church had come to feel that, since they were new creatures in Christ, they had already begun to reign with him in a full sense (4:8–13). Such a decision had immediate consequences for their theology. What about the body? Surely it has not reached a final state! It was concluded that death freed them from the crude and disintegrating body (15:12, 35). But the final dismissal of the body does not resolve the question of its present use. Should the Corinthians dissociate themselves from it in the present by adopting an ascetic life-style (1 Cor. 7: sexual asceticism) or should they conclude that the body really does not matter any longer and that the manner of its use is a matter of indifference (1 Cor. 6: prostitutes)? Further, if the body is unrelated to the 'true' (spiritual) person, should distinctions based on it be set aside (1 Cor. 11: marriage roles)?

Paul faced a serious problem at Corinth. He did not share the view of either side. He believed that the body was important to man and to God, bought with a price (6:20; 7:23), presently a member of Christ, the temple of the Spirit (6:15, 19), and destined to be wonderfully changed and raised from death (15:35–41). Christ's body cannot be joined to a prostitute (6:15) and ascetic denial of its functions are wrong (7:2–7). Paul's task was to win both sides to a different basic view and to different positions on specific issues. His task was all the more complicated by the fact that the Corinthians seem to have viewed their own insights as having the same authority as Paul's apostolic teaching. This draws frequent assertions of authority from Paul (3:10; 4:21; 5:13; 7:25; 9:1–2; 14:37–38). It is against this background that chapter 7 is to be understood.

2. Asceticism in 1 Corinthians 7

We are able to reconstruct some of the Corinthian attitudes behind 1 Corinthians 7 from Paul's comments. The chapter begins with a quotation from the Corinthians' letter to Paul: 'It is good not to touch a woman [a euphemism for intercourse]' (7:1).[4] The discussion moves on to divorce in various situations and to the advisability of remaining single. We may surmise that the Corinthians

---

[4] This is one of a number of quotations found in the letter. See J. Hurley, *Man and Woman in 1 Corinthians*, pp. 86–92, 112–115 for a discussion of Corinthian slogans in the letter. See J. Hurd, *The Origin of 1 Corinthians* (London, 1965), p. 68 for a list of commentators finding a quotation in 1 Cor. 7:1.

thought sexual relations wrong. They were therefore divorcing one another and arguing that those unmarried should remain so. Did Paul agree? In the course of the discussion, he said, 'It is good for them to stay unmarried, as I am' (7:8). 'Those who marry will face many troubles in this life, and I want to spare you this' (7:28). 'In my judgment, [a widow] is happier if she stays as she is' (7:40). A closer look at the chapter helps.

3. Abstinence and divorce among the married

The Corinthians objected to sexual intercourse as intrinsically wrong. Their slogan, 'it is good not to have intercourse', has as its counterpart the implication that intercourse is bad.[5] The consequences of this view resulted in abstinence within marriage (7:2–7), disapproval of the remarriage of the widowed (7:8–9), and divorce by believers to avoid defilement by intercourse (7:10–16). Paul's handling of these matters helps us to see his view.

The Corinthians seem to have been concerned with ceremonial defilement through sexual relations. In verse 14 Paul indicates that unbelieving spouses, like unbelieving children, are both made ceremonially clean by their relation to a believer. Many versions have misleadingly translated Paul's words. *Hagiastai* and *hagia* are usually translated 'sanctified' and 'holy'. This translation is legitimate, but it should be noted that the opposite of the terms is *akatharta*, 'unclean'. The 'sanctification' or 'holiness' in view is ceremonial cleanness. It may be that the Corinthians, aware of their daily contact with God in prayer and through 'gifts', were confused by their thoughts of being raised with Christ and were trying to maintain a permanent state of ritual cleanness. Priests serving in the tabernacle and the Israelites who met God at Sinai were called upon to maintain ceremonial cleanness by abstaining from intercourse (Lv. 22:4; Ex. 19:15). If the Corinthians considered themselves *constantly* before God (risen with Christ), the natural consequence would be *permanent* abstinence. Such abstinence would amount to 'making oneself a eunuch for the sake of the kingdom of heaven' and would naturally lead to divorce as a way of avoiding temptation. The Corinthian view might thus be

---

[5] The NIV paraphrases Paul at this point, rendering his words, 'It is good for a man not to marry.' This free rendering is a serious error in that it misdirects the reader. Although marriage was involved, the next verses make it clear that intercourse was the root of the problem. It has the further drawback of making 'have a husband or wife' in verse 2 appear to mean 'be married'. Verses 3–7 make it clear that 'have' means 'have sexual relations with'.

summed up as follows: 'We are a nation of priests. We are already raised and stand daily before God, as evidenced by our spiritual gifts. Those who stand in the presence of God must be ceremonially clean and abstain from intercourse as the priests and indeed the whole nation of Israel did when they met God. Our permanent presence before God demands permanent abstinence. Wives and husbands therefore have no sexual relations and the unmarried do not marry. Many already married divorce to avoid temptation as do those married to unbelievers, who are naturally "unclean". In doing this we are obeying the Lord Jesus who taught us to make ourselves eunuchs for the sake of the kingdom. We find it a moral necessity to abstain from sex. It is sinful to have intercourse. It is good not to touch a woman.'

Paul did not share the Corinthians' view at all. He favoured the single estate, not as 'morally necessary' but as allowing freer devotion to the Lord (7:29–35). He stressed this fact, saying, 'I am saying this for your own good, not to restrict you, but that you may live in a right way in undivided devotion to the Lord' (7:35). The service of God, he taught, does not require the rupture of marriages or a refusal to contract them.

> I think it good for you to remain as you are. Are you married? Do not seek a divorce. Are you unmarried? Do not look for a wife. But if you do marry, you have not sinned; and if a virgin marries, she has not sinned. But those who marry will face many troubles in this life, and I want to spare you this' (7:26–28).

It would be hard for Paul to have made his view more clear. Marriage is not a sin!

The heart of the Corinthian misunderstanding is addressed in verses 17–24. Whereas some of the Corinthians had come to feel that obedience required abstinence and a change as great as divorce, Paul directs that 'each one should retain the place in life that the Lord assigned him and to which God has called him' (7:17). In these verses he makes it clear that externals such as race, circumcision, or even bondage (notably he omits gender in this chapter) do not affect one's relation to God. The rest of the chapter makes the same point for various issues related to marriage.

Paul's concern was not only for marriage as such. He considered sexual relations within marriage requisite and good: 'Because of temptation to immorality each man should have [sexual relations with] his own wife and each woman [with] her own husband' (7:2). Whereas the Corinthians had withdrawn from sexual relations within marriage (perhaps unilaterally), Paul saw it as a matter of mutual obligation (7:3). Over against the Corinthian concept that holiness required permanent abstinence, Paul insisted that prolonged abstinence led only to Satanic temptation. Abstinence was permitted by him for brief periods, on condition of mutual consent and for the sake of special times of devotion to the Lord. Even this, he insisted, was a matter of concession rather than command (7:5–6).[6]

4. 'I say this (I, not the Lord)'

As Paul approached the matter of divorce, he became very aware of the relation of his teaching to that of Jesus (7:10). Paul typically spoke as an 'apostle' of Jesus Christ, as one commissioned by Christ to speak for him. He considered that as such he did not need to find a gospel quotation to support his views. There are therefore many places where the words of Jesus can be seen 'behind' Paul's teaching, but they are almost never cited as such. Paul took a similar approach to the Old Testament. In contrast to the rabbinical method of argumentation, Paul is not constantly defending his views from Old Testament text. We have already noted the fact that there are a number of places in 1 Corinthians in which Paul asserts his authority. None is more clear than 1 Corinthians 14:37–38: 'If anybody thinks he is a prophet or spiritually gifted, let him acknowledge that what I am writing to you is the Lord's command. If he ignores this, let him be ignored.' Despite his apostolic authority, we find Paul carefully (and uncharacteristically) distinguishing his teaching from that of Jesus in 1 Corinthians 7:10, 12 and 25. What is the reason for this unusual procedure?

It would appear that the Corinthians were sensitive to the teachings of the Lord on the matter of marriage and divorce. We have hinted above at a line of thought which may well have been present. By abstaining from sexual relations, they made themselves eunuchs for the sake of the kingdom. For some this meant

---

[6] Some have taken marriage as Paul's 'concession'. Jewish usage of the command/concession combination undercuts this. For further discussion, see J. Hurley, *Man and Woman in 1 Corinthians*, pp. 167–171 and D. Daube, 'Concessions to Sinfulness in Jewish Law', *Journal of Jewish Studies*, 10 (1959), p. 121. Daube applies the concession to the wrong verse.

abstention within marriage, and for others divorce. Paul did not share their exegesis of Jesus' teaching in Matthew 19. He carefully applies Jesus' prohibition of divorce in 1 Corinthians 7:10–11, indicating that the Lord, not he, forbade divorce. In verses 12–16 he makes a perfectly straightforward application of the Lord's principle to a new area, but makes it clear that the Lord did not speak directly to the issue.

At first sight some have felt that Paul was acknowledging in verse 12 that he could not speak with authority to this matter in which he had no saying of the Lord to give him authority, *i.e.* that he was acknowledging that he was not 'inspired' or authoritative at this point. Comparison with verse 25 and 14:37–38 makes it clear that Paul had no such qualms. Speaking of the marriage of single persons he said, 'Now about virgins: I have no command from the Lord, but give a judgment as one who by the Lord's mercy is trustworthy' (7:25). This verse is introduced by *peri de* ('now concerning . . .'), an expression which Paul uses in this letter to introduce topics raised by the Corinthians in their letter to him. They had asked him, therefore, about 'virgins'. We surmise from the context that their question had to do with virgins marrying.[7] Corinthian exegesis of Matthew 19 made Jesus' words important and it was necessary that Paul be precise. In 7:25 he denies having a quotation (commandment) of Jesus regarding the issue at hand (could it be that the Corinthians thought they did in the Lord's teaching about being eunuchs?) but then explicitly carries on to render his judgment.

Modern readers are prone to read 'opinion' or 'judgment' (*gnōmē*) as though it meant 'private opinion' and thus to interpret Paul as saying, in effect, 'I don't know what the Lord thinks about this matter, but I will give you my thoughts, for whatever they are worth.' Paul's actual statement is dramatically stronger. He specifically claims that *by the mercy of God* his rendered judgment in the matter is trustworthy (*pistos*). Far from disclaiming authority in the matter, he has claimed to speak with the authority of God in an area in which he makes it clear that Jesus did not speak! This, of course, stands in complete harmony with his claim in 14:37–38 that his words are the Lord's commandments. And with his general stance as an 'apostle', one sent out by the Lord to act

---

[7] This section is treated in detail in J. Hurley, *Man and Woman in 1 Corinthians*, pp. 180–195. Space prevents a close exegesis at this point.

authoritatively on his behalf (*cf.* his common introduction, 'Paul, an apostle . . .', Rom. 1:1; 1 Cor. 1:1; 2 Cor. 1:1; Gal. 1:1; Eph. 1:1; Col. 1:1; 1 Tim. 1:1; 2 Tim. 1:1; Tit. 1:1). When Paul identifies himself as an apostle of Jesus Christ, he is not using the term 'apostle' in a general sense. He is identifying himself as one who can speak with the same authority as the twelve because, although 'born out of season', he was personally commissioned by the Lord to speak authoritatively for him. I conclude that this passage reveals both Paul's concern to teach what Jesus taught and his strong view of his distinctive apostolic authority to speak for his master. He saw himself as an ambassador, a *plenipotentiary*, rather than as a herald who could but read out the words of the king.

5. Marriage: a second-best option?

One other topic in 1 Corinthians 7 demands attention before we pass on to the other texts. In verses 7–9 Paul speaks to widows as follows:

> I wish that all were as I am. But each has his own gift from God; one has this gift, another has that. Now to the unmarried and the widows I say: It is good for them to stay unmarried, as I am. But if they cannot control themselves, they should marry, for it is better to marry than to burn with passion.

On the basis of these verses, Paul is often criticized for seeing marriage only as a way of curbing lust. He is seen as saying, in effect, that the single life is the ideal but that if one is filled with lust, it is better to have a spouse with whom to vent one's lust. Marriage is thus cast as the lesser of two evils. Such a position is grossly unfair, although very common.

At the most superficial level, it is important to note that this chapter is not setting forth a theology of marital bliss but speaking to Christian ascetics. It is the wrong place to look for Paul's estimate of marriage. Ephesians 5:21–33 is better. On a more careful exegetical level, the text of the chapter rejects the crude views often attributed to it. Paul carefully expressed in verse 7a his personal preferences that all persons should be single as he. His reasoning will be further explained in verses 25–35. Verse 7b, however, qualifies his statement in an important way. Introduced by the strong oppositional form of 'but' (*alla*), verse 7b makes it clear that some are gifted *by God* to celibacy and some are not.

Paul viewed celibacy as a gift from God for those so gifted. There is no depreciation of marriage here, for Paul's language indicates that while some are gifted by God for celibacy, others are gifted by him for marriage.

Having made it clear (contrary to Corinthian sentiment) that celibacy is a gift not a requirement, Paul went on to revise the Corinthian statement that abstinence was 'good' in a morally absolute sense by saying that it was 'good' for the widowed to remain single as did he, but 'better' to marry if celibacy were not their gift and they were burning (with lust).

First Timothy sheds interesting light on Paul's teaching at this point. In 1 Timothy 5:11–14 he counsels that the younger widows remarry because of the strong sexual desires of youth. Only older widows are to be enrolled on the church's welfare rolls. He recognized that sexual drive is related to age (*cf.* also 2 Tim. 2:22, 'flee youthful lusts') as well as the gift of God. In 1 Timothy 4:1–3 we find Paul specifically warning Timothy against a hardened version of the sort of problem which he had faced at Corinth, 'The Spirit clearly says that in later times some will . . . forbid people to marry.' It was not marriage which Paul saw as wrong, but the forbidding of it.

6. Jesus and Paul: 'for the sake of the kingdom'

It is appropriate, at this point, to pay attention to the similarity between the theology of Paul and that of Jesus. We noted that Jesus understood the arrival of the kingdom to issue in two patterns of relations between the sexes: permanent marriage, and celibacy for the sake of the kingdom. The same pattern has begun to emerge in Paul. Paul's defence of celibacy is clearly grounded in a theology of 'gift'. According to him, God gives a gift of celibacy to some and not to others. We are reminded, of course, of Jesus' words about those 'to whom it is given' to receive his teaching (Mt. 19:11–12). Paul's view of the goal of celibacy is also similar to that of Jesus. Both see devotion to the kingdom rather than ascetic intent or flight from sin as the proper motive; 'for the sake of the kingdom' (Mt. 19:12) receives eleven verses of explanation in Paul (1 Cor. 7:25–35). We shall see in later studies that Paul is like Jesus in yet another way. Not only does he build his theology of celibacy from the concept of kingdom devotion and the gift of God, but he builds his theology of marriage from the pre-fall Genesis narratives rather than from the Mosaic concession to the fallenness of man.

7. Conclusions

Our examination of 1 Corinthians 7 has indicated that Paul's discussion of marriage in the chapter must be seen within the context of an interaction with asceticism. Paul's personal preference for the single estate, for the sake of greater devotion to the kingdom, is made clear, yet his explanation also makes it clear that he viewed single life as made possible through a gift of God and not as a requisite for God's people. Those who were married were to continue their marriages. Those still single or widowed were encouraged to consider the single life, but not required to seek it. Neither course was to be viewed as sin. In outline and theology, Paul's teaching on divorce, permanent marriage, and celibacy for devotion to the kingdom can be seen as to parallel that of his master. For Paul, as for Jesus, both permanent marriage and celibacy were valid patterns within the present form of the kingdom.

In the exchange with the Corinthians, Paul's relation to Jesus receives some elucidation. He knew and cited sayings of Jesus, but considered himself, by God's mercy, authorized to speak in areas in which there was no directly applicable saying. Thus his 'concessions' that at certain points he 'not the Lord' spoke or that he had no command of the Lord but 'gave his judgment' are not disclaimers, but rather assertions of apostolic authority.

Addendum: Paul's marital state

Paul's marital state has been a matter of considerable debate. While it is not crucial that we know about this issue, 1 Corinthians 7 does give us some useful information. As we have seen, the first portion of the chapter is addressed to married persons and the last to those unmarried. Verse 8, belonging to the first part, reads, 'To the unmarried and the widows I say: It is good for them to stay unmarried, as I am.' Who are the 'unmarried'? They may, perhaps, be all persons not yet married; but then why are widows brought in for particular attention? A suggestion may be made which sheds light on the matter.

The Greek language has no word for 'widower'. A 'widow' (*chēra*) was a person 'without' or 'left without'. While a woman might be 'left without' a husband and have to await the good offices of her kinsmen or the affection of a new man, a man could quite easily take steps to procure a new spouse. Further, a widow was often left 'without' money as well as 'without husband'. The term *chēra* has a strong social and financial overtone more appropriate to a widow than a widower. Thus the more passive and needy status of women meant that a Greek woman who was left without a spouse was left a 'widow', a 'person without a source of support'. A man in a comparable state was simply a man who chose not to marry, 'unmarried'.

If we accept that the first part of the chapter addresses the married, the 'unmarried' of verse 8 who are paired with the widows are in fact 'widowers' in modern language. Paul's 'as I am' in verse 8 thus indicates that he too was a person who had lost his spouse to death.

D. RELATIONSHIPS BETWEEN HUSBAND AND WIFE

We have noted in previous chapters that both Jesus and the apostolic church considered that women should be included among the people of God in a way which set the church apart from the Jewish community. Women learned, joined in worship and served in the church. Marriage, we observed, was held in honour as one of two patterns to be expected among the believers. In this section we must ask a new question: What effect, if any, did the new situation of believers have upon the relationship between husbands and wives? Was marriage to be egalitarian? Were husbands to continue 'lording it over' their wives? Are there any other options?

We shall focus our attention on two primary texts: Ephesians 5:21–33 and 1 Peter 3:1–7. We shall first examine these passages and then consider their relevance to the present era. First Corinthians 11:2–16 is also relevant, but we shall consider it below (chapter 7) in the discussion of women and men in worship.

1. Between Christian partners: Ephesians 5:21–33

Ephesians 5 and 6 discuss relationships between various categories of believers. Husbands and wives, parents and children, slaves and masters are discussed. The discussion of husbands and wives in 5:21–33 is one of the clearest Pauline discussions of marital relationships. It is worthy of careful study in its own right. Space limitations require that we consider it from the viewpoint of roles. Paul writes,

[21]Submit yourselves to one another out of reverence for Christ. [22]Wives, submit yourselves to your husbands as to the Lord.

[23]For the husband is the head of the wife as Christ is the head of the church, his body, of which he is the Saviour. [24]Now as the church submits to Christ, so also wives should submit themselves to their husbands in everything. [25]Husbands, love your wives, just as Christ loved the church and gave himself up for her [26]to make her holy. . . . [28]In this same way, husbands ought to love their wives as their own bodies. He who loves his wife loves himself. [29]After all, no-one ever hated his own body, but he feeds and cares for it, just as Christ does the church – [30]for we are members of his body. [31]'For this reason a man will leave his father and his mother and will be united to his wife, and the two will become one flesh.' [32]This is a profound mystery – but I am talking about Christ and the church. [33]However, each one of you also must love his wife as he loves himself, and the wife must respect her husband.

a. Mutual submission?

Verse 21 has been the subject of much controversy. Does it conclude Paul's discussion of the Spirit's work in verses 18–20? Does it call upon husbands and wives to be mutually submissive, or is it an introduction to the discussion of husband/wife, parent/child, slave/master? One way the verse calls husband and wife to submit to each other; the other ways it calls for submission of believers to one another in various relationships. The immediate context shows that the text applies at least to the wife in the wife/husband relation, for verse 22 has no verb, assuming the verb 'submit' from verse 21. The broader context demands that we should view verse 21 as a general heading for the section, applicable to the slave/master and parent/child relations as well. The following points are of importance:

1. Paul sometimes makes transitions from one topic to another by means of a transitional verse, which is both the conclusion of one discussion and the start of another. Verse 18 calls upon the Ephesians to be filled with the Spirit rather than being drunken. Verses 19 and 20 expand on the implications of being Spirit-filled. In a series of participial phrases Paul directs them to be *speaking* to one another in psalms, hymns and spiritual songs (verse 19), *singing* and *making melody* in their hearts to the Lord, *giving* thanks always (verse 20) and *submitting* themselves to one another from reverence to Christ (verse 21). Verse 21 is thus grammatically a part of verses 18–20. Various Bible translations and Greek Testa-

140

ments reflect this grammatical fact by paragraphing verse 21 with verses 18–20.

A further grammatical fact, however, prohibits a water-tight separation of verse 21 from the discussion which follows it. Verse 22 has no verb. It presumes the verb expressed in the participle of verse 21 ('submitting'). We must therefore argue that verse 21 is grammatically related to both the preceding and the following material. It is in fact a transitional verse. Its role is visually laid out in diagram 1.

DIAGRAM 1

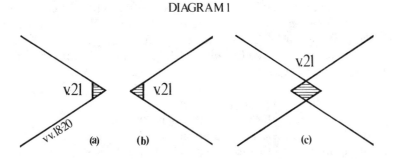

Diagram 1a shows verse 21 as the culmination of verses 18–20. Diagram 1b shows it as the starting-point for 5:22 – 6:9. As we have seen, the grammar requires that it be seen as functioning in *both* of these roles, as in Diagram 1c. This sort of 'both-and' transition is not unusual in Paul. First Corinthians 11:1 provides a particularly clear parallel.

2. Paul's discussion in 5:22 – 6:9 is concerned with relations demanding submission of believers to one another. In each such case he first discusses the submissive partner. Wives are to submit, children and slaves to obey. Parallel sets of relations occur in Colossians 3 and 4 and 1 Peter 2 and 3. The grouping of such relations elsewhere and the fact that verse 21 is manifestly appropriate to all three relations make it quite unnatural to restrict the idea of mutual submission to the husband/wife relation alone.

3. 'Mutual submission' can be understood meaningfully, in English, as Paul's instruction for both partners of the husband/wife and of the parent/child pairs. It is not appropriate for his words to the slave/master pair, and, as we shall see, this idea does not fit in with the New Testament use of *hypotassō* (to make subject) and the idea of submission. The idea of mutual submission

is, however, appropriate if it is addressed to the congregation at large and exemplified in these three relations in which one member must yield to another.

We conclude that verse 21 should be seen as both the conclusion of 5:18–20 and as an introduction or heading to the section which extends from 5:22 – 6:9; it ought not to be thought of as calling for mutual submission of both partners in the husband/wife, parent/child and slave/master pairs. This point will be developed further below.

The frequent mention of husband/wife, parent/child and servant/master relations by different writers in their epistles is significant. It suggests that they were continuing problems and possibly a set form of address. With respect to the marital relationship it is likely that the problem was, at least in part, related to the differences between Jewish, Greek and Christian ways of viewing women. The Christian church visibly set aside many old ways. On what basis was this done? What other customs should be set aside? In the area of man/woman relations, what guidelines should help formulate Christian patterns? We saw that the Corinthian congregation was called to build upon the apostolic foundation (1 Cor. 3:10) but warned of the danger of not doing so faithfully (3:10b–14). Paul's handling of marital relations is visibly intended to provide a rationale as well as instructions. He expected them to apply his words creatively and to work out (the present meaning of) their own salvation, knowing that it was God who worked in them to will and to act (Phil. 2:12–13). We saw in an earlier discussion that the Corinthian congregation strayed from the apostolic guidelines in its development and had to be reminded that it had to build faithfully upon Paul's foundation or suffer loss (1 Cor. 3:10–14; cf also 14:37).

What then does Paul say to the Ephesians? He taught the women of Ephesus to understand their relation to their husbands in terms of their relation to Christ: 'The husband is the head of the wife as Christ is the head of the church, his body, of which he is the Saviour. Now as the church submits itself to Christ, so also wives should submit themselves to their husbands in everything' (Eph. 5:23–24). In these verses Paul has drawn on a familiar biblical parallel. Throughout the Old Testament God's relation to his people is likened to that of a husband to a wife. The New Testament discussion of marital roles consistently draws upon this parallel.

i. Submitting oneself

The precise terminology of Paul's discussion is important for our understanding of this text and will be important for our study of 1 Corinthians 11:2–16. Paul defines a relationship between being 'head' (headship) and 'submitting oneself'. Recent discussion of these terms has explored the range of meaning of each term. We must do the same.

Paul uses the verb *hypotassō* to describe the relation of the church to Christ. The root meaning of *tassō* and its various forms is 'put in order', 'arrange', or 'put in place.'[8] *Hypotassō*, the form Paul used, means 'put in order under', or 'sub-ordinate' and is best translated by forms such as 'to make subject' or 'to subdue' in active uses and by forms such as 'to submit oneself' or 'to be obedient to' in passive or reflexive uses. Each of the more than forty New Testament uses of the verb carries an overtone of authority and subjection or submission to it. The use of the verb necessarily carries with it a concept of exercising or yielding to authority.[9] A few typical examples make the matter clear.

Romans 13:1, 5: 'Everyone must submit himself to the governing authorities. . . . Therefore, it is necessary to submit to the authorities, not only because of possible punishment but also because of conscience.' There can be no question of the sort of submission which Paul has in view here. It is that of a subordinate to one placed over him. Interestingly, Paul perceives the matter as one of conscience.

1 Corinthians 14:32, 34: 'The spirit[ual gift]s of prophets are subject to the control of prophets. . . . They [women] are not allowed to speak, but must be in submission, as the Law says.' We shall devote space to the exegesis of this passage later. At this point it is important only to note that 'submission' is not yielding to the needs of another but rather yielding to the authority of another.

1 Corinthians 15:27 (RSV) reads: 'For God has put all things in subjection under his feet.' But when it says, 'All things are put in subjection under him,' it is plain that he is excepted who put all things under him. When all things are subjected to him, then the

---

[8] For a general discussion of the word, see G. Delling, *TDNT*, 8, pp. 27–48.

[9] *Hypotassō* occurs at the following places: Lk. 2:51; 10:17, 20; Rom. 8:7, 20 (twice); 10:3; 13:1, 5; 1 Cor. 14:32, 34; 15:27 (three times), 28 (three times); 16:16; Eph. 1:22; 5:21–22, 24; Phil. 3:21; Col. 3:18; Tit. 2:5, 9; 3:1; Heb. 2:5, 8 (three times); 12:9; Jas. 4:7; 1 Pet. 2:13, 18; 3:1, 5, 22; 5:5. A survey of them will give a good indication of the strength of the word in the New Testament vocabulary.

Son himself will also be subject to him who put all things under him. . . .' This passage is worth careful attention. In it we see Paul's concept of the role of Christ as second Adam coming to fruition as Christ, in that role, subdues all things and then, as head of the new race, submits to God. We shall note this idea of Christ being subject to the Father when we consider 1 Corinthians 11. Paul's figure of speech warrants our attention. He describes God as placing everything under Christ's feet. This regal imagery portrays a victorious king above his conquered foe or subjects. It may have in mind a raised throne with subjects arriving and prostrating themselves at the feet of the king, or it may have in mind a conquering king symbolically placing his foot on the neck of a conquered foe. The same image recurs in Ephesians 1:22.

Other uses of *hypotassō* are equally clear in their employment of the term to describe yielding *to authority*. This grammatical observation is important.

Some recent discussions of Ephesians 5 have interpreted *hypotassō* (submit) in verse 21 as though it called upon husbands and wives, parents and children, slave and masters to submit *to the needs of* one another, *i.e.* to allow the needs of the other to come before their own needs and to alter their behaviour for the sake of the other. Used in this way the word points in the direction of self-sacrificing love. This, of course, is the pattern of Christ's love for the church, the pattern held out by Paul for husbands in Ephesians 5:25–31. This interpretation would provide a sense in which both husband and wife are 'submissive' to (yielding to the needs of) one another. Attractive though it would be, it is not compatible with the use of the word anywhere else in the New Testament. In the active voice, the verb always means 'subdue' or 'make subject'. In the reflexive voice it always means 'make yourself subject'. If the debated use in Ephesians 5:21 is held aside, there is no example at all of the partner with initiative being asked to submit himself to the subordinate. Conversely, the subordinate is always so asked. The idea of bending to meet the needs of a stronger or weaker partner in a relationship *is* present throughout discussions of relations involving subordination, but other words than 'submit' (*tassō, hypotassō*) are used for the partner to whom submission is due. That partner, be it God, a husband, a parent, the state, or a master, is never asked to 'submit' to the subordinate. Review the appropriate passages in Ephesians 5–6; 1 Peter 3:1–7; Romans 13, *etc.* to see the actual terms used with respect to the dominant partner. Active verbs such as 'love', 'be considerate', 'respect' are used.

The conclusion to be reached is that when the New Testament speaks of the self-giving love of Christ and calls believers to emulate this, it does not use the verb *hypotasso* (submit oneself). When we are called upon to bend ourselves to the needs and desires of another, *hypotasso* is not the verb because it directly implies making oneself subject to authority, rather than responsible to needs. Let me repeat myself for the sake of clarity: I am not saying that husbands should not imitate Christ's self-giving love or that they are free to forget Paul's call to spare no effort for the building up of their wives (Eph. 5:22–23). Husbands *are* to love their wives as their own selves. I *am* saying that the New Testament does not use 'submit' (*hypotasso*) to convey this idea and that submitting to one another (mutual submission) is not an appropriate term to use in describing the mutual obligations of husbands and wives, parents and children, slaves and masters.

Verse 21, 'submit yourselves to one another out of respect for Christ', is thus to be understood as a general heading indicating that there will be various situations in which certain believers will have to yield to the authority of others. The following text (5:22–6:9) sets out three particular relations in which this will be the case: wives will need to submit themselves to husbands; children will need to obey their parents, and slaves their masters. The idea of mutual submission has to do with various members of the congregation rather than with the two partners of each pair.

ii. A preliminary study of 'headship'[10]

Ephesians 5:22 not only calls upon wives to submit themselves to their husbands, it also identifies a husband as 'head' of his wife. What exactly does Paul mean? Paul's use of 'head' (*kephale*) is more complex than his usage of *hypotasso*. The term can refer to a literal, physical head (1 Cor. 11:7) or to a person possessing authority (Eph. 1:22), or to something which is the source or beginning of something else (Col. 1:18). Certain recent discussions of Ephesians 5 have suggested that 'head' does not imply authority in verse 23, but only 'origin' or 'unity'. The implication of this would then be that Paul was not suggesting that the man was 'in charge of' or 'having authority over' (=head over) his wife, but

---

[10] The idea of 'headship' receives extended treatment in chapter 7.

rather her 'source' or 'united to her' and that he should therefore be especially concerned for her as 'his body' (*cf*. verses 28–31). While it is surely correct to point out that Paul saw the fact that Eve came from Adam as significant,[11] it is a great mistake to try to remove any sense of submission from his use of 'head' in verse 23, which verse presents the model of Christ's headship as the reason for a wife's submission.

The concept of origin is not Paul's intended meaning here in Ephesians. If 'origin' is used to translate 'head' (*kephalē*) the passage says that Christ is the origin of the church, that the husband is the origin of the wife, and that the derivative role carries with it an obligation to submit. We shall examine Paul's use of this sort of reasoning in connection with our study of 1 Corinthians 11 and 1 Timothy 2 (see below, chs. 7 and 8). We should note, however, that in both cases where he uses the origin idea he does so by means of an appeal to Eve's being taken from Adam rather than to the 'head' motif. This fact in conjunction with a study of other uses of head (*kephalē*) offers no warrant to infer that 'head' means 'origin' in Ephesians 5.

Better arguments can be advanced in favour of the view that 'headship' language is meant to be a metaphor pointing to the closeness of husband and wife as paralleling the closeness of body and head. In favour of this it may be noted that chapter 4 portrays Christ as the head into which the body grows and in whom it finds unity (4:15–16). Further, Ephesians 5:31 points out that the husband and wife are a one-flesh unity.

Although the themes of unity and closeness are indeed present in the letter to the Ephesians, they are not the best tools for the analysis of verses 22 and 23. Paul uses the 'one flesh' idea from Genesis 2 in a variety of contexts. In Ephesians 5:31, as elsewhere, he points to the integrity of the married couple. This unity becomes a part of his argument to show why husbands should love their wives. It is not actually a part of his discussion of the wife's pattern of conduct. If we, nevertheless, import the 'one flesh' idea into the discussion of the wife's role, we portray Paul as arguing that the fact that the husband and wife are part of a single united body should lead her to submit to him. This tortuous line of reasoning can be discarded if we adopt the Hebrew and Septuagintal pre-

---

[11] *Cf.* 1 Cor. 11:2–16 and 1 Tim. 2:8–15 where Paul derives male 'headship' from the fact that Adam was 'first formed'. We shall discuss these texts later.

cedents for understanding *kephalē* (head) as meaning 'head over'. On this basis submission is a perfectly natural response to authority.

It is of great significance for the interpretation of 'head' in Ephesians 5:23 that the combination of headship, authority and union is not new to the Ephesian letter in chapter 5. It appears earlier in Ephesians 1:19–23. In that earlier context union with Christ and Christ's rule over all creation are closely joined. Paul spoke of 'that power . . . which he [God] exerted in Christ when he raised him from the dead and seated him at his right hand in the heavenly realms, far above all rule and authority, power and dominion, and every title that can be given, not only in the present age but also in the one to come. And God placed all things (*hypotassō*) under his feet and appointed him to be head (*kephalē*) over everything for the church, which is his body.' As always, *hypotassō* implies a relation of authority, in this instance the whole creation being made subject to Christ. The context makes it abundantly clear that Paul means to talk of authority. Note that Christ has the seat of authority at the right hand of the sovereign. He is above all forms of created authority that are or can be. Everything is made 'subject' to him (passive form of *hypotassō*) and symbolically put under his feet.

In the context, saturated with the language of authority, Paul parallels his assertion that things are subject to Christ with a declaration that Christ is appointed to be head (*kephalē*) over everything. There can be no escaping the idea of rule and authority. It would make no sense at all to import the idea of origin (God seated Christ over all authority, put everything under his feet and appointed him to be the *origin* of it all?). The idea of union is equally nonsensical as a description of Christ's relation to all things. The only satisfactory interpretation of 'head' (*kephalē*) in Ephesians 1:22 is 'head over'.

Paul's development does not, however, stop at this point. The idea of 'head' does lead to a second concept, a second meaning of head which does not relate to the creation but to the church. Christ's rule is *for the sake of* his body, the church. Here the idea of love, unity and rule for the sake of another are introduced. Paul draws the rule of Christ and Christ's love for his church together by means of two meanings of the word 'head' (*kephalē*).

The language of headship, subjection and rule in Ephesians 1:20–22 is paralleled in 5:22–23. In each Christ's headship is responded to by subjection. This model provides the pattern for a wife's relation to her 'head'. Christ's actions as head provide the pattern for the husband. Christ's self-giving love is to be imitated by the husband who uses all his resources for her good. Ephesians 1:20–23 and 5:22–33 have in common the head/body relation, subjection to the head, and self-sacrificing rule for the sake of the body. Only with violence to the text can it be asserted that the idea of authority is absent from the language of headship and submission in Ephesians 5:22–33.

However, a significant difference between the two passages must also be noted. Chapter 1 stresses that by God's design all creation has *been subjected* to Christ for the sake of the church. In chapter 5 Paul sees God's design as calling upon women to *subject themselves* (=submit) to their husbands as the church subjects itself to Christ. Husbands are *not* told to make their wives be subject. Both Peter and Paul follow this pattern whenever they speak to persons called upon to be subordinate, whether wives, children, slaves or citizens. Submission for the sake of the love of Christ is set before the one who is to submit. The one to whom submission is due is reminded of his or her relation to Christ and of its implications for the particular relation in view. He (or she) is not reminded to make the other subject to himself. The modern church must carefully imitate both Paul's sensitivity to human abuse of power and his insistence upon viewing both leadership and submission in a distinctively Christian and theological perspective.

We surmised from the frequency with which the issue arose that women in many of the congregations had problems submitting to their husband's judgments, which were no doubt sometimes as poor as Jacob's (Gn. 38) or Jephthah's (Jdg. 11:30–40). Paul's handling of submission set the matter in another realm altogether, making it independent of the immediate cultural or social situation. The women were not asked to submit for the sake of the superior wisdom of their husbands, but for the sake of Christ. The matter thus became one of theology rather than sociology.

Paul's words to the husbands reveal an awareness of men's shortcomings as well. It would seem that the men thought authority a thing to be exercised for personal satisfaction. Paul pointedly calls them to consider what it means to imitate Christ, who gave his own self up so that the needs of the church might be met (5:25–30; *cf.* 1:22–23). Here again the marital role is theologically rather than culturally defined. The husband's responsibility too is a function of divine pattern and appointment rather than personal qualification.

b. The exercise of authority

It is interesting to note the extent to which Paul's discussion is in keeping with the tone of Jesus' teaching about the nature of authority. Jesus taught his disciples that the rulers of the Gentiles saw authority as a way to set themselves over others. Using his own willingness to wash their feet as an illustration, he taught them that, among his followers, authority was for the purpose of service: the greatest should be like the least and the one who rules like one who serves (Lk. 22:24–27). Jesus' words did not argue against the disciples having authority; they regulated the exercise of that authority. Paul calls husbands to imitate the Lord, not by setting aside authority but by serving the needs of their wives.

Modern Christians tend to consider authority in the manner of the Gentile kings against whom Jesus warned. It is easy to consider only 'rights' or 'authority'. Our culture is very much concerned with such matters. The model of Christ and the church, however, has more to offer than bald 'right to command'. It is interesting and often valuable to ask husbands, who are 'overly' concerned to 'maintain their authority' and do so by suppressing their families, about their prayer life. Often they testify that they feel free to make their wishes and feelings known to the Lord and are confident that he both hears and responds for their good. If asked whether they feel constrained or demeaned by serving him, they will frequently indicate that being a bondservant of God is true freedom and makes them feel 'whole'. It is a pity that their actual relations with their spouses are frequently not in line with their Master's example and produce opposite effects.

Further communication with men whose 'authority' is rigidly or 'woodenly' imposed often reveals that they are not quite so sure of the Lord's provision as they say and that they are not quite as confident of their own ability as they make out. 'Wooden' suppression of others often represents an effort to achieve order by imposition, originating from fear of inability to guide in other ways. Deeper confidence in the Lord places less overwhelming responsibility on our poor shoulders and allows greater freedom to admit weakness, to hear the counsel of others and to consider the needs of others. The example of the Lord's leadership is helpful. He does not crush us or impose his will in a way which denies our humanity or initiative. The Christian is called to pray and to *act* with obedient initiative, to ask so that we may receive (Mt. 7:7–11, *etc.*) and to act so that we may work out the present meaning of our own salvation (Phil. 2:12). Husbands must learn that form of sacrificial leadership which fosters the growth of others. Wives must learn that form of active obedience which is not self-demeaning but joyfully upbuilding. Among fallen humans, even those in whom the image of God is being restored (Col. 3:10), this process calls for humility and mutual encouragement.

Practical help for both husbands and wives is offered by the intriguing model employed by Paul in 1 Corinthians 6. Verses 12–17 oppose sexual union with a prostitute as incompatible with union with Christ. In them Paul draws the following parallel, 'he who unites himself with a prostitute is one with her in body . . . but he who unites himself with the Lord is one with him in spirit' (6:16–17). The physical relation is parallel to the spiritual relation.

Some husbands and wives who cannot learn about leadership from prayer can learn about it from sex. Sexual fulfilment in marriage involves the genuine self-expression of both partners. If a husband insists upon being 'authoritative' and that his wife just 'take orders', *i.e.* on suppressing her self-expression during intercourse, his pleasure soon wanes and she is quickly embittered. Conversely, if she sullenly refuses to participate or (generally speaking) seeks to take over his leadership in the exchange, their relation soon disintegrates and is not fulfilling. Within the military model of authority, a general may be authoritarian and a private bitter or passive without destroying their relation. This model simply will not work for sexual relations.

A married couple may not understand this issue, but will soon wrestle with the problem. As they begin to make progress in this area, it can be of real value for other areas of their marriage. The husband must learn that his own fulfilment and satisfaction are enhanced rather than undercut when he learns to understand and to fulfil his wife's personality and her needs in their physical relationship. This lesson may be transferred to other aspects of their relation. A wife may also learn from the sexual relation. Given a husband who does care and who will seek her out, she can learn that the responsive role is not necessarily destructive of personal meaning, self-respect or fulfilment. It is interesting (but not surprising for those who receive the biblical teaching that God created the marriage relation in such a way that it mirrors his relation to his people) to note that human physiology is such that, generally speaking, when both partners are expressive in their physical relationship, the man will still be the one taking the active initiative and the wife the one making active response. Neither initiative nor authority necessarily crushes or distorts self-expression or personal fulfilment. Christians need to develop their ability to exercise and to respond to authority in such a way that this possibility will increasingly become realized fact.

The exercise of authority and leadership in any organization will be most effective if it is done in such a way that the abilities of those under authority are developed to their fullest rather than suppressed. This demands that the leader be aware of the thoughts and abilities of those under him. They in turn must be satisfied that their input is heard and respected. Authority must be delegated and initiative must be given to subordinates. If they can never act without first checking out their actions, progress will quickly be stifled. Resentment and suspicion will take its place. Christians must consider carefully how to administer and how to respond to authority in their home and in their church life. Failure to do so will inevitably produce destructive results.

c. The exercise of authority when agreement cannot be reached

Headship and leadership most often involve initiative rather than command. There are, however, situations in which differences come between a leader and those who respond to him or to her. These can often be resolved by communication. For Christians in such situations there is the added guidance of the Scripture and the peaceful work of the Holy Spirit. Prayer and Scripture have their place alongside talk. Our sinfulness, ignorance and sheer diversity will nevertheless still lead to situations in which differences are not resolved and in which neither side is willing to yield to the other. In marriage, such situations can be severe crises if the situation is such that a decision must be made even if there is no agreement.

The Scripture is the guide for faith and life in the Christian home. A husband's authority in the home is derivative: as a servant of God, his authority comes from God. He is, therefore, subject to Scripture in all that he does, and has no freedom to guide his family in ways which contradict it. Should he clearly do so, individual members must follow God before man. The example of Sapphira's willing sin and personal accountability makes this clear (Acts 5:9).

There are, however, other situations, *not* involving contradiction of biblical teaching, in which husband and wife, even after discussion, prayer and consultation with others, remain irreconcilably committed to different courses of action and are not prepared to give way for the sake of the other. There need not be many such cases, but in a fallen world there will be some. In them, the responsibility of the husband to lead and of the wife to respect his initiative requires her to yield to his decision.

The manner in which such situations are handled is crucial. The husband may not be high-handed and stubborn, knowing that she will finally have to give way. That is not the model of Christ's headship. Neither may the wife be grudging and resentful. That is not the manner of our response to Christ. In the last analysis, when the two can devote no more time to individual and joint seeking of the grace of God to permit them to come to one mind or to be willing to yield to the other, an exchange along the following lines is in order:

Husband: 'Not because I am inherently wiser or more righteous, nor because I am right (although I do believe I am or I would not stand firm), but because it is finally my responsibility before God, we will take the course which I believe right. If I am being sinfully stubborn, may God forgive me and give me the grace to yield to you.'

Wife: 'Not because I believe you are wiser in this matter (I don't) or more righteous, nor because I accept that you are right (because I don't or I would not oppose you), but because I am a servant of God who has called me to honour your headship, I willingly yield to your decision. If I am wrong, may God show me. If you are wrong, may he give you grace to acknowledge it and to change.'

Such decisions must be made. They can be steps of commitment to God which cement a relationship and assure both partners of the other's loving commitment. They can alternatively be times which show sinful abuse. The sort of commitment outlined above can be used to preserve the dignity and honesty of both partners by setting matters in their proper context.

The gravity of such disagreements points up the importance of a decision to marry. A husband takes on an accountability to God for his family. His wife places herself in a position from which she must sometimes yield to him. Hers, in the estimate of this male author, is the more difficult role, emotionally. She must be well satisfied that she trusts his judgment before entering into marriage. Both partners must be satisfied that they have developed the ability to handle serious disagreements through communication and prayer before making a marriage commitment. If they are married and have not developed such abilities, they do well to begin doing so and, if necessary, to seek help from a qualified person. For the Christian, times of irreconcilable difference between marriage partners need not lead to bitter stalemate, crushing abuse or 'trench warfare'. They can lead to a deeper love, growth and assurance of mutual commitment.

2. Relating to an unbelieving spouse: 1 Peter 3:1–7

a. *Submission in suffering*

Submission within the body of Christ was the general context of Paul's discussion of marriage in Ephesians. Both partners were called upon to consider and to imitate the pattern of Christ and his church. Marriage is seen within a very different context in 1 Peter. Peter wrote to a suffering church about the meaning of Christian life under oppressive governments, oppressive slave masters and oppressive husbands. Before them he holds the example of Christ, who 'did not retaliate' and 'made no threats', but 'instead entrusted himself to him who judges justly' (1 Pet. 2:23). He encouraged them to 'live such good lives among the pagans that, though they accuse you of doing wrong, they may see your good deeds and glorify God on the day he visits us' (2:12). In practical terms Peter's instructions meant: 'Submit yourselves for the Lord's sake to every authority instituted among men'; 'Slaves, submit yourselves to your masters with all respect, not only to those who are good and considerate, but also to those who are harsh'; 'Wives, in the same way be submissive to your husbands' and 'Husbands, in the same way be considerate as you live with your wives' (2:13,18; 3:1,7). Our concern in this section is with his instructions to marriage partners.

Then, as now, women married to unbelievers were faced with an especially difficult situation. Their husbands often resented their faith and could make life miserable for them. The women to whom Peter spoke had no doubt learned what many modern believers have also learned, that all the words which may be spoken are soon forgotten and that evangelism must finally proceed by life rather than by words. The husbands must see Christianity in their wives rather than simply hear about it. Peter says,

> Wives,. . .be submissive to your husbands so that, if any of them do not believe the word, they may be won over without talk by the behaviour of their wives, when they see the purity and reverence of your lives (3:1–2).

b. The 'situational' nature of Peter's advice

Why does Peter urge women to be submissive wives? Should we view his advice as applicable to the twentieth century? Should it be considered a tactic for converting pagan husbands rather than a pattern for modern women? Should we view the submission of wives as we view slavery, *i.e.* as something which we should work to get rid of but must regulate if present? We shall first look at his actual teaching on submission and then consider its relation to slavery.

i. Just a strategy?

Peter was obviously concerned to give advice which would achieve the conversion of pagan husbands. A look at his discussion, however, shows that the advice was not just a strategy shaped only by that consideration. The behaviour which he commended is justified on other grounds. He said,

> [your beauty] should be that of your inner self, the unfading beauty of a gentle and quiet spirit, which is of great worth in God's sight. For this is the way the holy women of the past who put their hope in God used to make themselves beautiful. They were submissive to their own husbands, like Sarah, who obeyed Abraham and called him her master. You are her daughters if you do what is right and do not give way to fear (3:4–6).

The behaviour which Peter urged was not justified by its effect on husbands. It was rather presented as 'of great worth in God's sight', as the way of 'women who put their hope in God', and as 'what is right' (*to agathon*).

ii. Sarah and Abraham

The example of Sarah and Abraham underscores this point. Sarah was not married to an unbeliever, but to 'the father of the faithful'.

Her example is offered as one to be imitated even by a woman in the terrible position of being married to an unresponsive unbeliever. The specific aspect of Sarah's behaviour which is pointed out is her submission (*hypotassō*) to Abraham as shown by her obedience (*akouō*) and her calling him her 'master' or 'lord' (*kyrios*).

In our discussion of Ephesians 5 we noted that the roles of both the husband and the wife were defined from the model of Christ and his church without regard to the social setting or to the qualifications or performance of the partner. Peter's discussion amplifies this by calling for the same sort of response in the worst possible context for a wife. She is to continue to live a godly life even with an abusive pagan husband who can in no way be considered to demonstrate Christ's love for the church. If we superimpose Paul's imagery upon Peter's we can make the following observations: (1) the suffering wife of an unbeliever is called by God, even in her painful situation, faithfully to demonstrate the obedient love of the church for Christ by her submissive love for her husband (Eph. 5:22–24; 1 Pet. 3:4–6), and (2) her willing, suffering love for her husband not only shows the church's love for Christ but also shows the willing suffering and love of Christ for his church (1 Pet. 2:21–25). It is not an easy calling which Peter lays before the Christian wife of an unbeliever!

iii. 'Sarah. . .called him. . .master'

A word is in order at this point about the fact that 'Sarah. . .called him "master" (or "lord")'. To modern ears Peter's words are both abrasive and objectionable. It is unthinkable to modern wives to call their husbands 'master' and would seem impersonal to most husbands. We would consider the term appropriate to a slave/master relation. This is one of those cases in which the cultural context is very important. In some ways it parallels our previous discussion of Jesus' use of the term 'woman' in reference to his mother. Peter evidently refers to Genesis 18:12 in which Sarah doubts the Lord's promise of a child and says to herself, 'I am past the age of childbearing and my master (*ba'al*, lord/husband/master) is old.' Sarah's use of the word shows how she understood her relation to Abraham. He was the master of the house. That was a social role and implied authority, as is indicated by 'master'. The term need not, however, imply the distance and impersonality which we attribute to it.

A modern analogy may help. In the southern United States, it is not uncommon for a child to call its parents 'Sir' and 'Ma'am'. The use of the terms shows personal respect and respect for authority but is in no way a sign of servile relation between parent and child. Although a household servant and a son both use the terms, their implications are entirely dependent upon the status of the speaker. Respect for position and role makes possible frank communication without rebellion. An adult Southern son may voice his opinion with great force and candour without disrespect for his father. 'Sir, I think you are wrong. . .' both speaks plainly and acknowledges role. Peter's example of Sarah is not to be cast in the military context of a private shouting, '*Yes, Sir!*' to show blind, mindless obedience to his sergeant. Peter's comments make it very plain that when he refers to Sarah he is talking about a loving respect rather than blind, servile or fearful obedience (1 Pet. 3:1–2,6). Twentieth-century Christians must be careful about reading things into the text which do not belong there or, worse still, beginning to act upon such things. A wife is not a slave and a husband is not a tyrant or slave-master. Christ's example must be brought to bear or his people will imitate the pagans.

c. Weaker vessels and fellow-heirs

Peter's discussion shows that he was well aware of the dangers which faced men. His example of a godly wife leads him into an address to husbands. He says,

> Husbands, in the same way be considerate as you live with your wives (*sunoikontes katagnōsin*), and treat them with respect as the weaker partner and as heirs together with you of the gracious gift of life, so that nothing will hinder your prayers (1 Pet. 3:7).

Our study of Ephesians showed that Paul was particularly concerned to have husbands imitate Christ by giving themselves for the well-being of their wives. He was no doubt aware of our sinful tendency to abuse prerogatives. Peter uses other words and images to communicate the same basic message. Peter's actual language is difficult to translate into English. He calls upon husbands to 'live together [with their wives] according to knowledge'. 'According to knowledge' may refer to knowledge of God's design or to knowledge of his wife and her role. The two are not mutually exclusive, as his further explanation shows. Husbands are to 'honour' or 'respect' their wives as 'weaker vessels' (AV) and 'fellow-heirs'.

The term 'weaker vessel' may be interpreted in various ways. The term is comparative with the man; he is the 'stronger vessel'. Some have suggested that this means that women are less intelligent or morally capable. Neither the words themselves nor the context offers the least support for such a view. The context has been discussing slaves and wives with respect to physical suffering and subordinate roles. Peter's expression ought then to be interpreted either as indicating the physical weakness of a wife as compared to her husband or as pointing to her weaker position with respect to authority. Either reading indicates that men are to be aware of and respond considerately to the situation of their wives. Although commentators have generally preferred the physical reference, a reference to authority fits context more naturally and makes more sense. It would seem unlikely that Peter would be saying, 'Remember that she is physically weaker and cannot lift as much as you', or 'Remember that she cannot take as much beating as you'. It is quite likely that he would say, 'Remember that hers is the subordinate position and don't abuse your stronger position of authority.'

The woman is not only the weaker partner, she is also a 'fellow-heir of the gracious gift of life' (3:7). Peter's instruction to husbands calls for consideration of the wife's weaker position of authority, but also stresses the equality of the partners before God. In his day, as in ours, there was tendency for those in strong positions to despise or to look down upon those in weaker ones. Indeed, we tend to value highly those qualities which we possess in abundance, and to belittle qualities which we lack. Consider, for instance, the rivalry between athletes and scholars in many educational institutions: each exalts his forte and discounts that of his adversary. Peter speaks against this by reminding the men of the fact that their wives are equally heirs of God's gift of life.

Peter's final comment to believing husbands reminds them that their marriage is not independent of God and that their relation to their wives will affect their relation to God. Considerate behaviour toward wives allows the couple to serve God together. He is to respect his wife as a fellow-heir of God's grace, with the result that their joint prayer be not hindered. Anyone who is married and has gone through periods in which one partner has felt abused by the other knows the consequences for joint worship and devotion to God. Peter's instructions are as appropriate today as they were when he wrote.

Looking back over Peter's words to suffering wives and to Christian husbands, we conclude that his approach is not the same as Paul's, in that Paul's words to women built from the example of Christ and his church, while Peter spoke of imitating holy women who did 'what is right' and 'of great worth in God's sight'. The two different men spoke to two different situations, which helps to explain the diversity of their discussions. Despite the differences of approach, however, both present a hierarchical view of marriage and neither grounds that view in issues which are culturally relative. The crucial theological elements of Peter and Paul include the relation of Christ and the church, the suffering of Christ, the self-sacrifice of Christ, the lives of holy women which are of great worth in the sight of God, doing what is right, and the fact that husbands and wives are fellow-heirs. Significantly, none of these are culturally relative. The actual views of Peter and Paul, as reflected in the texts studied, offer no ground for viewing the 'headship' of the husband as a first-century application of the gospel message which is not applicable to the present. The apostles show an awareness of the sort of abuses of authority which are well known to us and are to be rejected today as they were then. Despite them the apostles taught a structured view of marriage.

3. Slavery, kingship and marital authority: outdated?

Recent debate has raised questions about the relevance of marital authority from a different perspective. It has been noted that submission and authority receive a great deal of attention in the New Testament. The categories discussed are of particular importance. It appears to some that the lists of relationships in which subordination is called for are themselves culturally dated and irrelevant to the present. Ephesians discusses relationships within marriage, parenthood and slavery (5:22 – 6:9). Colossians presents a parallel list (3:18 – 4:1). First Peter includes rulers and subjects, slavery and marriage (2:13 – 3:7). First Timothy mentions only slavery (6:1–2) and Romans only the state (13:1–7). Authority and response to it was obviously an important issue to the apostolic church.

The contemporary debate is asking whether and in what way these relations are relevant to our lives.

Some feel that if we insist on marital authority we must also defend the authority of kings and the rightness of slavery. Others are selective, holding that some but not all of the relationships should be maintained. A few argue that kings and slavery are indeed approved and ought to be established.

'None', 'some' or 'all': these are the choices. Which is biblical? Careful consideration of the nature of the relationships mentioned and of the manner in which they are handled in the New Testament helps to answer the question.

a. Parenthood

The relationships mentioned involve marriage, parenthood, slavery and the state. Parenthood stands out as one which will necessarily continue as long as children are born. Parental authority is not subject to dismissal as being culturally relative, for children need their parents' leadership. Children appear in the lists of Colossians and Ephesians, being placed by both between husband/ wife and slave/master. The lists therefore cannot be treated as entirely relative to their culture. The 'none (applies today)' position is therefore to be discarded, even without closer examination of the text. It remains to be judged whether those who accept the New Testament as authoritative are bound to fight for slavery, kingship and marital authority as well (all), or whether there is warrant for being selective (some). Consideration of the New Testament's approach to the various areas provides a definite answer. Let us consider the areas individually.

b. Slavery

Slavery is discussed in six primary passages: 1 Corinthians 7:20–23; Ephesians 6:5–9; Colossians 3:22–25; 1 Timothy 6:1–2; Titus 2:9–10; 1 Peter 2:18–25, and Philemon. The instruction of these texts guides Christian slaves in relation to their masters and sometimes guides Christian masters in relation to their slaves. Ephesians, Colossians, 1 Timothy and Titus call upon the slaves to honour, obey and serve their masters whole-heartedly and indicate that such behaviour is pleasing to the Lord. Ephesians and Colossians speak to the masters, calling upon them to do good to the slaves in their turn and to give up threatening. Masters are to treat the slaves with fairness and justice, showing no partiality, for they serve a heavenly Master who shows no partiality. Peter speaks particularly to Christian slaves who are suffering. Philemon deals with Onesimus, an escaped slave.

The crucial question for our purposes has to do not only with instructions to slaves but also with the nature of the institution. The New Testament treats parent/child and husband/wife relations as ordained of God. Nowhere, however, does it suggest the same for slavery. In 1 Corinthians 7:20–23 we find Paul viewing it as a life situation which does not affect one's relation to God. His urging is to serve God in whatever situation in life a man may be. The instructions of Ephesians, Colossians and 1 Timothy elaborate how to do so. In 1 Corinthians, however, we get a bit more information. He urges, 'Were you a slave when you were called? Don't let it trouble you – although if you can gain your freedom, do so' (1 Cor. 7:21). He would never give such advice to wives, citizens or children. Paul's instructions to slaves tell them how to live as Christians in the reality of their situation. He does not endorse slavery, but rather regulates it and indicates its undesirable nature.

The structure of Christian faith actually led to steps toward the abolition of slavery within their ranks. As we have noted, slavery was a matter of indifference for membership in the church. Within Judaism a quorum of ten *free men* was necessary for the establishment of a synagogue. Christianity knew no such rule. Philippi began its church with women. Moreover, the requirements for elders and deacons within the church make no mention whatever of bondage. Slaves could be elders of or with their masters (as tradition has suggested in the case of Onesimus). Paul's letter to Philemon suggests quietly that Philemon free Onesimus, who has become a brother and been such a help to Paul (Phm. 10, 12, 14, 15–17, 21, esp. 16, 21).

We would suggest that the New Testament, and Paul in particular, handles slavery in a manner which parallels Moses' handling of divorce: a practice which was not prescribed is regulated. Slavery is nowhere presented as the divine plan for human relationships.

c. The state

Matters of government are treated differently. The New Testament makes numerous references to officials of the state. Peter talks of a king (1 Pet. 2:13, 17); Jesus speaks of Caesar (Mt. 22:21); Paul speaks of governing authorities more generally (*e.g.* Rom. 13:1). Does Peter's command to 'honour the king' (1 Pet. 2:17) require that there be kings? The immediate context makes such a claim ridiculous. The passage begins, 'Submit yourselves for the Lord's sake to every authority instituted among men: whether to the king, as the supreme authority, or to governors, who are sent by him . . .' (2:13). The king is an example, not a prescribed category. Paul's discussion makes matters yet more clear.

Romans 13:1–7 specifically identifies governing authorities as ordained of God for the good of men and for the curbing of evil in this fallen world. They are 'God's servant to do good'. In the Roman empire 'governing authorities' were sometimes kings, governors, tetrarchs, and, of course, caesars. The New Testament does not require kings, but it does present government as a divine institution and does regulate the Christian's response to it. It is not viewed in the same way as slavery.

d. Marriage

Our examination of New Testament arguments concerning marriage has shown that the marriage relation was viewed as ordained by God at creation, with a particular structure as a continuing element of that relation. With the exception of 1 Peter 3, the major apostolic discussions of marriage all appeal to the divine institution of marriage at creation as a ground for the present ordering of it (1 Cor. 11:7–12; 14:34?; Eph. 5:31; 1 Tim. 2:13–14). These discussions not only prescribe the institution of marriage, but also demand a particular structure within it.

If we consider slavery and parental, civil and marital authority in parallel, the differences between the New Testament handling of them readily appear. The four institutions should be compared with respect to three issues: (1) divine establishment (is the institution seen as positively ordained by God?); (2) divine specification of roles and assignment of them to individuals (did God designate set roles and specify categories of persons who should fill them?); (3) regulation of conduct (is the conduct of those in given roles regulated?). The tabular presentation below makes the differences plain.

The slave/master relation is not divinely instituted, roles are not assigned by God, but the conduct of Christian slaves and masters is regulated. Civil authority is divinely instituted, does not involve precise forms, titles or roles specified by God or assigned by him to individuals; the conduct of Christians in the relationship is regulated. Both the marital and the parental relations are divinely instituted, and involve roles specified by God and assigned by him

	institution divinely established?	roles divinely specified?	conduct regulated?
slavery master/slave	– no	– no	+ yes
civil ruler/citizen	+ yes	– no	+ yes
parental parent/child	+ yes	+ yes	+ yes
marital husband/wife	+ yes	+ yes	+ yes

to individuals by gender or age; the conduct of Christians in the relationships is regulated.

We conclude that the apostolic lists of relationships in which submission to authority was urged are intended to regulate behaviour within the relationships but not to convey equal approval of them or to imply that they are essentially of the same order. Examination of the apostolic attitudes toward them quickly reveals that slavery is not approved but regulated, that civil authority is approved but its precise form is not specified, that parental authority is approved, the roles of parent and child being carefully assigned by age, and that marital authority is also approved, the roles of husband and wife being assigned by gender. It is not necessary to defend slavery or kingship in order to accept the structured view of parenthood and marriage which the New Testament teaches.

7

Women and men in worship

We have seen the minimal role of women in the worship of Judaism and the greatly enlarged role of women in Christian worship. In this chapter we must ask further questions about the enlarged role of Christian women. In the last chapter we considered distinctions between husband and wife in the marriage relation. Does that distinction carry over to the public worship? If so, to what degree? This problem confronted Pauline churches on a number of occasions as they tried to work out the meaning of their faith for conduct during worship. We shall consider two primary texts in this chapter: 1 Corinthians 11:2–16 and 14:33–36. The first of these might have been considered in the previous chapter on marital relationships but is better included here as it specifically reflects upon the implications of the marital relation for worship. First Timothy 2:8–15 might also be discussed under the present heading, but will be deferred until our discussion of church office.

A. HEAD COVERINGS AND AUTHORITY: 1 CORINTHIANS 11:2–16

We have already discussed the various factions which grew up at Corinth. In 1 Corinthians 11:2–16 Paul addresses a question about hair and hair coverings raised in a communication from the Corinthians. We do not have the letter from the Corinthians, but we are able to discern much of its content from Paul's response. As we study the passage we shall build up a picture of the Corinthian question. Paul wrote,

> [2]I praise you for remembering me in everything and for holding to the teachings, just as I passed them on to you. [3]Now I want

you to realize that the head of every man is Christ, and the head of the woman is the man, and the head of Christ is God. [4]Every man who prays or prophesies with a covering [of long hair] dishonours his head. [5]And every woman who prays or prophesies with no covering [of hair] on her head, dishonours her head – she is just like a 'shorn woman'. [6]If a woman has no covering [of long hair], let her clip it short. And if it is shameful for her to have her hair clipped short or shaved, let her be covered [by it]. [7]A man ought not to have [long hair as] a covering on his head, since he is the image and glory of God; but the woman is the glory of the man. [8]For the man was not taken out of the woman, but the woman out of the man; [9]neither was the man created for the sake of the woman, but the woman for the sake of the man. [10]For this reason a woman ought to have a sign of authority on her head, because of the angels. [11]In the Lord, however, woman is not independent of man. [12]For as woman was taken out of man, so also the man is born of woman. And everything is from God. [13]Judge for yourselves: Is it proper for a woman to pray to God with her head not covered [by her hair]? [14]Does not nature itself teach you that if a man has long hair it is a disgrace to him, [15]but if a woman has long hair, it is her glory? Her long hair is given her instead of a veil. [16]If anyone wants to be argumentative about this, we have no such practice – nor do the churches of God (1 Cor. 11:2–16, my own rendering).

Paul's response is complex and raises many different points. We shall therefore have to look at a series of issues if we are to derive maximum benefit from it. Patience must be exercised as we consider each topic. It will be helpful to look back over the biblical text as a whole whenever attention to detail begins to cause the whole to get out of focus.

1. The meaning of headship

Paul opens this discussion with a word of praise for his church. It was very much his practice to offer positive words where he could, a practice which was no doubt effective in showing his concern. In this case it has a bit more importance than usual. He praises the Corinthians for holding his teachings, and wishes to build upon some of his teachings to persuade them to alter a practice of theirs. All parties would have agreed that Christ is the head of every man. It is not as clear what they would have thought about the man as the head of the woman. Presumably they would have had little problem with understanding God the Father as head of Christ. From this series of 'headship' relations Paul will draw conclusions about head coverings. It is necessary to examine the meaning 'head' (*kephalē*) in some detail.

In our day, the head is known to be the seat of thinking and the 'executive' of the body. In ancient times, however, this was not the case. The head was merely the uppermost organ of the body. Its uppermost position, however, led to its use to identify that which is most visible, 'on top', 'at the beginning' or 'prior'. In English we speak of the 'head' of a river to refer to its point of origin. This was a typical usage of 'head' (*kephalē*) in classical Greek. By Paul's day, however, a change had occurred. The Greek versions of the Bible used *kephalē* (head) to translate the Hebrew word r'osh, which also means 'head'. The Hebrew word, however, was used to indicate one in a position of authority or command as well as origin or 'priority'. In Paul's day, therefore, the Greek word 'head' (*kephalē*) could mean a physical head, a person with authority, or the source of something. Head (*kephalē*) was used in first-century Greek as a synonym for the more common words for 'ruler' (*archōn*) and for 'source' (*archē*).[1]

To say that a man is head of a woman may thus be to say that they are intimately connected as parts of a single body, or to say that he is her origin (*i.e.* her beginning is in him), or to say that he is in a position of authority with respect to her. These various

[1] S. Bedale's influential study, 'The Meaning of *kephalē* in the Pauline Epistles' (*Journal of Theological Studies*, 5 (1954), pp. 211–215), provides careful documentation of the meaning of *kephalē*. He suggests that the word should be understood as 'origin' in 1 Cor. 11. His conclusion is frequently cited by persons who do not see 'authority' in Paul's use of 'head' in this passage. Indeed, some authors seem to imply that it is ignorant to take 'head' as pointing to authority because it really meant 'origin' to the first-century mind. In such cases Bedale has either been misunderstood, cited at second hand, or misused. He argued that Paul *derived* man's authority over woman from the fact of his priority. Bedale may be allowed to speak for himself. Having made the point that Paul saw man as *kephalē* (head) of the woman in the sense of being her *archē* (beginning, *i.e.* the one from whom her being is taken), he goes on to say, 'in St. Paul's view, the female in consequence is "subordinate" . . . (*cf.* Eph. 5:23). But this principle of subordination . . . rests upon the order of creation. . . . That is to say, *while the word kephalē (and archē also, for that matter) unquestionably carries with it the idea of "authority"*, such authority in social relationships derives from relative priority (causal rather than merely temporal) in the order of being. St. Paul makes it plain, of course (. . . Gal. iii:28), that he is here speaking of men and women in their respective sexual differentiation and function, not of their spiritual status or capacities' (pp. 214, 215; italics mine). It is obvious that Bedale offers no support for the idea that *kephalē* (head) does not imply authority if it means 'origin' instead of 'head over'. As will be clear from the ensuing discussion, I think 'head over' is the better translation in 1 Cor. 11. What should be absolutely clear is that it is an abuse of Bedale and his point to cite his article to disprove the idea that authority is inherent in Paul's use of *kephalē* (head).

meanings are, of course, not mutually exclusive. We must therefore ask, on each occasion of its use, which sense of 'head' is intended. We must be prepared even to accept the possibility of two or three meanings being applicable simultaneously.

Which meaning is to be preferred in 1 Corinthians 11:3? Until recently, scholars were uniform in preferring 'head over' to 'origin of'. The question cannot, however, be solved by appeal to numbers of authorities. Nor can it be solved by appeal to lexicons. It must be answered from the context and from analogy in other Pauline writings. The following considerations are relevant:

1. Paul's use of head elsewhere. Our previous study in chapter 6 of Ephesians 5:23 and 1:22–23 showed that Paul used 'head' in those passages to point to Christ and husbands as possessing authority and as being ones to whom subjection is due. A second meaning, head (Christ) united to a body (the church), is also present in both texts. We have seen that in as much as all things are said to be under Christ's feet and he is said to be 'appointed' or 'given to be' (edōken) head over all things for the sake of his body the church (1:22–23), it is difficult to see room for the 'source' concept to enter the discussion. Paul did not say that Christ was given to be source of all things, but ruler over them. Ephesians 1:22–23 builds from the body language of head and feet to the idea of head as ruler.

A different direction can be discerned at Colossians 2:19 and Ephesians 4:15. In these passages Paul builds from the body/head imagery to the idea of Christ as the pattern (full-grown head) into which his body, the church, is growing. To this he adds the idea of Christ as the source of strength for its growth. The concept of authority is not introduced in these two passages using head (kephalē) in the sense of source. In addition it should be noted that neither passage makes use of marital imagery alongside the head-as-source imagery.

'Head' (kephalē) as 'authority' and 'source' may coalesce with the idea of union as in Colossians 1:15–20, where Christ is the source of all things, the head of his body and supreme over all the things which he has created. As with the other head-as-source passages, the marital imagery is not brought into play. Interestingly 'headship' is not even used about the marital relation in Colossians 3:18–19.

We conclude that Paul used head/body language to describe the relation of Christ to his church. In Ephesians 1 and 5 'head' meant 'head over'. In Colossians 1 and 2 and Ephesians 4 it was related to bodily imagery and to the idea of 'source'. It is significant that in those passages which clearly use 'head' (*kephalē*) to mean 'source' Paul does not introduce marital imagery. In passages in which he does use 'head' as 'head over', he uses the head language to illustrate the marital relationship. We concluded that Paul's other usage of 'head' (*kephalē*) would favour the idea of 'head over' being present at 1 Corinthians 11 where marriage is being discussed.

2. Paul's appeal to man as the 'origin' of woman in other places. Paul does view the prior creation of Adam and the fact that Eve was drawn from him as significant in the relation of men and women. He mentions these facts in 1 Timothy 2:13 and 1 Corinthians 11:8. In these verses he does not say that Adam was Eve's 'head' (*kephalē*) or even her source (*archē*). Instead he speaks of her coming 'out of' (*ek*) him or of his being 'formed first'. Paul does not introduce 'head' language when he is talking about origins.

3. If 'head' means 'source' in 1 Corinthians 11:3, Paul's parallelism is poor and he virtually teaches that God made Christ. This is most clearly seen if we consider the implications of the head-means-source view for each of the three relationships sequentially:

a. Man/woman. (i) Adam is the source of Eve in that she was physically taken out of him. (ii) She had no existence prior to that time. (iii) Adam had no part in making her.

b. Christ/man. (i) Christ is not the source of Adam if by that we mean that Adam was physically taken out of him. (ii) Adam did come into existence through the creative work of Christ. In this sense Christ is his 'source'.

c. God/Christ. In this case an effort to maintain parallelism with other parts of the series leads to strange conclusions. (i) Does Paul wish to say that Christ was physically created from a piece taken out of God? (ii) Does he mean to indicate that Christ did not exist before that time? (iii) Does he mean that God was the Creator of Christ? These conclusions were specifically rejected by the early church at the time of the Arian controversy and are not compatible with other Pauline teaching. There is no way to construct a satisfactory set of parallels if we take 'head' to mean 'source' in 1 Corinthians 11:3.

If, on the other hand, 'head' means 'head over', a set of parallels can be established:

a. Man/woman. In the home, the husband is the head over his wife. In the church, the religious sphere, certain men act as heads by being elders, teachers and leaders of the worship (assuming that women elders and teachers are prohibited by 1 Timothy 2–3, which will be discussed later).

b. Christ/man. In the home, Christ is head over all husbands. They are to model their behaviour after his. In the religious sphere, Christ is the head over all elders and teachers.

c. God/Christ. God the Son became man and acted on behalf of Adam's race. As 'second Adam' (*cf.* 1 Cor. 15:45) he was obedient to God's authority (headship), even to the point of death (Phil. 2:8). In his capacity as the second Adam, the head of a new mankind, Christ will acknowledge God as 'head over' mankind by handing over 'the kingdom to God after he has destroyed all [other] dominion, authority and power' (1 Cor. 15:24).

This set of parallels, in contrast to the set assuming that 'head' (*kephalē*) means 'source', is self-consistent and does not do violence to either Pauline or other New Testament theology.

4. Head coverings were at issue in 1 Corinthians 11. In the first century these were not understood as having anything to do with woman's origin from man. They were signs of her relation to his authority. This remains the case whether we conclude that Paul was talking of veils or the length and style of a woman's hair. Even the text of 1 Corinthians 11 makes it clear that the issue under debate at Corinth was authority (verse 10). Reading 'head' (*kephalē*) as 'head over' in 1 Corinthians 11:3 is therefore more consistent with the central problem at issue in the chapter.

The best conclusion seems to be that in 1 Corinthians 11:3 Paul was teaching that a hierarchy of headship authority exists and that it is ordered: God, Christ as second Adam, man, woman. Paul saw this as relevant to the question of head coverings.

Two further comments need to be made: (1) We have noted that, if Paul taught that God is the origin of Christ, he taught what the church has condemned as Arian Christology. It has been argued by some that, if Paul taught that God is head over Christ, he taught subordinationist Christology, which the church has also condemned. This charge must be rejected because it is manifestly Christ *as head of mankind* who is in view in 1 Corinthians 11:3. The Corinthian letter itself teaches that it is *precisely as such* that he will acknowledge the headship of God by handing over the kingdom (1 Cor. 15:24). It is not as the eternal second person of the Trinity but as head of mankind that he is subordinate. In theological jargon, the relation is economic, not ontological. (2) As we noted above (note 1, p. 164), even if 'head' were taken to mean 'source' in 1 Corinthians 11:3, the conclusion to be reached is *not* that Paul did not teach subordination, but that he did so *by means of* such an argument. Thus, although we think it quite unlikely, the choice of 'source' as the meaning of 'head' (*kephalē*) in 1 Corinthians 11:3 does not shift the focus of the chapter from the question of authority in the marriage relation.

2. What did Paul want on women's heads?

Contemporary Christians have wrestled with the meaning of obedience to Paul's requirement concerning women's heads. Older translations have generally understood him to have meant veils, and have therefore supplied the term in 1 Corinthians 11. Paul does not in fact mention veils except in verse 15, where he says, 'Her long hair is given her for (*anti*, instead of) a veil.' Lifted out of this chapter, this verse would be universally rendered as teaching that long hair is given *instead of* or *to take the place of* a veil. That is always the force of *anti*. 'For' is an adequate translation, *if* it means '(as a substitute) for'. Most Bible versions, convinced that Paul taught the necessity of veiling, have supplied the word 'veil' earlier in the text and allowed *anti* to be translated by 'for' or 'as', implying that a woman's long hair is given her as a veil and that it points to the necessity of putting another veil on top of her hair, *i.e.* that her 'natural' veil shows that she needs another one. It is easy to understand the motivation for this; it seems unlikely that Paul would argue strongly for the necessity of veils from verse 2 to verse 14 and then insist that long hair is really quite sufficient! A close examination of Paul's language suggests another way of approaching the problem which does not require weakening the force of *anti*.[2]

Throughout the earlier part of the passage, the words usually translated 'covered with a veil' or 'veiled' are *kata kephalēs echōn* (11:4) and *katakalyptos* (11:6, 7, 13), literally 'having upon the head' and 'covered'. The word usually translated 'uncovered' or 'unveiled' is *akatakalyptos*, which literally means 'uncovered'. None of

---

[2] A more detailed development of the view about to be presented can be found in J. Hurley, 'Did Paul Require Veils or the Silence of Women? A Consideration of 1 Cor. 11:2–16 and 1 Cor. 14:33b-36', *Westminster Theological Journal*, 35 (1973), pp. 190–220. The exegesis of the passage in this book is essentially similar, but has a few significant changes.

these words specifies what sort of covering is in view and it is perfectly reasonable to supply a general word such as 'veil'. As we have seen, however, verse 15 casts doubt on the propriety of this. Further reflection on verses 4–6 in the light of our previous study of veiling customs and of a study of *akatakalyptos* (uncovered) in the Greek Old Testament suggests a better alternative.

Our consideration of veiling customs and hair-styles in the Old Testament and in Judaism noted that veiling was not practised as a requirement in Old Testament Israel and that it is doubtful that it was required by Jews at the time of Christ except perhaps among the wealthy of the large cities.[3] We also noted that hair length and the way in which it was worn was of significant importance. Greek, Roman and Jewish women grew their hair long and wore it put up in various styles. In all three cultures long hair flying loose, dishevelled hair or hair cut off was a sign that its wearer was set off from the community.

One particular case of loosed hair is of importance to our present question: the loosed hair of a suspected adulteress undergoing the 'bitter-water' rite of Numbers 5:18. Her hair was publicly loosed to mark her off as one suspected of being 'unclean' by virtue of adultery, of repudiating her relation to her husband by giving herself physically to another man. If the rite showed her to be innocent, her hair was once again put up. This procedure was not assigned for a woman actually accused of adultery. Such a woman was tried and either acquitted or executed without undergoing the bitter-water rite. By the New Testament period, however, the Jews could not execute and the punishment for an adulteress was the shearing of her hair and expulsion from the synagogue.[4] It is against this background that Paul's words to the Corinthians are best understood. The relevance of the background can be seen from a look at Paul's discussion and his particular word choice for 'uncovered'.

Let us consider first Paul's actual discussion. In verse 4 he indicates that a man who prays or prophesies with long hair or a veil on his head dishonours his head. Presumably, the second use

---

[3] See appendix for a fuller discussion of this point.
[4] On capital punishment, see our previous discussion and T. Reinach, 'Diaspora' in I. Singer (ed.), *The Jewish Encyclopedia* (London, 1893), 4, pp. 566–567. On the shearing of the hair, see Wettstein, *Novum Testamentum Graecum* (Amsterdam, 1752), *ad. loc.*, and Buchler, 'Das Schneider des Haares als Strafe der Ehebrecher bei den Semiten', in *Wiener Zeitschrift für die Kunde des Morgenlandes*, XIV (1905), pp. 91–138. The practice of cutting the hair of an adulteress has continued even into this century as a folk punishment.

of 'head' means Christ and perhaps also the man's own self as well. How does he dishonour Christ or himself? And how does an uncovered woman dishonour her 'head' (presumably meaning her husband or men generally and perhaps herself)? How also does her being 'uncovered' make her like a woman who has had her hair clipped short or shaven off and bring her shame? Let us assume for a moment that the covering (whatever it was) is a sign of the authority of a man in relation to his wife (*cf.* 11:10). The removal of the sign by the wife would then constitute a repudiation of her husband's authority, of his 'headship'. If a man's wife publicly repudiated his authority, it is easy to see how this would dishonour him, her 'head'. It is not clear that her action would dishonour or shame her. In our day it might even make her a liberated heroine. Let us move on to consider the dishonour caused by a man with his head covered. If a man, whose head is Christ, puts on his head the sign of being under a man's authority, it is easy to see how Christ is thereby dishonoured; one who should be under Christ alone publicly announces that he is submissive to another 'head'.

While it is not likely that the Corinthian men were in fact putting coverings on, it would seem quite likely that the Corinthian women had concluded that, having been raised with Christ (1 Cor. 4:8–10), their new position in Christ and their resultant freedom to participate in the worship by prayer and prophecy was incompatible with wearing a sign of submission to their husbands! Paul defends their right to pray and to prophesy, but does not see it as doing away with the marital relation. The already realized aspect of the kingdom leads to women's participation; it does not do away with marital submission, but rather should restore it to its proper form. Only at the resurrection will marital patterns be done away completely (Mt. 22:30). The Corinthians had not grasped the both/and of the present stage of the kingdom.

How does all this relate to a woman without a covering being shamed as a woman who is clipped or shorn? Paul's actual word choice helps us here. We have noted that he did not specify the nature of the 'covering'. He spoke instead of 'having on the head' and of being 'uncovered' (*akatakalyptos*). It is this word which provides a help. The suspected adulteress of Numbers 5:18 was accused of repudiating her relation to her husband by giving herself to another. As a sign of this, her hair, which was done up on her head, was let loose. The Hebrew word which is used to describe both the letting loose of the hair and being unveiled (*pr'*) is translated in the Greek Old Testament by *akatakalyptos*, the word which Paul uses for 'uncovered'. Could it be that Paul was not asking the Corinthian women to put on veils, but was asking them to continue wearing their hair in the distinctive fashion of women? Let us follow out the implications of this for the passage and in particular for the shorn hair.

If the Corinthian women were 'letting their hair down' to show that marital patterns no longer applied, that they were no longer subordinate to their husbands, the sign of their independence was also the sign of a woman suspected of adultery. In Jewish practice of the day, a woman convicted of such a charge had her hair clipped short or shaved off and was put out of the synagogue. The clipped or shaven hair thus became a highly visible sign of her shame, rather like the famous 'scarlet letter' of Nathaniel Hawthorne's Hester Prynne. We can now understand Paul's remarks. If a woman accuses herself by putting on herself the sign of a suspected adulteress, of a woman who has repudiated her husband's authority, she should go on to put on the sign of one who has been convicted. Her long hair is thus itself the sign either of her dignity as a wife or of her shame. A review of the translation of 1 Corinthians 11:2–16 on pages 162 and 163 will show the implications of this understanding for our text. This 'long-hair' view has been adopted as an alternative by the NIV. We will discuss the implications of Paul's instructions for our day at the end of our study of 1 Corinthians 11.

3. Who is the image of God?

The eleventh chapter of 1 Corinthians has borne the brunt of much criticism over the last few decades, and even before. Paul's insistence on 'coverings' has often been seen as an absolutizing of a passing local custom (defended by Paul through faulty exegesis of Gn. 1) as though it were a requisite of the faith. A recent commentator has said of Paul's teaching in this chapter, 'The apostle elevates the relativities of culture to the absolutes of Christian piety.'[5] The ten verses (11:7–16) which develop Paul's rationale for the coverings have been the focus of such attacks. We must therefore consider them in some detail. To do this successfully we shall have to consider not only 1 Corinthians, but also some passages

---

[5] P. Jewett, *Man and Woman*, p. 118.

from Genesis. Some of these matters will be raised again in connection with 1 Timothy 2:8–15.

Verse 7 reads, 'A man ought not to cover his head (with long hair), since he is the image and glory of God; but the woman is the glory of man.' Furore has often attended the reading of this verse. Many commentators have forcefully pointed out that the text of Genesis 1:26 will not permit such an argument as Paul apparently wishes to make. Paul argues that the man is the image and glory of God and that the woman is the glory of man. Does he mean that the woman is *not* the image of God? Or that she is the image of man? Genesis says that both men and women are the image of God. A simple comparison of Genesis 1:26 and 1:28 sustains this point in the form in which it is usually raised. Genesis 1:26 informs us that God determined to create man (*adam*, a man/ Adam/mankind) in his own image, with *dominion* over the earth. Verse 28 relates God's actions and indicates that he blessed *them* and told them to increase in number and to *rule* the earth. Unless changes in the manner of reproduction have taken place and unless God made some other males who are unmentioned, it is inescapable that the plural 'them' of verse 28 is the man and his wife and therefore that *adam* in verse 26 is a collective reference to mankind rather than to males or to Adam alone.

Further reflection on the structure of Genesis 1 reveals that the chapter is not intended to give us information about the presence or absence of hierarchical relations within the species mentioned. A central stress in that chapter is the rule of God over his creation and his forming of various realms with rulers over them; thus the sun and moon rule the day and night, the fish rule the sea, the birds rule the air, *etc.* Not surprisingly, when the creation of man is reported, it is said, 'Let us create man [-kind] after our image and let him [*i.e.* mankind = them] have dominion [exercise rule] over . . . *all* the earth, and over *all* the creatures that move along the ground' (Gn. 1:26). Mankind is thus set apart from all of the other creatures. The others rule a given realm, by divine appointment; mankind images God by ruling over all of the realms and all of the kinds. It is especially with respect to this universal rule over the creatures that mankind is identified as the image of God in Genesis 1:26–28. Because the text of the chapter is nowhere concerned to speak of hierarchies *within* species, it would be an abuse of the verses 26–28 to cite them *either for or against* the 'headship' of one partner or the other. To do so is to introduce something which the text ignores. Animal species for instance very definitely have dominant sexes. The text completely omits reference to such facts, stressing only that each 'kind' is to multiply and to rule its sphere. With respect to mankind, therefore, it can and must be stressed that both sexes are called to multiply and to rule all of the earth. To go on to suggest the subordination of one sex or the equality of the sexes would be to abuse the text of Genesis 1. Other texts must be examined to determine how the sexes are to relate. We conclude, therefore, that if Paul, in 1 Corinthians 11, meant to argue from Genesis 1:26–28 that men rather than women are the image of God, he has not faithfully exegeted the text of Genesis.

But *has* Paul in fact appealed to Genesis 1:26 and did he wish to deny that a woman is the image of God in the sense intended in Genesis 1:26–28? Consider for a moment the context of the chapter and Paul's actual words. The chapter is concerned for authority relations: social, functional relations in which God is head, Christ is head, and men are head. Paul has not been discussing personal dignity or worth (ontological value). Man, in his authority relation to creation and to his wife, images the dominion of God over the creation (a central theme in Gn. 1) and the headship of Christ over his church (Eph. 1:20–22; 5:22–23, *etc.*) The woman is not called to image God or Christ *in the relation which she sustains to her husband.* She images instead the response of the church to God and Christ by willing, loving self-subjection (Eph. 5:22–23). In *this particular sense* of authority relationships, the main topic of 1 Corinthians 11, it is absolutely appropriate to say that the man images God and that the woman does not. I want to stress that in saying this there need be no implication whatsoever that women are not the image of God in *other senses.* Paul did not say that man was the image of God and that the woman was the image of the man. Indeed, as we shall note when we consider verse 10, Paul himself points out her rule over creation. The same point can, of course, be made from Colossians 3:10–11 in which Paul says that all believers are being renewed according to God's image. The context of 1 Corinthians 11, then, does not point to Genesis 1:26 as the basis of 'image' in 1 Corinthians 11:7. It points instead to the 'dominion' theme of Genesis 1 as a whole, of the Old Testament as a whole, and to the headship idea as expressed in 1 Corinthians 11:3 in particular as the basis of man's role as image in 1 Corinthians 11:7.

This point is emphasized by Paul's actual word choice. Paul did *not* follow the Greek Old Testament when he said that man is the image and glory of God, although most commentators and virtually all critics have assumed that he did. All our Greek Old Testaments translate the Hebrew words for 'image' and 'likeness' in Genesis 1:26 as *eikōn* (image) and *homoiōma* (likeness), appropriate words. Paul shows in Romans 1:23 that he is aware of this fact. In 1 Corinthians 11:7, however, he used *eikōn* (image) and *doxa* (glory). He has deliberately not used the terminology of Genesis. It is important to pursue the meaning of *doxa* (glory) if we are to understand him.

We have seen that man imitates or images God and Christ in his headship role. How does that relate to man's being the 'glory' of God and to the woman being the 'glory' of the man? What does 'glory' mean? We often think in terms of 'reflection', *i.e.* that man's 'glory' reflects God's. This brings 'glory' back into the sphere of 'image' in that an image and a reflection may be virtually synonymous. Paul does not use the term quite this way. The word *doxa* (glory) had a variety of shades of meaning. Paul's use of it in 1 Corinthians 15:40–41 is helpful here. In that text he speaks of the differing 'glories' or 'splendours' of the sun, moon and stars. The glory of the sun is that brightness which corresponds to, points to and emerges from its station. The brightness of the moon points to or manifests its station. The glory of a thing is thus that which points to or manifests its dignity, honour or station. Man is relationally the glory of God when he is in an appropriate relation to him: under God, thereby pointing to God's dominion; over creation, thereby manifesting in his action that dominion. Correspondingly, a woman would be the 'glory' of her husband as she stands in a proper relation to him, thereby manifesting his station. To use the terminology of Ephesians, the husband is to manifest or visibly demonstrate God's role (= be the glory of God) by taking responsible initiative and by being the loving, self-sacrificing head. The woman is to manifest or demonstrate the church's role by being the self-subjecting wife who acknowledges the man's calling (= being the glory of the man). Paul's pattern of thought may or may not be congenial to the twentieth-century way of thought, but he is not guilty of denying Genesis' teaching concerning male and female as the image of God in his remarks in 1 Corinthians 11.

4. Woman for the sake of man?

Paul follows his comment on roles with two supporting comments about the creation of the sexes in Genesis 2. He says that the man was not taken out of (*ek*) the woman, but vice versa, and that the man was not created for the sake of the woman but vice versa. His obvious point is that these two facts imply that the man should be the 'head'. Modern critics have not been happy with his reasoning. Why should the fact that she was taken from him make her subordinate? Should it not show them to be equal, of the same stuff? Why could it not be said that she was made for the sake of his need rather than for the sake of his having someone to command? The question of the legitimacy of Paul's use of Genesis is once again raised. It will be raised again when we consider 1 Timothy 2:8–15, in which Paul appeals to the same texts and to the same themes. At risk of inadequately treating our subject, I shall defer consideration of Paul's use of Genesis until we come to the appropriate place in the discussion of 1 Timothy 2:8–15.[6] Whether or not all agree with Paul that woman's derivative origin and her creation to be man's 'helper' imply that she should be subordinate, virtually all agree that that is what he thought.

5. A sign of authority because of the angels

1 Corinthians 11:10, literally translated, reads, 'Because of this the woman ought to have [a sign of] authority on her head because of the angels.' This cryptic remark has been the subject of much discussion. Three basic views have been advanced: (1) the woman ought to have a sign of a man's authority over her so that angels, also present at the gathering of the church, will not be sexually aroused by the women; (2) the woman ought to have a sign of man's authority so that she will not offend angels, who are the guardians of the divine order; (3) the 'sign of authority' is both a sign of the man's authority with respect to the woman and a sign of her authority with respect to the rest of creation, in particular angels. Let us consider them one by one.

The 'aroused angels' theory has a long pedigree in theological thought.[7] Its root lies in Jewish speculation that the 'sons of God' in Genesis 6:2 were evil angels. The sons of God are better understood as men faithful to God. Quite apart from the question of Old

---

[6] Chapter 8, pp. 197ff.
[7] For a good bibliography, see J. Hurd, *The Origin of 1 Corinthians*, p. 184, n. 1.

Testament exegesis, such a view is quite foreign to the New Testament. Satan and his hosts were defeated by Christ's victory. Christian women need not live in fear that they will be sexually assaulted by them. Further, the angels present with God's people are obedient to God (*cf.* Heb. 12:22; Rev. 5:11); and why are the angels more likely to be aroused than the Corinthian men? There is little to say in favour of the 'aroused angel' theory.

The 'out of respect for the angels' theory has more to support it. As we have noted, the New Testament church did think in terms of the presence of angels with the assembly of God's people. The Corinthians evidently considered that some of their tongues were those of angels (13:1).[8] In addition, the Corinthians showed a particular concern about their relations to angels. More than all the other letters of Paul, this one discusses relations with angels. There is good indication that the Corinthians thought that their state of being raised with Christ had put them on a par with angels (4:8–9; 6:1; 13:1). Paul was concerned to say that they were not yet reigning with Christ (4:8) but were at present a spectacle for the universe to see (4:9), although they would ultimately judge the angels (6:1). Interpreted in this light, the 'out of respect for the angels' view calls upon the Corinthians to respect their relation to the angels as well as the relations between the sexes by wearing a covering.

There is one serious drawback to this view: the word *exousia* (authority), translated here 'sign of authority'. The term does not mean 'sign of (someone else's) authority'. It has instead an active sense and, apart from the context, would be taken as pointing to the authority of the woman herself, not that of her husband.[9]

The third way of understanding Paul's remark in verse 10 picks up the active meaning of *exousia*. Up to this point in the chapter, the women have been told to recognize the authority of others. The woman seems to be told, 'You are low man (!) on the totem pole!' One is reminded of the saying in which the eldest brother kicks the next, who kicks the next, until the smallest '. . . and he went and kicked the dog'. It almost seems that the careful balancing note which we previously found is missing. In Ephesians 5:22–33 we found careful instructions to the husband, checking his

<hr />

[8] For a more extended discussion, see J. Hurley, 'Did Paul Require Veils?', pp. 210–211.

[9] Paul uses *exousia* (authority) nine other times in 1 Cor. (7:37; 8:9; 9:4, 5, 6, 12 (twice), 18; 15:24). All nine are active in meaning. For further discussion, see J. Hurley, 'Did Paul Require Veils?', pp. 206–212.

abuse of authority and reminding him of his close union with his wife. The same note was struck in 1 Peter 3:7, where husbands were reminded that their wives were fellow-heirs of the gift of life (note the parallel with Paul's thought at Galatians 3:28). In my estimate, verse 10 marks the beginning of just such a stress on mutual relation in 1 Corinthians 11.

The flow of the chapter to this point would lead us to expect the conclusion that a woman should wear her hair as an acknowledgment of the continuing relevance of her relation to her husband. This helped to check Corinthian confusion about the implications of the present state of the kingdom. Paul's assertion that her long hair is a sign of authority which she possesses comes as quite a jolt. How can the sign of her relation to her husband be a sign of authority which she possesses? 'Because of the angels,' Paul says. The woman's hair marks her as a woman. The manner in which she wears it marks her as a woman embracing her role in the creation of God in this given moment of the course of redemptive history . . . or as a woman rejecting it. The place of a woman in Christianity was not the empty, valueless place of many Eastern women. Her place was above all creation (angels included), barring only her father or husband (and this too would change with the return of Christ). Her hair is thus a sign of tremendous authority as well as a sign of a particular relation to her husband.

The Corinthian women no doubt saw the loosing of their hair as a sign that they possessed authority equal to that of the men. Paul pointed out that their action was in fact a rejection of the order of God and of the role of women; loosed hair was a sign of rebellion and disgrace. When that hair was *not* done as a man's but as a woman's it became that which marked her as one possessing authority, as vicegerent of creation, one who would join in the judgment of rebellious angels, rather than be judged with them (1 Cor. 6:1). Paul's cryptic remark about angels, thus interpreted, is related to the remark in Ephesians 5:28–31 about the union of husbands and wives and to the stress in 1 Peter 3:7 on the two as fellow-heirs.

The next two verses are not at all cryptic or unclear. The theme of the inter-relatedness of the sexes stands out clear and strong: 'In the Lord, however, woman is not independent (*chōris*) of man, nor is man independent of woman. For as woman came out of (*ek*) man, so also man is born of (*dia* + genitive, 'through') woman. But everything is from God' (1 Cor. 11:11–12). The husband may

not consider himself the ruler of his wife and abuse his authority.
By God's design he is dependent on her for birth; they are inter-
dependent by God's design. As in each of the other passages
calling for a social, functional (economic) subordination of women,
we find a strong counterbalance to check male abuse and disregard
of the unity of the sexes.

6. Long hair and glory

Paul returns to his central thrust with a rhetorical question, asking
them to judge the matter for themselves (in the light of what he
has said; 11:13). He then goes on to a final set of remarks which
shift the focus somewhat. He says,

> [14]Does not nature itself teach you that if a man has long hair, it
> is a disgrace to him, [15]but that if a woman has long hair, it is
> her glory? Her long hair is given to her instead of a veil. [16]And
> if anyone wants to be contentious about this, we have no such
> custom – nor do the churches of God (11:14–16).

Many contemporary readers of Paul wonder just how 'nature'
teaches these things. It is likely that Paul is using 'nature' (*physis*)
here in the same sense that he used it in Romans 1:26; 2:14, 27,
etc., where it means God's design for nature rather than simply
the way things happen to be or what society is doing. He may be
thinking of the discussion of the purpose of hair (according to
God's design) which he has just completed, *i.e.* 'Does not nature,
as I have just explained it, teach. . . .' If he had not mentioned
nature, we would understand him simply to be calling them to
notice that long hair was in fact a disgrace to a man in that time.
He was no doubt aware that convention was in conformity with
his point.

We do well, however, to remember his earlier discussion. He
has explained that a man with a woman's hair dishonours his
'head'. He has also discussed 'glory'. The man points to the station
of God (is his glory); the woman points to the station of the man
(is his glory); here we learn that a woman's hair points to her
station (is her glory). This, of course, stands in line with his earlier
remark that what she has on her head is a sign of her authority,
that her hair marks her as vicegerent of creation. Not only by
social custom, but also by divine design, a woman's hair marks
her high role in the creation of God.

7. Veils

The final sentence of verse 15, 'Her long hair is given to her instead of a veil', has already been mentioned but requires somewhat further comment. Paul's Corinthian congregation was a sea of contrasts. Some wished to divorce their wives to avoid ceremonial defilement through intercourse (7:1–14); others felt free to use prostitutes (6:12–20) or to marry their father's wife (5:1–3). Some felt free to enjoy meat at idol-feasts (10:14–22); others had scruples about the butcher's meat (10:25–30). In the chapter at hand we have seen that some felt free to discard signs of marital authority. What might have caused Paul to follow his words about a woman's hair being her glory with a strong command that she needs no veil because her hair is given to her instead of one? The word which is translated as 'veil' is *peribolaion*. It means 'a thing which is wrapped or thrown around'. It does not describe a facial veil or a light head-covering such as a hat. It would be used of a cloak, a shawl or the garment known as a *himation*, a long lightweight rectangular shawl which could be draped over the arms and head of its wearer. Paul is specifically rejecting the idea that women must have an additional covering over their hair. So strong was his feeling about the sufficiency of hair that he went on to say that if anyone wished to argue about it, neither he nor the churches of God had any *such* custom (*toiautēn sunētheian*). Most translations substitute 'other' for 'such' because they think that Paul required veils rather than forbade that they be required. It may be that Paul's remarks have a broader reference than just verse 15. He may have in view the custom of uncovering the head by letting the hair down as well as that of adding to the hair by requiring a shawl as a covering. His use of the singular noun ('custom' instead of 'customs') argues against this. I would suggest that Paul's strong closing remarks are directed to a very conservative group which sought to impose not only distinctive hair, but also veiling upon the women. This group may perhaps have been ultra-Jewish, or perhaps simply over-zealous as were those who supported divorce and required celibacy. At any rate, Paul denied them their stance.

8. Which women were in view?

This exposition has thus far avoided dealing specifically with an important issue: which women did Paul expect to wear long hair? I have generally illustrated with husbands and wives. This is appropriate, as the vast majority of the women will have been wives, married from their early teens. We must, however, consider other women as well. This is particularly fitting for the Corinthian congregation, which had some who were single for the sake of devotion to the Lord. Did Paul expect single women to have long hair? What about widows?

A careful reading of the chapter shows that his discussion may be applied to married persons, but it is difficult to restrict it to them.[10] This raises another question: exactly who is the 'head' of a widow or of a single woman? In tribal life a newly single woman would generally have reverted to the protection of her paternal household or married into that of her husband. This was not the case in urban first-century Greece. From the point of view of marital authority, single adult women had no male 'heads'. Would their conduct in this matter of veils have mattered? A recent parallel is helpful. Think back to the period (say) of the 1890s and consider the impact of a woman joining the football team, or putting on a man's suit and hat. Her behaviour would be seen as a blatant rebellion against her sexual identity. Consider, for instance, the impact of her having her hair cut like a man's. That too would have been a clear-cut rebellion. Although we may or may not wish to have women adopt the social roles of women in the 1890s, it should be clear that actions have implications beyond one's immediate marital situation. A specific woman's actions can make a general statement about the role of her sex.

Although appropriate, this line of thought is not finally convincing or sufficient. Paul was not speaking about the attire of women on the street (although he does do so in 1 Tim. 2:9). His specific discussion related to a situation in which women were praying and prophesying, to some sort of meeting of the church. The setting is relevant and to explain its relevance we must here anticipate material which will receive more careful discussion later.

We have seen that Paul clearly understood the husband to be the one appointed to be head of the family. From other passages I conclude that he saw male headship as appropriate within the formal structure of the church as well. We shall discuss this at greater length when we discuss 1 Timothy 2 and 3. If this be accepted as Paul's view (I know none who challenges this except by denying the Pauline authorship of 1 Cor. 14:33–36 and of the pastoral epistles; many, however, feel that Paul's view should not

---

[10] I am, at this point, moving away from a view which I defended in an earlier publication.

be applied today), then it helps us to see why Paul's language is not restricted to marital situations alone. The women's rejection of the appointed headship role of men was apparently focused in the worship service, or at least in a time when the group was praying and prophesying (*cf.* 1 Cor. 14 for Paul's desire to have careful regulation of other excesses at such times). It is easy to see how these women and the men who supported them could feel that, especially at such times of charismatic expression, sexual differentiation was irrelevant. However understandable, Paul considered it wrong. If the leadership of the congregation was divinely placed in the hands of men, a rejection of sexual differentiation was a rejection of the divine pattern.

I conclude, then, that Paul spoke, in 1 Corinthians 11, to a situation which had several fronts. Headship in marriage and in the church were at issue. His discussion reflects primarily upon the situation of a married couple, the situation of the majority of his readers then (as now), but it also affects the generic situation of women in worship. In his answer he was concerned to set out his understanding, to curb the behaviours resulting from Corinthian misunderstanding of the present stage in the arrival of the kingdom, and to prevent the formalists from imposing shawls in addition to long hair.

9. The relevance of Paul's instructions today

What is the 'cash value' of Paul's instructions today? An answer to this question is crucial, but ought not to be given in a single, easily misquotable sentence. Biblical ethics do come to specific application; a variety of considerations must, however, enter in. Even a basic decision about (1) the divine principles (God's commands) must be accompanied by understanding of (2) the history of redemption (Are we under the Mosaic regulations for the state of Israel? Or has the kingdom begun? Or is the kingdom fully realized?), of (3) the social context of an action (Will my action be perceived as dishonouring to my parents?), and of (4) personal motives (Am I honest in my expression of love to my parents or am I seething inside?). Most people take these into account more or less automatically. Such considerations do not lead to 'relativism', in the sense that there are no standards, but to precise application of biblical truth. It should, however, be noted that history, social structure and individual personality enter in. How do these apply to the question of hair?

Let us begin with the question of principles. 1. The basic command or principle at issue is the appointive headship of men in certain situations. Paul argues his case from the creational relation of Adam and Eve and from a headship hierarchy which includes God, Christ and believers of both sexes. These considerations were considered relevant for first-century believers. Are they to be so today? 2. The church of the twentieth century stands alongside the church of the first century in the history of redemption. Both are after the resurrection and Pentecost, and both await the return of the Lord. 3. Paul's setting out of the hierarchy which includes Christ (11:3) gives no hint that it is in any way tied to its culture alone. There is no reason within the text itself to set it aside as 'culture bound'. Any effort to do so would have to import reasons at which the text does not hint. The references to the creation of Adam and Eve are also as relevant today as they were then. They have the additional support of the pattern to which Jesus appealed. As we saw, he considered that the kingdom which he brought would renew the ability of mankind to obey the creational patterns for marriage. The question of the idiosyncrasies of our particular society does not affect the relevance of Adam or of Christ either. 4. What of individual motive? Paul applied his view both to people sympathetic to him and to persons committed to an opposite course; so motive is not an issue. We conclude that none of these suggests another conclusion than that Paul's principle is applicable today.

How is the principle of headship to be applied? Should we ask women to wear long hair or veils? The answer to this question is largely dependent on whether Paul saw long hair as a matter of divine principle, as he did view the headship/submission issue, or as a cultural expression of the principles involved in headship and submission. Paul has answered the question of veils directly: No, her hair is given to her instead of a veil. Veils are not a requisite (although other factors might lead individuals to *choose* to express their relation to their husbands by wearing a veil).

What of long hair, distinctively styled? The following points need to be made:

1. Paul appeals to 'nature' as showing that women should have longer hair and says that it is a woman's glory. If 'nature' means 'social custom', Paul's comment is cultural and may or may not be relevant in a given culture, depending on the attitude of that culture toward men with long hair and women with short. If he

means 'God's design for nature' as explained in his teaching and reflected in the culture of his day, then longer hair for women ought not to be seen as culturally relative. In the former case, we could look for a parallel social symbol which would mark a man as man and a woman as woman. The new sign, rather than her hair, would then be her 'glory'. In the latter case, we should urge believers to adopt this particular symbol, noting carefully that *relative* rather than absolute length is in view and that styles are not stipulated. Absolute length and styles may vary as they will from group to group and time to time. Christians will disagree as to this matter. It is my opinion that a study of Paul's use of 'nature' (*physis*) strongly favours the latter alternative.

2. The earlier portions of the chapter appeal to the Jewish background of Paul's congregation (shorn woman) and to their sense of social embarrassment (If it is shameful. . .). This first-century Jewish background is clearly socially and culturally relative. The shorn hair remark and the idea of embarrassment are thus illustrative rather than normative. They are particularly effective for people with such backgrounds, and less so for those without. However, the lessened impact of these points does not affect the principles which Paul sought to establish.

3. If one decides that Paul was employing hair as a useful cultural symbol of a relationship rather than commanding that only that symbol should be used, it becomes crucial to consider carefully the culture in which one lives. If, in our culture, certain hair-styles are distinctively male or female, their gender association should be respected. If certain other signs are in common use, they too should be respected in order to maintain the clear distinction between the sexes which both Testaments call for.

4. If Christians live in a culture which lacks such signs or in which they are fading, it would be well worth considering the establishment of (tasteful) distinctive marks. Christians should not be fearful of being cultural innovators, especially as we are convinced that God's pattern is that which is right. The manufacturer's instructions are worth following.

5. Attitude and motivation are important to Christian obedience. Strong convictions about hair and veils do exist. Christians holding differing views must explore the Scripture together and beware both of forcing external conformity without commitment and of tempting one another to act against conscience. Romans 14 speaks to such an issue, as do 1 Corinthians 8–10.

6. The points which have been made above would still be basically applicable if one were to hold that the chapter is discussing veils rather than hair. Although it seems less likely to me, such a conclusion would not affect the principal points which Paul made about the basic relation of men and women, nor would it make more than incidental changes regarding the relevance of the practice in view.

10. Conclusions

Our examination of 1 Corinthians 11:2–16 has shown a continuity between Paul's words to marriage partners about their relation in the home and about their relation in church. The headship which we saw in Ephesians 5 stands as the background for 1 Corinthians 11. Paul taught the Corinthians that the appointive headship of the man applied in worship as well as in the home. The new freedom of the Christian women during times of worship did not overthrow, but rather stood alongside a structured marital relationship and also alongside a pattern of male leadership in the church itself. The newness of the kingdom did not do away with the creational patterns but called for their genuine fulfilment.

Upon examination, we found that the basis of Paul's view of the headship of men was not in an area which is culturally relative. His appeal to a Christological hierarchy and to the creational relation of Adam and Eve are independent of the actual cultural setting of the Corinthians. He does not, for instance, indicate that the women's lack of training or the possibility of offending certain cultural groups influenced his hierarchical teaching. His specific application of the hierarchy involved the women and men of his congregation in practical ways. The two were to retain their appointed roles and the symbols thereof. This, in my understanding, was specifically directed to the women who had begun to wear their hair loose in the manner of the men. Paul understood this rejection of their relation to men as rejection of a divine structuring of relations. Its consequence was not the pride of equality but the shame of rejection of divine ordinance. A woman's hair, he directed, should continue to be a sign of her place within the creational hierarchy of God, Christ, man, woman (and then angels and the rest of creation). In addition, he directed that her hair is a sufficient sign; no shawls are needed.

B. THE SILENCE OF WOMEN IN THE ASSEMBLY:
1 CORINTHIANS 14:33b–35

At first sight, Paul's presumption that women will pray and prophesy (1 Cor. 11:5) seems to stand in stark contrast to his command of 1 Corinthians 14:33b–35, which reads,

> As in all the congregations of the saints, women should remain silent in the churches. They are not allowed to speak, but must be in submission, as the Law says. If they want to inquire about something, they should ask their own husbands at home; for it is disgraceful for a woman to speak in the church.

These verses appear to be so strong that it is doubtful whether Paul would have allowed women even to make known a prayer request or to share some spiritual lesson, to say nothing of the prayer and prophecy mentioned earlier. How are they to be handled?[11]

Four basic methods of dealing with the passage have been proposed: 1. It does not belong here and was put in by someone after Paul. 2. Paul is inconsistent and contradicts himself. 3. Paul did not really give women permission to speak in chapter 11. In that chapter he dealt with the basic issue of authority and here in 14 he silenced the women altogether. 4. Chapter 14 does not contradict chapter 11, but gives instructions for another problem, for instance, talkative women, women speaking in tongues, or women judging men by their speech. Let us consider these one by one.

1. 'The text is not authentic'

A variety of recent commentators have felt that this passage is so difficult that it must be seen as an interpolation by someone other than Paul. The textual evidence for such a view, however, is nil. A few manuscripts which elsewhere tend to edit the text do place it later in the chapter (after verse 40), but none omits it.[12] Except for the difficulty of the text, there is no reason to remove it. A principle of interpretation which carves up text because the inter-

---

[11] For further discussion of this passage, see J. Hurley, 'Did Paul Require Veils?', pp. 216–219.

[12] The group is headed by D G 88*. The transposition of 14:33b–35 is obviously for the purpose of easier reading. Scholars appealing to this as 'textual uncertainty' or remarking on 'doubtful authenticity' have either not done their homework or are allowing their prejudice to sway their judgment. None would defend such a conclusion on a non-controversial text. For a more detailed discussion, see J. Hurley, 'Did Paul Require Veils?', p. 216.

preter cannot satisfactorily deal with it cannot claim to be scholarly or to respect the text. It must finally be seen as subjective, making the ability of the interpreter to follow the text the true measure of its authenticity. This is not a way to resolve difficulties; it is a way to remove them, and is to be rejected.

2. 'Paul is inconsistent'

We have noted that the removal of 1 Corinthians 14:33b–35 makes the ability of the interpreter the measure of the authenticity of Scripture. A similar problem arises if the second basic approach to the text is adopted. A variety of recent interpreters have been unwilling to edit the text arbitrarily and have frankly admitted their inability to reconcile 1 Corinthians 14:33b–35 with 11:5. Some have then gone on to determine that Paul was simply inconsistent in his application of the gospel. This approach is more candid, but once again makes the ability of the interpreter the measure of Scripture. From the scholarly point of view the conclusion that a man such as Paul was grossly inconsistent on so practical a matter, contradicting himself within the space of three chapters, is suspect. Such a conclusion should be adopted as a last resort. From the point of view of anyone committed to the Scripture as a guide to faith and life or to the Scripture as inspired of God, such a conclusion is self-destructive. To judge Paul inconsistent in the application of faith to life is a straightforward denial of the sufficiency of the Scripture for faith and life and sets the interpreter once again above the author and the Scripture.

3. 'Chapter 11 did not give permission for women to speak'

This approach has a long pedigree in Christian interpretation. It has the virtues of facing the apparent contradiction and of accepting biblical authority. Its drawback is that there is little warrant for supposing that Paul meant to allow an objectionable practice (women speaking) to go by for the sake of argument in chapter 11. He does not seem to have any objection at all to the women praying and prophesying. He presumes that such activity would be acceptable if their heads were covered. In the absence of other solutions this would be viable, although essentially poor.

4. 'Chapters 14 and 11 are discussing different situations'

This position is in fact manifold, as a variety of suggestions about the setting of each passage have been made. I will deal with only a few of the most common and with the one which I think most likely.

a. Formal or informal meetings?

It has sometimes been suggested that chapter 11 has informal meetings in view, perhaps mid-week prayer meetings (or some such thing), and that chapter 14 has the Sunday worship in view. This option presumes a differentiation of kinds of worship service which is impossible to demonstrate from the New Testament. In addition, 1 Corinthians 14 teaches that prophecy (*cf.* 11:5) is a gift for use in public worship and gives regulations for it on that basis. The flow of chapter 14 from prophecy to silence suggests that the verses regulating women's speaking are to be understood as making it all the more unlikely that two radically different kinds of service are in view. It must be rated as possible but improbable that the tension between 1 Corinthians 11 and 14 is to be resolved by assuming that Paul is making an implicit differentiation between the formal worship service on Sunday and informal meetings of one kind or another.

b. Wives are to be silent

Some commentators have felt that chapter 14 has wives in particular in view. On this basis women in general might pray and prophesy in services, but married women would be silent, their husbands speaking for them. Paul's word for women (*gynaikes*) may also be translated as 'wives', and his mention of husbands lends support to such a distinction as applicable in chapter 14. Certain objections must, however, be raised: (1) chapter 11 also has wives in view (although more than they are talked of) and it permits them to speak; (2) chapters 12–14 assume that all of the members of the body, men and women, will participate in the worship (*cf.* especially 14:26); (3) it is difficult to see why married women should be singled out and required to be silent (this is, of course, the weakest argument).

c. Women were uneducated or badly behaved

Cultural factors have been seen as the cause of Paul's remarks. Women were not well educated in his day and may well have been seated apart from the men in the church. It has been suggested that they called out questions to their husbands, disrupting the worship, or that they became noisy in times of charismatic expression by the congregation, not having the sense of order which their husbands had. The plausibility of this explanation fades somewhat when the following observations are made: (1) there is no indication elsewhere in the letter that the women in particular were unruly; (2) Paul does confront unruly situations in the letter (11:33–34; 14:27,29,31). He meets them by establishing order rather than by silencing the unruly completely; (3) the rule which Paul sets out is one which he says applies in all his churches (14:33b). It seems unlikely that the problem of noisy women had arisen in all of them; (4) it seems unlike Paul to silence all women because some are noisy or disruptive. His actual handling of other disorderly people provides concrete grounds for arguing against wholesale action when only some individuals are in fact violators.

d. Women may not judge prophets

It seems preferable to me to understand the verses to be concerned that women do not participate in the evaluation of the prophets. On this view, the verses in question (14:33b–35) must be carefully interpreted within the context of their chapter. The chapter as a whole discusses disorder in Corinthian worship. From verse 26, it is concerned to regulate tongues and prophecy. Verses 33b–35 are within the section regulating the 'judging' of the prophets. On this basis the end of the chapter may be outlined as follows:[13]

14:26 GENERAL TOPIC:
When you come together. . .let all be done for edification.

14:27 I. SPECIFIC ISSUE 1: Tongues:
  If anyone speaks in tongues
  A. Restriction on number speaking: *Let it be two or at most three*
  B. Ensuring the edification of the congregation:
    1. *And let one interpret*
    2. *If there is no interpreter*
14:28   a. *Let him keep silence in the church*
           b. *And let him speak to himself and to God*

---

[13]I am indebted to Dr Wayne Grudem for the idea of presenting Paul's argument in outline form. Our interaction on these verses has been fruitful in sharpening and extending my work on them.

14:29 II. SPECIFIC ISSUE 2: Prophets:

    A. Restriction on number speaking: *Let two or three prophets speak*

    B. Ensuring the edification of the congregation: *Let the others weigh what is said*

    C. Further explanatory comments about prophets speaking (II.A) and the weighing of their words (II.B):

14:30–31   1. Regarding (II.A) prophets speaking. *If a revelation is made to another. . .let the first be silent*

        a. *For you can all prophesy one by one*

          (i) *in order that all may learn*

          (ii) *and be encouraged*

14:32   b. *And the spirit[ual gift]s of the prophets are subject to the prophets*

14:33a   (i) *For God is not a God of confusion*

          (ii) *but of peace*

14:33b–34a   2. Regarding (II.B) the weighing of what was said by the prophets: *As in all the churches of the saints, let the women keep silence in the church* (during the judgment of prophets)

14:34b   a. *For they are not permitted to speak*

          (i) *but they should be subordinate*

          (ii) *even as the law says*

14:35   b. *If there is something they want to know,*

          (i) *let them ask their husbands at home*

          (ii) *for it is shameful for a woman to speak in church*

Let us consider the structure of Paul's instructions as set out in the outline. The general topic of the section has to do with edification of the congregation through charismatic exercises in tongues and prophecy (14:26). Paul is concerned to regulate the two forms of expression along similar lines. In each case he restricts the number who may speak and takes steps to ensure that their contributions will in fact be edifying to the congregation.

Verses 27 and 28 regulate tongues. Only two or three may speak and all speaking is prohibited in the absence of an interpreter, whose service allows the tongues to have an edifying effect upon the hearers. Verses 29–35 deal with prophets. Verse 29 closely parallels the instructions given with respect to tongues. The number of speakers is restricted to two or three and steps are taken to ensure that what is said really does edify the congregation. In this case there is no need of an interpreter, but the words of the prophets are to be weighed (literally, 'judged', or 'assessed', *diakrinō*) to ensure conformity with the apostolic message. It seems likely from verse 35 that the implications of the messages were also explored by discussion.

Verses 30–35 offer further words of explanation concerning the regulation of prophets. Verses 30–33a address the matter of order in the speaking of the two or three prophets: 'If a revelation is made to another. . .let the first be silent. . .' Verses 33b–35 address Paul's other instruction concerning prophets, the evaluation and exploration of their message. His point is that the women are not to participate in this exercise of ecclesiastical authority. It can be seen from the outline that this analysis of the text provides an orderly structure for the entire passage, a structure in which the discussion of women has a natural place and does not appear as a sudden intrusion or as a shift of topic. It appears instead in the appropriate place for further discussion of the evaluation of the prophets.

The weightiest argument against this view is the fact that it is not obvious at first sight. This is primarily caused by the length of the instructions concerning the interruption of one prophet by another (14:30–33a) and by the unrestricted use of the term 'be silent' in verse 34.[14] The former is unavoidable and in fact is of the same length as the comment about the silence of women (14:33b–35). The latter demands comparative study. Other Pauline and New Testament comments on silence help us to understand Paul's unrestricted use of it here. Paul left it to his readers to grasp the context. It was not difficult for them to assess the context, knowing the situation, although it can be difficult for us. Consider, for instance, verse 30, discussing the speaking of the prophets. Paul said, 'if a revelation is made to another sitting by, let the first *be silent*.' The obvious contextual meaning is that the first is to cease speaking and allow the other to speak. There is no intention that the first should speak no more in the worship service. He or she may certainly sing hymns, pray, *etc*. A similar point may be made about the tongues-speaker of verse 28. Paul wrote, 'If there is no

---

[14] I am indebted to Dr Grudem for much of the discussion on these particular points.

interpreter, let him *keep silent* in the church, and speak to himself and to God.' It would be a mistake to assume that Paul was prohibiting him to sing hymns, pray in an intelligible tongue, or enter other verbal exercises appropriate to the congregation generally. In both cases the context rather than Paul's words limits their application. If verses 33b–35 are about the judging of the prophets, their context would naturally restrict their application to that context and not at all indicate that women should remain silent in other contexts, such as prayer, the singing of hymns, or even prophecy itself. Chapter 11 would provide a natural example that this interpretation is correct.[15]

If we accept the conclusion that 1 Corinthians 14:33b–35 refers to the evaluation of prophets, we must then go on to consider the actual instructions given by Paul about the matter. He did not see it as insignificant. All the churches of God, he said, were uniform in this practice (14:33b). Verse 34b provides his rationale: 'They (women) are not permitted to speak, but should be subordinate, even as the Law says.' The issue at hand is once again that of subordination. The speaking in view constituted some sort of exercise of authority and was therefore inconsistent with the subordinate or submissive role which Paul believed women should play in the assembled church body. It is hard to see how this could be applied to just any form of speech; it is not difficult to understand if the evaluating of the message of a prophet is in view. The participation of women in an activity which involved a judgment of male and female prophets within the context of the church is certainly an exercise of authority.

We have seen in our discussion of 1 Corinthians 11 that Paul was concerned about male headship in the worship service. His discussion here in chapter 14 is explicitly intending to discuss women 'in the church'. In chapter 11 Paul appealed to creational patterns and to a Christological hierarchy for support for male headship. He appealed to the creation, and to the new creation in its present realization. In chapter 14 he does not develop a lengthy rationale for his position, perhaps because of his lengthy remarks three chapters previously. He does, however, remark that 'the Law' too requires his view. It is difficult to figure out how it could be said that the Law (*i.e.* the Old Testament) taught that women

---

[15]For other examples of verbs of speaking or silence with contextual limitation, see Lk. 18:39; Acts 21:14,18; Mt. 13:34; Mk. 4:34; Jn. 18:20; Rom. 15:18; 1 Thes. 1:8; 1 Tim. 2:12.

should be silent at all times in worship. It teaches the opposite
(Ex. 15:20–21; 2 Sa. 6:15,19; Ps. 148:12). It is *not* difficult to see that
the Old Testament would support the silence of women in the
judging of prophets, as its whole structure teaches male headship
in the home and in worship.

Some commentators have thought Paul was appealing to Genesis 3:16 ('Your husband. . .will rule over you') when he spoke of
'the Law'. Although it is conceivable that this text was in Paul's
mind, the analogy of Paul's other discussions of submission argues
against it. In those cases in which the texts to which he appealed
can specifically be identified, he uniformly appealed to the relation
of Adam and Eve *before* the fall rather than after it, to Genesis 2
rather than to Genesis 3. (Paul's use of the first three chapters of
Genesis will be discussed at greater length in connection with
1 Tim. 2:8–15.) We have discussed the Old Testament teaching of
male headship in the home and in worship in chapter 2. Paul's
appeal to 'the Law' need not have any particular text in view. It
is enought that he reminds them that men were called to exercise
authority and to render judgment in matters in the home and in
the 'church in the wilderness', in the religious life of Israel. From
his appeal, however, we may deduce that he considered that the
Old Testament pattern of male headship in religious matters
should continue in the church *alongside the new freedom of women to
participate in the worship*. This is no more than we found in his
other teaching and implicitly in that of Jesus when he recognized
both marriage and celibacy as proper kingdom responses.

A final issue needs attention. Paul seems to have a particular
sort of situation in view in verse 35 where he directs that women
should ask their husbands questions at home (as opposed to asking them of the prophets in church). Here we see a frank acknowledgment of women's interest and ability in learning. This, as we
have seen, sets the New Testament apart from Judaism in its day.
Paul may be concerned to prevent the possibility that women
would 'just ask a few questions for information' and in fact enter
into the congregational judgment of the prophets.

We might ask about single women or widows. Whom should
they ask? And what of the husband who does not know the
answer? Do we presume that every husband can answer all of his
wife's questions? To such particular questions, the best answer is
simply that Paul was not writing an exhaustive manual for en-
quiring women but rather addressing a problem. The principal

issue under discussion was not who should answer women's questions, but rather whether women should examine the prophets. Married women (which category included the vast majority) served as an example. We may presume that they and other women might speak to elders, husband, family or friends about the things of the Lord. The Scripture commands this in numerous places.

Verse 36 deserves at least a brief comment. It reads: 'Did the word of God originate from you? Or are you the only people it has reached?' These words are often taken as directed to arrogant Corinthian women who presumed to speak in the assembly. Many versions of the Bible paragraph them with verse 35 and introduce a new paragraph with verse 37. But Paul's language *prohibits* applying the words to women alone, indicating that they should not be included with the discussion of women but with the following discussion of prophets and 'spiritual persons'. The *monous*, translated 'only', is a masculine plural form. It may apply to men only or to men and women. It cannot apply to 'arrogant' women only; the feminine plural would be used in such a case. Paul's comment in verse 36 is better understood as the beginning of a paragraph which calls upon Corinthian 'spiritual persons' and prophets to acknowledge Paul's authority (verse 37) and confess that the Word came to them through him and that it went out to many. It is not, and indeed cannot be, his closing blast against women who speak in the church.[16]

5. Conclusions

We conclude from our examination of 1 Corinthians 14:33b–35 that the intent of this passage is to teach that women ought not to participate in the examination of prophets, an exercise which Paul understood as incompatible with the subordinate role which he considered God had assigned to women in the home and in the church. The passage does not in any way stand in opposition to 1 Corinthians 11, which specifically presumes that women will speak to pray and to prophesy in the church. Nor is it in conflict with the teaching of chapters 12–14, which assume that the various members of the body of Christ will all participate in the corporate meetings.

From the perspective of those modern churches which do not

[16]For further discussion, see J. Hurley, 'Did Paul Require Veils?', p. 218.

practise charismatic exercises such as prophecy and tongues-speaking, these words have no direct application to daily practice. Our negative conclusion, that they do not prohibit women from vocal participation in worship, has obvious positive implications for all churches. The principle of headship which the text embodies stands alongside our previous discussion of marital authority and will be relevant for our subsequent discussion of the role of women in ecclesiastical authority.

8

Women and men in church office

We have considered the relationship of men and women within the body of Christ, within the marriage relationship and in the worship of the church. In this chapter we shall discuss it in the context of church office. Our study will focus upon a few major texts: 1 Timothy 2:8–15; 3:1–13; and Romans 16:1–2. In order to deal with these texts we shall also have to consider Paul's use of the first three chapters of Genesis and the nature of church office as set out in the New Testament. The topics which we shall examine are not new. They have been the subject of much controversy in recent years. The discussion will not be in the direction of examining and interacting with the current literature, although those familiar with it will recognize responses to various positions. I shall, instead, try to lay out the teaching of these crucial texts within the context of Paul's thought and that of the day. From this base we shall consider their application in the present.[1] My conclusions will not please everyone. It is my hope, however, that none will feel that violence has been done to the text of Scripture.

A. THE ANNOUNCED PURPOSE OF 1 TIMOTHY

We noted earlier that much of the debate over the role of women in the Christian church has come from an abuse of Galatians 3:28. In that text Paul stressed the unity of all believers in Christ Jesus. He did not intend his discussion to be used to obliterate all dis-

---

[1] Some contemporary scholars do not consider the letters to Timothy and Titus to be genuinely Pauline. This is not the place to debate the issue, but it is important to note here that I do consider them genuinely Pauline, perhaps by the hand of an amanuensis whom he asked to write under his direction. An increasing number of scholars have been encouraged to reconsider their opposition to these letters as a result of J. A. T. Robinson's deliberately provocative volume *Redating the New Testament* (London, 1976). More substantial grounds have been provided by scholars such as Spicq, Jeremias, Guthrie and Kelly in their recent commentaries.

. tinctions within Christ's body. He taught both the unity of the body and the diversity of its members. Before considering the specific argument of 1 Timothy 2 and 3, it is appropriate to ask whether it is fair to its author's intent to use the letter to learn about differentiations in the body of Christ and whether it was his intent to have the specific instructions of the book applied generally within the church.

It is universally accepted that 1 Timothy was intended to provide a clear statement concerning certain issues which its author, whom I take to be Paul, felt needed attention. The letter forms a 'spiritual will' from Paul to Timothy. In the letter Paul indicates that he hopes to be able to come soon to Timothy, but fears that he will be delayed (3:14–15a). He writes, 'I am writing you these instructions so that, if I am delayed, you will know how people ought to conduct themselves in God's household, which is the church of the living God. . . .'

The precise wording is helpful in deciding whether his instructions are normative. Paul wrote *pōs . . . dei anastrephesthai*, 'how . . . it is necessary to conduct oneself'. *Dei* is an impersonal verb meaning 'one must' or 'one ought'. In Pauline and in general New Testament usage it points to a strong degree of necessity, generally involving divinely based moral obligation. Paul uses it twenty-four times, the majority referring to historical necessities required by God's rule over history (*e.g.* Rom. 1:27; 1 Cor. 11:19; 15:25, 53; 2 Cor. 2:3; 5:10; 1 Thes. 4:1; 1 Tim. 3:2; 2 Tim. 2:6, 24; Tit. 1:7, 11). Paul's use of *dei* here is presumptive evidence that he considered what he said normative beyond the immediate situation.

Anastrephesthai (to conduct oneself) is a present infinitive form. It takes no person or number and is best translated in this context by the generic or abstract rendering which most translations have adopted. Paul did not say, 'Timothy, here is how you personally ought to behave.' He deliberately said that he wished Timothy to know 'how one ought to conduct himself in God's household'. An alternative would be 'how people ought to conduct themselves'.[2] Paul's abstract language indicates that his instructions should have a general rather than closely limited application.

Despite the obviously general intention of the author, a large number of recent writers on the subject of the role of women have

---

[2] A survey of all the translations immediately available to me shows ten following this pattern, only the AV using an individual rather than an abstract form. A similar number of commentators were unanimous in favour of the more general translation.

suggested that the matters discussed and the instructions given in this letter ought to be seen as relevant only in its particular time period. Even a superficial reading of the letter shows, however, that its author would not accept such a view of it. He delivers 'trustworthy sayings worthy of full acceptance' (see 1 Tim. 1:15; 3:1; 4:9). He informs Timothy of things which will happen in the 'later times' (4:1). The subjects discussed are not passing issues. The opening chapter discusses Paul's life, the work of Christ and wandering from the faith. The second deals with prayers for rulers, personal conduct in church and teaching functions in relation to women. The third discusses qualifications for elders and deacons and begins a discussion of the mystery of the faith and its future rejection. Chapter 4 continues the discussion of 3. The fifth chapter regulates relations between various classes of persons within the church. The final chapter continues the topic of the fifth and warns against love of money. Only the last section of the sixth chapter is pointedly restricted to Timothy. The topics of the letter are not culturally relative, although they could be brought to particular application in Timothy's context. An attempt to discard the substance of the instructions of 1 Timothy cannot find support from the intention of the letter itself. Other, foreign considerations must be introduced if its principles are to be deemed not applicable to the present.

B. TEACHING AND THE EXERCISE OF AUTHORITY: 1 TIMOTHY 2:8–15

The second chapter of 1 Timothy deals with prayer and worship. The first half of the chapter calls for prayer for 'all those in authority, that [Christians] may live peaceful and quiet lives in all godliness and holiness' (2:2) and that even such rulers may be saved (2:3–7). From the topic of prayer for rulers in order that Christians may lead godly lives, Paul turns to discuss particular aspects of a godly life. He begins with the conduct of those who pray and goes on to related issues. He says,

> [8]I want men everywhere to lift up holy hands in prayer, without anger or disputing. [9]I also want women to dress modestly, with decency and propriety, not with braided hair or gold or pearls or expensive clothes, [10]but with good deeds, appropriate for women who profess to worship God. [11]A woman should learn

in quietness and full submission. [12]I do not permit a woman to teach or to exercise authority over a man; she must be silent. [13]For Adam was formed first, then Eve. [14]And Adam was not the one deceived; it was the woman who was deceived and became a sinner. [15]But women will be kept safe through (the?) childbirth, if they continue in faith, love and holiness with propriety (1 Tim. 2:8–15).

1. Behaviour which mars a Christian's approach to God

Verses 8 and 9 shift the focus of the chapter from the prayers which Paul wants offered to the offerers of the prayers. He is concerned that the prayers offered for rulers be acceptable to God and that Christians conduct themselves in a godly manner when they meet to pray. The injunction that prayers should be made for all those in authority (2:2) is matched by instruction that these prayers should be offered everywhere (2:8).

Paul's concern for the men (2:8) makes clever use of the prayer posture of the day and of biblical imagery for an obedient way of life: men are to lift holy (*hosios*) hands. This comment immediately brings to mind not only the uplifted hands of the posture of prayer but also the meaning of clean or holy hands in passages such as Psalm 24:3–5, in which we learn that he who has 'clean hands' and a pure heart will be able to stand before the Lord in his holy place (*cf.* also Jas. 4:8). Paul was concerned that the manner of life of the men should not mar their prayers. It would seem from the end of the verse that he had anger and quarrelling particularly in mind.

A different concern was expressed for women (2:9–10). In words which closely resemble those of Peter (1 Pet. 3:3–4), Paul directs that women should not focus upon fancy clothes as adornment which will commend them to God, but rather that they should be adorned by good deeds. The net impact of his instructions for women is parallel to those for men; both sexes are to live holy lives of obedient works. The difference between the commands to the two sexes gives us some indication of besetting sins of the day.

The particular wording of verses 9 and 10 is helpful as an example of contextual application of ethical principles. Paul makes it clear that he is calling for decency, propriety, modesty and good deeds. These are, of course, not at all culture bound. They are permanently appropriate and their opposite reprehensible. The specific examples offered are, to a certain extent, culturally relative.

Paul warns against 'braided hair *and* gold or pearls or expensive clothes'. He is not, in fact, speaking against all braids, gold wedding-rings and pearl ear-rings. He refers instead to the elaborate hair-styles which were then fashionable among the wealthy and also to the styles worn by courtesans. The sculpture and literature of the period make it clear that women often wore their hair in enormously elaborate arrangements with braids and curls interwoven or piled high like towers and decorated with gems and/or gold and/or pearls. The courtesans wore their hair in numerous small pendant braids with gold droplets or pearls or gems every inch or so, making a shimmering screen of their locks.[3] Pliny complains of the vast sums spent on ornamentation and various satirists comment on the hours spent in dressing the hair of women. When Paul wrote 'braided hair *and* gold *or* pearls' he probably meant 'braided hair decorated with gold or with pearls'.

Whatever his specific illustration, we have no trouble discerning that these practices were not modest or proper and *therefore* not to be practised. Obedience to this command of Paul's requires no subtle exegetical skill or knowledge of the customs of Paul's day; it requires only an assessment of what adornment is excessively costly and not modest or proper. Christians must allow for individual and social differences as they bring this to bear in their individual lives, but they have no need to set aside Paul's instruction as somehow 'culture bound'.

2. Teaching, ruling and women

1 Timothy 2:11 moves beyond clothing to another aspect of the lives of 'women who profess to worship God' (2:10): their role in situations involving teaching or the exercising of authority with respect to men. This section demands close attention.

Verses 11 and 12 should be taken together. Verse 11 makes a positive statement, and verse 12 a corresponding negative one. 'Women should learn in quietness and in full submission.' The general thrust of this command and several of its particular words merit comment. First of all it should be noted that Paul is not

---

[3] Useful information on hair-styles is to be found in J. P. V. D. Balsdon, *Roman Women*, pp. 252–258; J. Neil *Everyday Life in the Holy Land* (London, 1930), pp. 200–203; E. Potter, M. Albert, E. Saglio, 'Coma', in C. Daremburg and E. Saglio (eds.), *Dictionnaire des Antiquités Grecques et Romaines* (Paris, 1887); T. G. Tucker, *Life in the Roman World of Nero and St Paul* (London, 1910), p. 311; and L. Wilson, *The Clothing of the Ancient Romans* (Baltimore, 1938). Pliny remarks in his *Natural History*(9) that vast sums were being wasted on hair and body ornaments and jewels. See also appendix below, pp. 257–259.

expressing a matter of custom or of personal preference. This will be very clear from his subsequent explanation, but is also asserted by his use of an imperative verb, *manthanetō* (let (a woman) learn). Paul's instructions are cast as a command. Interestingly, his command specifically presumes that women will in fact learn. Some have felt that Paul's view of women was still 'rabbinic', yet, as we have noted before, his assumption that women can and will learn is *not* a typical rabbinic view.

We must consider now what Paul actually commanded. He calls for *hēsychia* (quietness, peacefulness, silence) and *hypotagē* (submission, subjection, from *hypotassō*). These concepts are familiar to us from our study of Ephesians 5, 1 Peter 3 and 1 Corinthians 14. They recur with great regularity in discussions of women in the Christian community. It is important to note that *hēsychia* is not the word used for being silent in 1 Corinthians 14. *Sigaō*, the word used in 1 Corinthians 14, means 'to keep silent' and stresses the silence. It may be used as a command to mean 'Hush!' or even 'Shut up!' *Hēsychia* does mean silence but carries with it connotations of peacefulness and restfulness. Its use in 1 Timothy 2 shows that Paul is not just calling for 'buttoned lips' but for a quiet receptivity and a submission to authority in his description of the manner of women's learning.

The actual structure of verses 11 and 12 helps us to understand what he was thinking of. Rendered literally, he said, 'A woman, in quietness (*hēsychia*) let her learn in all submission. And to teach a woman I do not permit neither to exercise authority over a man, but she is to be in quietness (*hēsychia*).' The components of these verses are sometimes separated, thus requiring that women (1) learn in silence, (2) be in all submission, (3) not teach, (4) not exercise authority over men. When they are separated in this fashion, the grammar and women are abused. The damage is further increased if they are taken out of context. In such cases, the prohibitions and injunctions become generally or universally applicable and men and women who wish to obey Scripture insist that women never, under any circumstances, teach, and that they always, in every circumstance, submit to men. A close look at the context and Paul's wording can set us free from such misunderstanding.

Consider first the context. Paul has been discussing the conduct of Christians in the gathered congregation in which prayers are to be made for rulers (verses 1–4), in which unholy conflict may mar the prayers of men (verse 8), and in which ostentatious clothes may damage those of women (verse 9). Paul's remarks are not directed to life generally, but to the gathering of God's people and even to a specific situation during that gathering. Women were certainly free to speak in the Pauline churches (1 Cor. 11). Paul is speaking only of teaching situations here in 1 Timothy 2.

The way in which Paul has constructed his sentences is a help. 'In quietness' and 'in full submission' are in apposition to one another. Verse 11 is concerned with one particular issue, the manner in which women learn. Paul employs two phrases to describe what he wants. 'In quietness' and 'in full submission' function adverbially to qualify and to explain his goal. The AV and the RSV have done better than the NIV at catching the flow of the text at this point. They read, 'Let a woman learn in silence with all submissiveness (subjection).' The NIV reads, 'A woman should learn in quietness and full submission.'

Verse 12 is sometimes taken as making two quite distinct statements: (1) a woman may not teach; (2) a woman may not exercise authority over a man. Paul's grammar permits this reading by inserting the 'or'. The preceding and following context, however, indicate that he was not thinking in that manner. Verse 11 calls for quiet and submissive learning. Verse 12 forbids teaching or exercising authority over men. The two are visibly parallel. Quiet learning inversely parallels (verbal) teaching and full submission inversely parallels exercising authority. Both verses have the same situation in mind, one in which women are not to teach authoritatively but are to learn quietly. The closing remark of verse 12 makes this clear by summing up both verses with a single short statement: 'she must be silent.' We conclude, therefore, that Paul intended that women should not be authoritative teachers in the church.

The question of what constitutes authoritative teaching or an exercise of authority is a vital question for practical life in the church. We shall explore it further in connection with our discussion of 1 Timothy 3. For the moment we must leave it without further development.

The strength of Paul's feeling on this issue may be gauged from the imperative verb ('let a woman learn . . .)' in verse 11 and his use of 'permit' (*epitrepō*) in verse 12. *Epitrepō* does not mean 'to advise' or 'to urge' but has overtones of command and is rightly translated 'to permit' or 'to allow'. It is the same verb which was used by Paul in 1 Corinthians 14:34 to say that women are not permitted to speak in the judging of the prophets.

The meaning of verse 12 pivots on our translation of 'to exercise authority' (*authentein*). The Authorized Version translates this by 'usurp authority'. It is clear that the authority in view is not proper in Paul's eyes, but this fact is to be learned from the context rather than from the verb used. Until recently there were only a few known uses of the verb and it was necessary to guess whether it meant 'exercise authority' or 'illegitimately exercise authority'. Further examples of its use have shown that it does not carry with it the connotation of illicit authority, nor does it carry the connotation of 'domineer' ('act imperiously' or 'be overbearing') as some translations and even lexicons have suggested. It simply means 'have authority over' or 'exercise authority over'.[4] What Paul disallowed therefore was simply the exercise of authority over men, which was incompatible with submission, rather than the abuse or usurpation of authority.

3. Why did Paul forbid women to teach or to exercise authority?

Paul's view of women and church authority is less debated today than is his rationale for his view. Paul offers two supporting arguments: 'Adam was formed first, then Eve. And Adam was not the one deceived; the woman, being deceived, became a sinner' (2:13–14). Paul believed that these observations support his case. Many modern critics have viewed them as irrelevant, 'rabbinic', distortions of the meaning of Genesis, and/or actually arguments against Paul's position. We shall make some preliminary observations about the nature of Paul's comments and then consider them in connection with the first three chapters of Genesis and his other appeals to them.

Recent debate has suggested that Paul's teaching in 1 Timothy 2 is designed for his own day and for the particular cultural situation which he faced. Some feel that, were Paul to have written in the twentieth century, he would have taken a different stand. From this it has been concluded by some that if we are to be

---

[4] Dr George Knight of Covenant Theological Seminary, St Louis, Missouri has done scholars the favour of examining every use of the term recorded in the current lexicons and of providing not only translations of those Greek texts, but also an analysis of the history of the interpretation and translation of *authentein*. At the time of this writing, his article '*Authenteō* in Relation to Women in 1 Tim. 2:12' has not yet appeared in print.

faithful to the 'genius' or 'central thrust' or 'greater vision' of Paul, we must reject his actual teaching. Is this legitimate as an approach to 1 Timothy 2?

The question of cultural relativity must be answered in connection with the text itself. Does Paul's teaching contain elements which should be modified in the light of changed historical circumstances? It is not difficult to see, for instance, that Paul's discussion of braided hair must be interpreted in terms of then-contemporary practice and ought not necessarily to be interpreted as prohibiting a woman having her hair in two braids. Paul's teaching in 1 Timothy 2 does not, however, lend itself to such reapplication. The (valid) observation has been made, for instance, that he spoke to a society in which the women were largely ignorant and uneducated, and therefore should not be in positions of authority. It has then been argued that 'new cultural factors', such as the education of women, should lead to new roles for women. Unfortunately for this point of view, Paul frequently had women 'fellow-workers', commended women as representatives from their churches (Phoebe), recognized the abilities of women such as Priscilla, thought that women could learn and should be taught, and, most telling of all, made no reference whatsoever to the relatively ignorant, uneducated state of women in his day as a ground for his position. His case in 1 Timothy 2 hinges instead upon his interpretation of events in the opening chapters of Genesis, with no reference whatever to culture, uneducated women, or even to possible cultural offence which might result if women were to teach. His argument does not allow the introduction of 'new cultural factors' which would have caused him to make other applications of his principles.

Some commentators have introduced 'cultural factors' of a different sort. They have held that Paul's ways of thinking and of interpreting Genesis are first-century, rabbinic ways and should not be followed today. In particular it is felt that his view of Genesis is not what the text actually teaches but represents instead an interpretation of it which he learned from his earlier days as a rabbi and never really integrated into his Christian way of thinking. In other words, Paul is not right about Genesis and is more Jewish than Christian in his thinking about women; he is not consistent with his best insights into Christian truth. This sort of position is to be commended for its candour, but its assumptions and consequences must be clearly understood.

From such a perspective the points under debate are no longer related primarily to the application of Paul's principles, but rather to (1) whether Paul made a mistake in his evaluation of Genesis, and (2) whether he was consistent in his application of Christian truth. By adopting this stance we have set ourselves as the judges of Scripture and as the ones who have the right to determine when the words of the apostle are authoritative. We thus claim to stand over the Bible rather than under it. If we may judge the apostolic understanding of the meaning of the gospel to be error at this point of application of faith to life, there is no reason why we should not do so at other points as well. The meanings of the death of Jesus, of the cross itself and of the person of Jesus also become topics on which the apostles may have been in error. The issues being debated are not inconsequential. The authority of Scripture is the issue which is finally under debate. Paul expressed his own understanding of the authority of his teaching and of those who would overthrow it. He said, 'If anybody thinks he is a prophet or spiritually gifted, let him acknowledge that what I am writing to you is the Lord's command. If he ignores this, he himself will be ignored' (1 Cor. 14:37–38). Paul claimed to write as 'one who by the Lord's mercy is trustworthy' (1 Cor. 7:25). Strikingly, he made these claims precisely in the context of his (presently questioned) teachings about women and men. Was he right?

I have tried to point out the consequences of dismissing Paul's teachings as culturally relative where he did not think that they were. This does not free us from the task of trying to understand and responsibly to explain them. We must ask whether, in fact, we are able to follow Paul's use of Genesis and to understand how it can be reconciled with an honest assessment of the meaning of Genesis.

An excursus on Genesis 1–3 and Paul's use of it

We have noted in our studies that both Paul and Jesus use the opening chapters of Genesis for support for their teaching about the relation of men and women. Let us review the important Pauline texts and then consider their use of Genesis:

1. 1 Corinthians 6:16. In this text Paul argues that sexual union of a believer with a prostitute creates a monstrous 'one flesh' relation (Gn. 2:24) and that a member of the body of Christ should instead be united to Christ in the Spirit. None considers this a misuse of Genesis.

2. 1 Corinthians 11:7–9. Paul argues for male headship because man is the image and glory of God and the woman the glory of the man (verse 7), because the man did not come from the woman but the woman from the man (verse 8; Gn. 2:21–22), and because the woman was created for the sake of the man (verse 9; Gn. 2:20). We have already considered the question of 'image' and 'glory'. We shall review them and consider his other points.

3. 1 Corinthians 14:34. Paul cites 'the Law' without making clear what he means. We have already discussed and dismissed the suggestion that he meant Genesis 3:16 and need not pursue this text further.

4. Ephesians 5:31. Paul cites Genesis 2:24 to point out the close unity of a husband and wife as 'one flesh'. None questions the appropriateness of Paul's point. We have already devoted considerable space to this text.

5. 1 Timothy 2:13–14. Paul appeals to the temporal priority of Adam's creation ('Adam was formed first'; cf. Gn. 2:20–22) and to Eve's having been deceived (Gn. 3:6; cf. 3:13) as showing that women should not teach or exercise authority over men. Both of these points need consideration.

The points at issue may be listed as follows: (1) What is the relation between Adam and Eve's equality as the 'image of God' and women's subordination as taught by Paul?; (2) Do the facts that Adam was made first, that Eve was taken out of him, and that she was made 'for his sake' or to be his 'helper' mean that she should be subordinate? and (3) Does the fact that Eve happened to be deceived mean that all women should be subordinate to their husbands? With these in mind, we must turn to the Genesis narratives.

a. Genesis 1 and Paul's use of it

As part of our discussion of 1 Corinthians 11, we considered Paul's use of the terms 'image' and 'glory' in relation to Adam and Eve. According to Paul, the man is the image and glory of God and the woman is the glory of the man. In that discussion we noted that Genesis 1 was not in fact being cited by Paul. For the purposes of this chapter, we need to review our conclusions concerning the actual meaning of 'image' in Genesis 1 and the meaning of Paul's use of the term in 1 Corinthians 11.

We noted that the entire first chapter of Genesis is concerned with the rule of God over his creation and with his establishing of a variety of realms with creatures to rule over them (day: sun, night: moon, sea: fish, air: birds, *etc.*). Mankind is distinct from all other kinds in its calling to image God by having dominion over *all* of the realms and their rulers. We noted that the chapter does not bring relationships within species into view. It does not comment on headship among animals, although there are clear dominant and subordinate roles among many of them. Our applications of Genesis 1 to Adam and Eve must therefore be carefully restricted to speak only where the text speaks. This means that the interpreter of the text can and must say that both men and women are to multiply and to rule over the creation as a joint task. The interpreter may not seek to read into the text any implications about the headship, subordination or equality of the sexes. To make Genesis 1 speak to such issues is a matter of projection of prejudice rather than of extraction of textual meaning.

We noted in our previous study that in 1 Corinthians 11 Paul was not discussing the idea of image in the sense of Genesis 1. The discussion of 1 Corinthians 11 does not focus upon the rule of mankind over creation, but upon the headship of the man in marriage and worship. Thus man 'images' God as 'head' and the woman does not. In a similar vein, we found that the concept of 'glory' deals with the showing or manifesting of the role or station of another. Man points to and honours the rule of God by being subordinate to him and by the manner of his headship with respect to his wife. The wife is the glory of her husband as she points to or honours his headship by her life and attitude. We concluded, therefore, that Paul did not teach that women are the 'image' of men, or that women are not the image of God in the sense of Genesis 1:26–28. He did teach that the relation of men and women in worship and in the home is such that the man images God and is his glory as he exercises his leadership role and that the woman is the glory of the man as she appropriately responds. In other words, Paul's use of 'image' and 'glory' is not an abuse of Genesis; indeed, it is not even an appeal to it.

b. Genesis 2 and Paul's use of it

We must now turn our attention to the teaching of Genesis 2 and to Paul's use of it. This chapter is the one upon which Paul draws to explain his view of the relation of the sexes. He develops three particular arguments to show that women should subject themselves: (1) Adam was formed first (1 Tim. 2:13; Gn. 2:20–22);

(2) Eve was taken out of him (1 Cor. 11:8; Gn. 2:21–22); (3) she was made for his sake (1 Cor. 11:9; Gn. 2:20). We shall consider these in order.

i. Adam was formed first, then Eve

As we have seen, 1 Timothy 2:8–15 teaches that men rather than women should teach and exercise authority in the church. Paul goes on to refer to the prior formation of Adam as supporting his conclusion. Recent debate has asked what the relevance of this might be and whether such a line of thought ought not to lead to the absurd position that land animals ought to rule mankind because they were formed first, or that the birds and fishes should rule all else by virtue of their formation on the fifth day, or even that the plants of the third day ought to be rulers over the animals and man. Reflection upon the meaning of primogeniture (being first-born) in the Old Testament and in Paul's writing suggests that such criticisms are not well founded.

In the Old Testament, as we noted in chapter 2, the first son inherited a 'double portion' of his father's goods (*i.e.* twice what his brothers received) and became the head of his father's house and leader of its worship upon the event of his father's death. The first-born inherited command of resources and the responsibility of leadership in the home and in worship. He became 'head' of the household. This law (Dt. 21:15–17) can be seen in effect in the cases of Reuben (Gn. 49:3) and Esau (Gn. 27:19) in the Old Testament, and is presumed in the New Testament in the parable of the prodigal son (Lk. 15:11–32). It appears figuratively in Elisha's plea for the 'double portion' of Elijah's spirit (2 Ki. 2:9). The oldest son had particular responsibilities for the younger ones, and to him was due certain respect. Paul's appeal to the prior formation of Adam is an assertion that Adam's status as the oldest carried with it the leadership appropriate to a first-born son (Adam, the first human, could not be 'first-born'. He was instead 'first formed').

The theme of the authority of the first-born finds expression elsewhere in Paul. Colossians 1:15–18 deliberately intertwines the themes of Christ's being temporally prior to the rest of creation and his having the authority of the first-born over it. It reads,

He (Christ) is the image of the invisible God, the firstborn over all creation. For by him all things were created: things in heaven and on earth, visible and invisible, whether thrones or powers or rulers or authorities; all things were created by him and for him. He is before all things, and in him all things hold together. And he is the head of the body, the church; he is the beginning and the firstborn from among the dead, so that in everything he might have the supremacy.

Space limitations make it impossible to try to unravel all of the cryptic imagery of this complex passage, but it is well worth noting the interplay of themes which we have considered throughout this book. Christ is set out as (1) the Image of God, (2) the First-born, (3) the Originator or Source of creation, and (4) the Head of the church. All of these are drawn together as the basis of his supremacy or authority over everything. From this supremacy comes blessing to the church. Our earlier study of Ephesians 1:22–23 and of the parallel passage, 5:22–33, has shown that Paul pointedly called attention to the implications of this pattern of thought about Christ's headship and authority for the role of 'head' which is to be exercised by a husband for the sake of his wife. Christ's authority, the model for husbands, is tied with his being the 'first-born'. We should not be surprised that Paul saw Adam's being 'first formed' as implying authority! In the light of the strong Old Testament background and of the clear-cut Pauline parallels, I conclude that Paul's comment that men should teach and exercise authority because the man was formed first fits within his familiar patterns of thought and is intended to say, in effect, that the man is to exercise the role appropriate to the first-born male.

We are now in a position to respond to the suggestion that Paul's argument leads to the conclusion that animals or trees ought, by right of temporal priority, to rule over mankind. Proponents of this argument rightly call attention to the fact that the Scripture says that people are to rule over the animals and trees; Genesis 1:26–28 makes this point forcefully. They fail, however, to take into account the important considerations of the Old Testament precedent and other Pauline teaching which we have just examined. Further, they lose sight of the differences between mankind and the animals. They finally make Paul to be saying, in effect, the first bull born in a man's house should be ruler of his son upon his death. The laws of primogeniture apply to humans born in a home. They do not apply in such a way as to confuse the first animal with the first son! The idea that Paul's argument makes mankind subordinate to the animals which were formed before him needs to be explored, and then firmly dismissed as inadequate.

We have noted Paul's view that Adam's priority of formation resulted in his being appointed to carry the responsibilities of the first-born. Is this view really compatible with the teaching of Genesis, or does it read in what the text would deny? The actual text of Genesis 2 makes clear the prior formation of Adam, but does not discuss its implications *as such*. Does it do so by implication? Some have suggested that the fact that the woman was made to be man's helper, to be a 'helper appropriate to him' ('*zr kngdw*), indicates that she was intended to be subordinate. This interpretation rests upon a misapprehension of the meaning of 'helper' ('*zr*). In English, the term can mean 'junior assistant'. It is highly questionable whether this is a legitimate reading of the Hebrew. The term is used to describe one who lends a hand or helps out, frequently in a context of need. It is most often used of God in relation to Israel. Woman's role as 'appropriate helper', therefore, does not carry with it an implication of subordination. She is the needed helper whom God supplies to end man's loneliness and to work alongside him, not the junior assistant.

Are there other textual considerations which suggest that subordination was in view? Adam's naming of the animals and of his wife, as well as the explanation of the name given her, suggest so. These are best taken up in conjunction with Paul's discussion of the fact that the woman was taken out of the man.

ii. The woman was taken out of the man
In 1 Corinthians 11:8 Paul defends the headship of the man from the fact that the woman was taken out of (*ek*) him. His point has seemed obscure to modern readers, who often ask what is to be proven from her origin except that the two were literally one flesh. As we have seen, some have asked whether this line of argument does not lead to the conclusion that the ground ought to have authority over man because he was taken from it. Those who do not see man as a special creation of God have often dismissed Paul's point as ignorant of the evolutionary origin of man or have (condescendingly?) commented on the fact that by Paul's argument mankind ought to be subject to the apes and other species from which he has descended ('out of' which he came). We have noted that this sort of argument is to be dismissed as failing to

recognize the biblical distinction between man and the animals and the explicit assignment of man to the role of ruler of the rest of creation. It still remains, however, to make a positive statement about Paul's meaning.

1. Origin and authority. Biblical thought knows a strong respect for the power to originate and for the role of being derivative. We have already seen this in connection with Paul's discussion of Christ as the beginning or originator of all things (Col. 1:15–18). The same train of thought is to be seen in the respect due to parents from children. The child is derived from both parents ('out of' the father; 'through' the mother; cf. 1 Cor. 11:12) and to honour both. The father, the male origin, is the senior with respect to authority. This background, of itself, is sufficient to generate the authority of which Paul spoke. Adam's historical situation prevented Eve's developing from his 'seed' in a woman. She was instead specially formed by God, from his body itself, to be Adam's helper and the mother of all mankind. Adam was her 'source' and to him was due appropriate honour. Although it would have been present in Hebrew minds, this line of reasoning is not developed by the text itself. It is by another line of thought that we come to see the relation between origin and authority more clearly.

2. Naming the animals. The text of Genesis 1 and 2 makes it clear that both mankind and the animals were shaped by God. Mankind, however, was made to rule over the others and to guard the garden of God. His rule is expressed in his naming of the animals. This idea is foreign to modern readers. It is therefore worth considering briefly the function of 'names' in the Old Testament.

For the Hebrew a name was not simply a group of vocables which correspond to a thing or person. The 'name' of something was related to its essence or function. The various names of God, for instance, describe different aspects of his person and action. Yahweh or Jehovah was his identity as the covenant God who promised his blessing to Abraham and to his seed. To 'know' a person or a God, for a Hebrew, might mean either to know about that one, or to have experienced a relationship with him. Thus, when God says to Moses that Abraham, Isaac and Jacob knew him as God Almighty but not as Jehovah, he was not saying that they had never heard the name of Jehovah (Ex. 6:2–3). He was rather saying that they had experienced his power, reflected in the name 'God Almighty', but had not experienced his fulfilment of the covenant promises which he had made. Moses, on the other hand, would 'know' him as Jehovah as he and the children of Israel experienced deliverance from Egypt and received the promised land. To them he 'revealed his name', *i.e.* acted in accord with his character as indicated in the name.

In the twentieth-century West we no longer give our children proper names reflecting their characteristics. We may, however, do so in people's nicknames: Shorty, Ginger, Fatty, *etc.* A friend of mine observed, 'Even people who don't name their children according to essence or function name their pets that way. Our Siamese cat is called Idle-wild because he *is*. Someone didn't understand and asked bewilderedly, "Why do you name your cat after an airport?" '

'Name' was associated with function and the power to assign or to change a name was connected with control. Jacob, whose name meant 'the supplanter', obtained his older brother's birthright by cunning (Gn. 27). In his later life he continued to operate by his own cunning rather than by trust in God. In Genesis 32 God meets with him in the form of an angel and wrestles with him. Jacob cannot prevail against his mysterious opponent, who ends the match by simply touching Jacob's thigh, putting it out of joint. Having thus shown his power over Jacob, God assigns him a new name, Israel, the one who wrestles with God. When Jacob asks God's name, God declines to give it. God is the ruler; he names Jacob but will not be named by him, nor even inform him of his name.

Within this context we can begin to see the importance of God's bringing of the animals to the man whom he has appointed to rule the earth 'in order to see what the man would call them' (Gn. 2:19–20). God was not waiting to see what sounds Adam would associate with each animal. The prerogative of assigning them names reflects control. He was allowing his vicegerent to express his understanding of and to exercise his rule over the animals by assigning them names. Adam does so, and demonstrates his control: 'whatever the man called each living creature, that was its name'.

There was, however, no animal which was appropriate to be Adam's companion. God therefore put Adam to sleep and fashioned a woman from Adam's own body (2:21–22). It is what happened next which demonstrates the authority of the man with respect to the woman. The text says

> Then Jehovah God made a woman from the part he had taken out of the man, and he brought her to the man. The man said, 'This is now bone of my bones and flesh of my flesh; she shall be called "woman" (*'iššah*), for she was taken out of man' (*'iš*) (Gn. 2:22–23).

Adam's response to the woman both stresses their unity ('bone of my bones and flesh of my flesh') and also stresses his rule over her in that he assigns her a name ('she shall be called. . .'). This stress on unity and subordination is familiar to us from the New Testament texts which we have studied.

The name which Adam gave, *'iššah*, means 'woman' and sounds like the word for man, *'iš*. A pun of sorts may have been intended. Yet who knows what language was spoken? It is also possible that the actual name given is not the only thing in view when Adam says, 'because she was taken out of man'. It may be that he is commenting on the reason that he has the privilege of naming one who is, after all, bone of his bone and flesh of his flesh. If so, what he said may be paraphrased, 'She is indeed my own kind, from my own body. She is, however, derivative and it is my privilege to assign her a name. Let her be called by the name I give, "woman", because she was taken out of me.'

Adam's responsibility to act as God's subordinate ruler, even after the fall, is reflected in Genesis 3:20 where he assigns the woman a new name in response to God's promise that, despite the sentence of death as the result of sin, the woman will bring forth live children to continue the race (3:15–16). We read, 'Adam named his wife Eve (*hwh*; literally, 'living'), because she would become the mother of all the living.' His headship continued after the fall. It would be a mistake to say that it began with the fall.

I conclude that Paul's cryptic remark that the fact that the woman was taken 'out of' the man is faithful to the teaching of the Genesis narrative, which reflects the headship of the man over the woman who was taken out of him in the accounts of the man's naming of both the animals and his wife. Paul's faithfulness goes beyond his observation of male authority. He reflects its teaching by his emphasis that the unity of the sexes stands alongside a hierarchical or headship relation.

iii. Woman for the sake of the man

We come now to the final conclusion which Paul drew from Genesis 2 in support of the headship of the man. According to Paul the woman was made for the sake of the man. It is not at all difficult to grasp his point or to verify it from the text of Genesis. Adam was made and no appropriate companion and helper was found for him. For the sake of providing such a companion and helper, God formed the woman. There can be no question that she was made for his sake rather than vice versa.

Problems begin to arise as men and women interpret this fact. Men are prone to abuse it and to conclude that women were made to be either their slaves or their playthings. Women often feel deeply resentful, inferring that the text suggests that women were made as an afterthought and that their sole purpose is to be 'used' by men. They sometimes feel the text gives them no valid existence except as an appendage to men. These attitudes of men and women are in error and are tremendously destructive.

The text of Genesis and the text of 1 Corinthians do not say that women are made to be men's playthings. They do say that women were made to share with men in the service of God and in the custodial ruling of the earth. The woman was indeed made for the sake of the man's need, but it was his need of a companion and fellow-worker rather than his need for toys which was in view. When men conceive of their wives as less than a God-given help which they need, or, worse still, begin to treat them in such a fashion, they are unfaithful to the teaching of Genesis. They are also falling short of the example of Christ's headship; he is head and brother and husband to the church. His leadership is for its benefit. It is not his toy, but his love. The church is not depersonalized in its relation to Christ but fulfilled in its humanity. For men to adopt a lesser model is unfaithfulness.

The headship of men in the home and in the church does not rob women of their purpose in life or make them only appendages of men. Both sexes are members of Christ's body. They share in the ruling of God's creation and in the publication of the gospel. As we have noted, all humans are to serve God in a structure which includes appointive headship. The arrival of the kingdom has introduced a new situation in which the validity of women's existence apart from men is clearly demonstrated. Some men and women will be gifted to be eunuchs for the sake of the kingdom. Their service to God does not involve marital structures. Further, in the resurrection marriage relationships will be done away with completely. Who then can be seen as an appendage?

c. Genesis 3 and Paul's use of it

We have now examined Paul's use of the first two chapters of Genesis. We have found that he does not contradict the teaching of Genesis 1 that both sexes are the image of God, called to rule the world and that he faithfully reflects the teaching of the second chapter in his teaching of male headship in worship and in the church. Paul's application of the teaching of these chapters which discuss events before the fall is in line with the teaching of Jesus that the arrival of the kingdom would enable humans to live out the Creator's original design for marriage. We must now turn our attention to his use of the third chapter and to relationships which resulted from the fall. This is of particular importance since numerous critics of Paul's teaching have argued that women's subordination was the result of the fall and that Paul, mistakenly, made the distorted relations after the fall to be normative. Our exegesis of pre-fall teaching has shown this view to be in error. It now remains to study the teaching of Genesis 3 and Paul's use of it.

i. It was the woman who was deceived

First Timothy 2:14 explains, 'Adam was not the one who was deceived; the woman, being deceived, became a sinner.' How did Paul think these cryptic words offered support for his view that women ought not to 'teach or exercise authority over men'? Did he mean that Adam knew better (was not deceived) and did not sin? Is he saying that women are therefore responsible for the fallen state of mankind and that, as a punishment for Eve's act, no women should be allowed to teach? Does he mean that Eve and other women are gullible and should not be allowed to propagate their ignorance?

Rabbinic schools and Jewish theologians debated the cause of the fall. Same laid responsibility at Eve's feet.[5] Romans 5:12–21 make it clear that Paul was not among their number. He placed the responsibility specifically upon the shoulders of Adam. Comparing Adam's sin to Christ's obedience, he said, 'Sin entered the world through one man'; 'death reigned through that one man'

---

[5] N. P. Williams' study, *The Ideas of the Fall and of Original Sin* (London, 1927), remains one of the most valuable sources of information in this area.

(Rom. 5:12, 17). Paul's clear statement leads us to discount the possibility that 1 Timothy 2:14 is saying that the fall was Eve's fault. A straightforward reading of the text suggests another possibility. Paul seems to be saying that Eve was *not* at fault; she was deceived. Adam, on the other hand, was not deceived but, deliberately and with understanding, chose to sin.

We may similarly dismiss the likelihood that Paul was saying that all women are gullible, as was Eve, and therefore are untrustworthy teachers. Titus 2:3 directs the older women to teach the younger. Paul urged Timothy to continue in the teaching of the Scriptures, which he had known from infancy (2 Tim: 3:15). Inasmuch as his father was a Gentile and Paul commended the sincere faith of his Jewish mother and grandmother (2 Tim. 1:5), we can only presume that it was they who taught Timothy from his infancy. In the same vein we note Priscilla and Paul's female fellow-workers. In the light of the central role of all these women, I think it very unlikely that Paul meant to say that the fact that Eve was deceived shows that all women are too gullible to teach.

Another simple reading of 1 Timothy 2:14 is possible. If we ask who was at fault in the fall, the verse answers: 'Adam was not deceived; the woman, being quite deceived (*exapatētheisa*), fell into transgression.' We know from Romans that Paul considered Adam at fault. The verse under consideration appears virtually to excuse Eve on the basis that she was in reality deceived by the serpent. Adam, on the other hand, is said not to have been deceived. His sin was therefore with understanding and deliberate! Christian men cannot indulge themselves by saying, 'Oh, that Eve had kept her mouth shut and not done it!' Paul says that Adam, not Eve, did it and that he did it knowing full well what he was doing.

But how, then, does Paul's point help his case about women in authority? Would you rather be led by an innocent but deceived person, or by a deliberate rebel? Our study of other Pauline uses of Genesis provides some help. In 1 Corinthians 11:8–9 and in 1 Timothy 2:13 we saw that Paul appealed to the divinely established relationship of the partners as supportive of his understanding, arguing that the *pre-fall* role relations should be normative for the church. Can verse 14, which discusses the fall itself, be understood from such a perspective?

Consider the topic under discussion in this section of the chapter: teaching and exercising religious authority. Paul points out in verse 14 that Eve was deceived by the serpent about the central theological issue of the truthfulness of God. Adam was not, and became responsible for their falling into sin. We have seen that Paul considered that headship (responsibility to lead and final accountability) was given by God to men in the home and in worship. Could it be that his point in verse 14 is that Adam was the one appointed by God to exercise religious headship, and that he was the one prepared by God to do so? On this basis there is no need to generalize to the preparation of other women to make religious decisions, as the divine assignment of headship in religious affairs to the husband is the point in view. Paul's point might then be paraphrased, 'The man, upon whom lay responsibility for leadership in the home and in religious matters, was prepared by God to discern the serpent's lies. The woman was not appointed religious leader and was not prepared to discern them. She was taken in. Christian worship involves re-establishing the creational pattern with men faithfully teaching God's truth and women receptively listening.' This interpretation brings Paul's remarks into line with his other uses of Genesis. It is yet another call to re-establish the creational relationship in the time before the return of Christ. How does this view stand up to the teaching of Genesis? An examination of the fall and of the curse sanctions in Genesis 3 offers further understanding.

ii. The curses of Genesis 3

The first part of Genesis 3 relates the temptation of Eve and the consequences of the fall in the hiding of the man and his wife from one another and from God. It is from verse 8 that the text is most relevant for our present purposes. In verse 9 God addresses the man to ask where he is and why he has hidden. While it is precarious to build much upon the fact, it is worth noting that it is the man who is addressed and questioned. It is apparently he who is the family spokesman. The exchanges with God and the curses give further insight into the roles of the man, the woman and the serpent.

We shall consider first the curse upon the serpent. Whereas both the man and the woman are questioned as to why they have acted as they have, the serpent is asked no questions, but only cursed. The first part of the curse (3:14) marks him as cursed beyond all animals and comments on the manner of locomotion which marks serpents. It is not clear whether this portion announces a new situation (*i.e.* that serpents, who formerly walked or flew, will now crawl) or whether the serpent's lowly posture and constant licking of the dust will now be a sign of God's curse (thus negatively paralleling the adopting of the rainbow which follows rain as a sign of God's promise to Noah). The latter seems the more likely.[6] The second half of the curse (3:15) discusses a new relation which will obtain between the woman and the 'serpent' and between their respective seed. It should be carefully noted that the new thing is not that they relate to one another but the manner in which they relate. It is not simply relations with snakes which are in view, but relations between Satan and mankind. Mankind should have ruled over Satan, but yielded instead to his seduction and will suffer at his hand as he seeks to destroy them. The warfare between Satan and the woman's seed comes to its climax in the death of Christ. That hour of Satan's apparent victory is in fact the hour of his defeat and the redemption of the fallen race. Returning, now, to the curse on the 'serpent', we see that the fall has distorted relations between actual snakes and humanity (real snakes strike people; people crush snakes) and between the one who used the serpent, Satan, and humanity (Satan seeks to destroy the race; Christ's victory will overcome Satan's effort). The curse on the serpent declares that the pre-fall relations of mankind and the 'serpent' will be (1) painfully distorted but (2) God will prevent the distortion from overthrowing his original plan.

The same basic pattern is discernible in the curse upon the man (3:17–19). It has often been noted that the man sought to evade his responsibility by explaining that the woman whom *God* gave him led him into sin (3:12). The curse upon the man denies his plea. He is cursed because he listened (*i.e.* yielded) to the voice of his wife. His responsibility was to obey God; it cannot be evaded. The curse itself is of importance. As a consequence of his disobedience the ground itself is changed and their relation distorted. Whereas he had previously dressed the garden and eaten of the earth with freedom (2:15–16), he would henceforth eat of it in sorrow (3:17). Although it would continue to yield its fruit and he would continue to eat of it, the ground would now resist his efforts and raise up thorns and thistles to cause him pain (3:18). Man's role as guardian of the garden in fellowship with God was changed to that of an exile labouring in the sweat of his face until

[6] For substantial yet readable discussion of the curse contents, see G. Vos, *Biblical Theology* (Grand Rapids, 1948), pp. 52–55. A less technical treatment is available in E. J. Young, *Genesis Three*, (London, 1966).

he dropped from his toil as a result of God's judgment upon his sin (3:19). It should be noted that what was new was not the relation of man to the ground. He had previously ruled over it and it had yielded its fruit peaceably. The new element introduced by the fall is the conflict and the pain. Once again we have (1) a painful distortion of an existing relation and (2) a divine promise that the disruption, despite the pain, will not overthrow the original plan.

Against this background, let us turn to the curse upon the woman. She, as her husband, is questioned about her disobedience (3:13). She explains that she was deceived and ate. It is striking that, while the serpent was specifically cursed because of his deed (3:14) and the man cursed for his deed (3:17), the woman is not told that her curse flows from *her* deed. If we bring to bear an idea of Adam's headship, we may *speculate* that her curse may be the first example of 'original sin', *i.e.* that her curse comes not only for her sin, but also because Adam, the head of mankind, has sinned and those whom he represented suffer as a consequence. Whatever the relation of her curse to original sin, we must consider its content.

The curse upon the woman divides into two parts. The first concerns child-bearing, the second her relation with her husband. The commands of creation (1:28) include a calling to multiply and to fill the earth. Childbirth was therefore a part of the pre-fall pattern for humans. As a result of the fall this process will become very painful (3:16). By the grace of God, however, the process will not fail and live children will be born. As before, (1) an existing relation has been distorted painfully, but (2) the grace of God will prevent its destruction.

We now come to the relation of the wife to her husband (3:16). Here God says, 'Your desire shall be to your husband; nevertheless he shall rule over you.' Does he mean that she will begin to want a husband and that a new relationship of subordination will be set up? The text is often understood in this way. It is thought by many that the previous relation had been that of partners with no subordination and that the change is her great desire for a husband which will lead her even to subject herself. The analogy of the preceding curses and an examination of the wording of this portion suggest another alternative.

All of previous curse sections involved the painful distortion of an existing relation and its preservation by God's grace. Can this section be seen in the same light? It might be said that her desire for her husband was new and his rule a painful distortion, but this approach leaves no gracious preservation despite the pain. A study of the words 'desire' (*šwq*) and 'rule' (*mšl*) provides a better insight. In what sense does the woman 'desire' her husband? We have already noted that the word can be interpreted as 'long for' or 'want' in a positive sense. Genesis 4:7 offers quite a different perspective. Cain is told, 'sin is lying in wait at the door and his desire (*swq*) is to (rule over) you, but you must rule over (*mšl*) him'. The parallel to the curse is obvious. Sin's desire is to overcome or overthrow Cain. If this negative meaning of *šwq* in Genesis 4:7 is brought back into the preceding chapter, the woman is being told that she will come to desire (*šwq*) to overthrow her husband, but that he will rule (*mšl*) over her. This meaning, warranted by the use of desire and rule in chapters 3 and 4, brings this curse in line with all the others. The relation of the man and woman will be (1) painfully distorted by her desire to overthrow him, but (2) she will not succeed; he will nevertheless rule over her. History shows that because of his sinfulness and her resentment his rule itself will often be painful and abusive.

The net result, then, is that God's words to the woman concerning her relation to her husband are not pointing to the establishment of a new marital hierarchy, but to the painful distortion of an already existing hierarchical relationship, the existence of which we have already noted in connection with Genesis 2. The latter half of the curse is intended to show that God will prevent her effort to overthrow her husband from succeeding.

With respect to the deception of Eve, to which Paul makes reference, note that she seeks to excuse herself on the grounds of her deception and, although cursed by God, is not contradicted on the point. She was, in fact, deceived and her husband was not. His judgment was for wanton disobedience. The exchange between God and the couple suggests throughout that the husband was presumed to be the one responsible for religious decisions and the spokesman for the couple with God.

iii. Multiple roles: a problem when interpreting the first pair
Interpreters of the first couple have a major problem: their relation involves an intricate superimposing of numerous roles. Adam functions as priest, husband, and perhaps as head of the social unit. It is impossible to separate one role from another. It is im-

possible to derive principles from their situation for application to more complex social arrangements without further information. It is in this context that the rest of Scripture becomes important. We have noted that the headship of men in domestic and religious affairs continues from the pre-fall period through the time of Christ's advent and will continue until his return and the end of marriage relations. In the religious sphere we found that the larger social units of the tribe and nation were accompanied by the appointment of certain representative males in the area of worship. This same principle evidently continues to hold true in Paul's arrangement of the church.

d. Conclusions

We have now surveyed each of the texts in which Paul drew upon the opening chapters of Genesis in support of his teaching about the relation of men and women. We have found that those chapters teach that both sexes are the image of God and called to rule the earth. They also demonstrate male headship in the accomplishment of that task. We noted, however, that this headship is not such that women are demeaned or made less worthy. It has to do with the service of God by mankind, not the service of men by women. Genesis 1 stressed the joint task of the race in ruling the earth. The second chapter described the formation of the man and his exercise of authority in the naming of the animals. Because no appropriate co-worker was found, a woman was formed by God out of the man. Her purpose was to share in man's rule. We found that his naming of her reflected his role with respect to her. In the third chapter we noted that the headship of the man was reflected in his being called upon to answer for the pair and possibly in the lack of explanation of the basis of her curse.

Our study of the curses themselves indicated that in each case an existing relation was painfully distorted by the fall but, by the grace of God, those relations were not allowed to be entirely destroyed. Thus the serpent was hostile to the woman, but would be destroyed by her seed rather than destroying it. The land, likewise, resisted the man's efforts to gain food, but would nevertheless yield it. Pain would accompany child-bearing, but live children would be born. In the marriage relation the woman would seek to overthrow the man, but would not achieve her end.

It is interesting to note that the temptation itself was connected with this matter of hierarchy. Satan through the serpent led Eve to persuade her husband that God had lied about the fruit for selfish reasons. The order of authority thus established is Satan, serpent, woman, man. The order which should have prevailed in this debate over religious authority (*i.e.* should God or Satan be accepted as the source of truth) should have been: *God* the definer of truth, who spoke first to the *man*, who communicated with his *wife*, who shares in the rule over creation, including the *serpent*, which may be in the garden-sanctuary of God, while *Satan* the liar is excluded.

It appears that Paul's cryptic references to the early chapters of Genesis are in line with the actual teaching of the chapters and in line with his own teaching elsewhere as well as with the teaching of Jesus that the present state of the kingdom calls for the renewal of the creational relationships by a renewed mankind. Contrary to much current thinking, we found that Paul did not build his view of the relationship of men and women from Genesis 3 and events after the fall, but rather appealed consistently to Genesis 2 and relationships prior to it.

4. Saved through childbirth?

We have found that Paul's prohibition of women teaching or exercising authority over men in the church is in fact a call to make things as they were 'in the beginning'. One more element needs attention before we complete our study of 1 Timothy 2. Verse 15 reads, 'women will be saved/kept safe through (the?) childbirth, if they continue in faith, love and holiness with propriety'. This verse is difficult to follow and presents two difficult linguistic problems.

First, it is difficult to know which of several things Paul meant when he wrote 'she will be saved through (the) childbirth'. His verb, *sōthēsetai*, may mean either 'she shall be saved' or 'she shall be kept safe'. If the former refers to salvation from sin, it is a flat contradiction of Paul's view of salvation by trust in Christ and thus raises impossible contradictions. The second option makes Paul's words say, in effect, that she will survive childbirth if she is pious. This seems almost totally irrelevant to the context and quite unlike Paul. Other options are available; we shall discuss them below.

A second interpretative problem with the verse has to do with 'the childbirth' (*teknogonia*). The expression which Paul uses is unusual. It is optional whether 'the' should be included. If it is, it suggests that a particular childbirth is in view. We shall explore this further.

A final problem with the verse has to do with the shift from a singular to a plural subject. Paul has been discussing Eve and moves in his discussion to women in general. The singular subject suggests that at that point in his sentence he had either woman-kind, 'woman', or Eve in particular in view. The plural subject at the end indicates a general application to women. Why the shift?

It is possible that Paul's reference to 'the childbirth' is a reference to the birth of Jesus, the promised child. In recent years this view has been challenged by many, but remains quite possible. It would be an obscure reference. Paul has, however, been discussing Eve and the fall. It would not be surprising for him to turn in his thinking to the remedy for the fall. His words would then be interpreted as meaning, 'Eve will be saved from the curse through the birth of the promised child, Jesus, and other women who exhibit obedient faith will similarly be saved.' This accounts for his shift from the singular to the plural subjects in quite a natural way, for other women will be saved on the same basis as Eve. The drawback of this reading is the fact that it breaks with the flow of the passage. Paul does make such shifts of thought, but a reading which maintains the flow might be preferable.

It is possible to understand this verse as a continuation of the discussion of women's role. The passage has been discussing patterns of conduct for men and women in prayer, in adornment and in teaching and worship. The interpretations thus far proposed have assumed that Paul meant that women would be saved either from judgment or from death in childbirth. I would propose the possibility that he is thinking instead that Eve and women in general will be saved or kept safe from wrongly seizing men's roles by embracing a woman's role. This allows the text to be read as it stands and keeps it in line with the issue at hand. It also raises a question: did Paul mean that all women should marry? That is a possible implication of verse 15. Lives of 'faith, love and holiness with propriety' can be for all women; childbirth is only for the married and, indeed, not for all of them. We know from 1 Corinthians 7 that Paul considered *both* celibacy and marriage divine callings and actually preferred the former. In the light of his attitude to marriage it is unlikely that he would call all women to marry. It is, therefore, more likely that he is speaking generally of a woman's role when he speaks of childbirth, using a typical part to represent the typical whole.

Twentieth-century cultural developments make the selection of child-bearing as the part to represent the whole seem inappropriate or strange. Public opinion is increasingly against the bearing of children. Both men and women often look upon children as a problem and a burden. In some circles the bearing and raising of children is viewed as a prime means of reducing women to bondage. This sentiment is sometimes expressed in the remark 'keep 'em barefoot and pregnant'. It is easy to see that Paul's remarks here will be abrasive if received from such a perspective. We have already considered biblical attitudes toward child-bearing. The bearing and raising of children were considered by women and men alike to be activities of surpassing personal and social worth. The bearing of children was a central element in the definition of womanhood and in the fulfilling of God's calling to mankind. The selfishness of our twentieth century, which does not want its enjoyment of pleasures undercut by the financial and personal obligations entailed in raising a family, was not common in the first century. In his day the bearing of children which Paul selected as a part to represent the whole of the high calling of women was a valued activity which women embraced with joy and with pride and for which they were deeply respected.

On the interpretation which I am proposing, we may paraphrase Paul as saying that women in general (and most women in his day) will be kept safe from seizing men's roles by participating in marital life (symbolized by childbirth), which should be accompanied by other hall-marks of Christian character (faith, love and holiness with propriety) which will produce the adornment of good deeds for which he called in 2:10.

C. ELDERS, DEACONS AND 'WOMEN': 1 TIMOTHY 3:1–13

Our study of 1 Timothy 2:8–15 has shown that Paul's use of the primogeniture concept and the roles reflected in the early chapters of Genesis is in keeping with both his and Jesus' view that the followers of Christ should follow the Creator's patterning of the relation of men and women. In the area of the church, this meant that certain men should teach and exercise authority and that women should learn responsively. The next chapter of 1 Timothy raises the question of formal offices within the church. The topic is as important today as it was in Timothy's day. Indeed, it is probably more of a battleground today than it was then. 1 Timothy 3 describes the qualifications required of persons who will be elders and deacons in the church. The requirements for elders are such that women cannot hold the office. The verses dealing with the office of deacon are less clear and will need close attention. Before considering these issues, however, a brief discussion of church offices is in order. This is particularly important in view of the difference in church government found among modern churches.

1. Church office in the New Testament

We noted in our examination of Jesus' ministry that he did not establish an ecclesiastical structure during his personal ministry on earth. It was only after the resurrection and ascension that the church began to wrestle with questions of that sort. The book of the Acts gives indications of an emerging structure, but does not give sufficient detail to gain a full picture. The letters provide more insight. Our study below of the 'eldership' will not be a balanced one. We shall be paying particular attention to the question of teaching and authority. This stress is *not* the dominant or central note in biblical discussions of the office. As we have noted, Christian authority is for the sake of service. The elders are to nurture, guard, teach, build up, and be examples to the flock. Deacons minister to it. Responsibility to foster growth and to ensure faithful teaching necessarily entails authority. Authority can be abused. We have already noted Jesus' concern to prevent abuse of authority (Lk. 22:24–26). His concern is reflected by Peter (1 Pet. 5:1–2). I hope that the concentration on authority in the study which follows will not mislead any into thinking that I am suggesting that the eldership should be conceived of primarily in terms of authority and the right to command. The eldership should be seen primarily in terms of shepherding.

In Acts we see apostles and 'elders' (Acts 11:30; 14:23; 15:2–23; 16:4; 20:17; 21:18) and the appointment of 'deacons' (*diakonoi*, men who serve needs) to ensure fair treatment of Hebrew and Hellenistic widows (Acts 6). We do not know if this last category represents a unique case or is to be related as prototypes to the 'deacons' of the letters of the New Testament.

Acts witnesses the appointment of 'elders' (*presbyteroi*) in cities such as Ephesus. We shall consider their tasks and then those of the deacons. We get some indication of their function when Paul charges them, 'guard . . . all the flock over which the Holy Spirit has made you overseers (*episkopoi*, 'bishops'). Be shepherds of the church of God . . .' (Acts 20:28). The elders (or bishops or presbyters; the terms are used interchangeably in the New Testament) were charged with the welfare of the congregations. Their shepherding responsibilities involved guarding their people against false teaching (20:29) and teaching them by word and example to live as Christians (1 Pet. 5:1–3; Eph. 4:1, 12). Acts knows other roles in the church such as prophet and evangelist. In many cases it is difficult to know whether a function (*i.e.* activity) or a formal role (*i.e.* office) is being mentioned. For our purposes it is not necessary to resolve questions about all of the offices.

The New Testament letters, especially those to Timothy, Titus and the Philippians, witness to the establishment of the categories of elder and deacon in a formal way. Paul and Timothy are teachers of the apostolic message and Timothy is charged to entrust that message to qualified men who will in turn teach others (2 Tim. 2:2). These men are not just congregational members, but have formal responsibility for passing on correct teaching, which teaching is to be lived out in the lives of the Christians (2 Tim. 1:13–14; 3:10–12). Such men are elders who direct the life and work of the church. Paul commands that 'the elders who direct the affairs of the church well are worthy of double honour [possibly 'honorarium', *i.e.* wage], especially those whose work is preaching and teaching' (1 Tim. 5:17). The author of the letter to the Hebrews comments on such men from a slightly different perspective. He calls upon his readers to be mindful of those who rule over them (13:7) and to 'obey those who rule over you and submit yourselves to them, for they watch over your souls, and they must give account' (13:17). Paul charged the elders/shepherds to watch over the sheep which God had placed in their charge. The author to the Hebrews charged the sheep to obey and noted that the shepherds are accountable for them. These texts from the letters to Timothy and Hebrews supplement what we have seen in Acts and provide a picture of the elders as men who are involved in the direction of the congregations and who are charged particularly with teaching, ensuring that the message is faithfully taught and directing the outworking of the message in the life of the church. These tasks involve distinctive leadership and authority, extending to formal actions to rid the flock of the 'savage wolves' whom the apostle warned would rise up within the flock (Acts 20:29; *cf.* 1 Cor. 5).

We need not pursue the work of the elder here at length. Sufficient has been said to show that his task of instruction, shepherding and discipline falls easily within the areas of 'teaching and exercising authority over men' which Paul reserved to men in 1 Timothy 2. These basic considerations will be of importance when we look at 1 Timothy 3.

The role of deacons is more difficult to define precisely from Scripture. Our task is additionally complicated by the complexities of various contemporary forms of church government and by their diverse understandings of church office. In many Baptist church governments, the 'minister' is also considered *the* 'elder' of the congregation. He sometimes shares in the disciplinary (although not necessarily in the preaching) responsibilities with a board of 'deacons'. Such 'deacons' are thus exercising some of the tasks which fell to the 'elders' of Acts 20 and to the qualified men who were 'elders' in the letters to Timothy.

We shall first consider the biblical data. The term *diakonos* means 'one who serves', 'servant' or 'minister'. It can be used to describe the activity of 'one who serves' the needs of another (Mk. 9:35; 10:43). It can also describe one who represents or acts on behalf of another as his servant or minister (Acts 6; Eph. 3:7). In this sense it takes on a slightly more formal meaning. The formal, representative aspect and the idea of serving others can come together, as with the deacons of Acts 6 who ministered to the needs of the widows as representatives of the church. The term 'deacon' points both to their representative role and to their actual function in serving. It is clear that the deacons of Acts 6 possessed a certain amount of authority in their distribution of food. A question arises, however, if we ask whether, for instance, this authority is of a sort which, if given to women, would violate the restrictions upon them as set by Paul in 1 Timothy 2:11. He seems to have had in view teaching and discipline rather than serving through distribution of goods. We shall discuss this further when we discuss 1 Timothy 3.

The biblical data are not the only data to be considered when using the terms 'elder', 'bishop', 'minister' and 'deacon' today. The terms are used differently in different forms of church government. Virtually all are agreed that the role of the bishop, elder or presbyter is one which involves responsibility to direct the life of the flock, teaching with authority, and the exercise of disciplinary authority to guard the faith. The term 'minister' is most frequently used of a man who preaches regularly and supervises the pastoral care of the congregation. His function is thus that of an elder. The term 'minister' can, however, be used in a less technical way to describe someone who meets the needs of others (ministers to their needs). In this sense it has little to do with church office as such. It is important to be careful to grasp which sense is intended in a given context.

The term 'deacon' is more varied in its meaning than the others. In some polities (forms of church government) the elders are concerned with the spiritual oversight of the congregation and for the faithful teaching of the apostolic message, while the deacons are responsible for ministering to the physical needs of the congregation and the practical demonstration of Christian love. In such situations the deacons, as other believers, may be involved in 'teaching' in the sense of sharing the Word, but are not involved in 'teaching' in the sense of having primary responsibility to ensure the faithful passing on of the Word and to correct or to discipline where that does not occur.

In other polities the 'deacons' do share in the spiritual oversight of the flock and are differentiated from the 'pastor' or 'elder' more by training and by the fact that they are not full-time servants and teachers in the church. In such cases, the activities of deacons overlap the activities of elders in the exercise of authority and even in teaching.

A third basic use of the term 'deacon' occurs in churches which ordain men as deacons as a first step to the eldership or priesthood. In such cases the authority involved depends upon the definition of the office by the particular church.

Other meanings of 'deacon' exist and some churches combine more than one of the above. Each reader must consider his or her own church situation and make appropriate allowances in the discussion which follows. It will become clear that I prefer the first of the three understandings.

We have noted that the central element in the role of the elder is related to the shepherding of the flock. The flock is to be directed and guarded so that it may be nourished and grow. Teaching and correction are included in the task. The 'deacons' of Acts 6 were men who were well respected in the congregations and would not be suspected of favouring either Jews or Greeks. Their task was not in directing the flock, but in distributing resources. The apostles, on the other hand, continued in prayer and the ministry of the word (Acts 6:4). This basic division is not identified as corresponding to that of elder and deacon in the letters to Timothy, but is very suggestive, especially when coupled with those passages in the letters to Timothy which call for the committing of the apostolic message to men who will faithfully teach and for special respect for elders who direct the church by teaching and by preaching (1 Tim. 5:17; 2 Tim. 2:2). This impression is strengthened by the coupling of apostles and elders in the authoritative decrees of the Council held at Jerusalem (Acts 15). Those elders were certainly carrying out functions parallel to those of the apostles.

If the elders preach and teach and shepherd, what did the deacons do? 1 Timothy 3 isolates elders and deacons as special classes of persons, with special qualifications, and also clearly distinguishes them from one another. In Acts 20 Paul met with the elders, but not with the deacons of Ephesus, addressing them as the shepherds of the flock (Acts 20:28). The deacons of Acts 6 did not teach and rule but served physical needs. Could it be that the deacons of 1 Timothy 3 are to be distinguished from the bishops by a similar division of labour? I think so.

The discussion which follows will presume that both deacons and elders are congregational representatives and are distinguished by their tasks. The elder's calling is to foster the spiritual growth of the congregation, and the deacon leads in ministering to its physical needs and showing the love of Christ to outsiders through meeting their physical needs. Elders teach with formal authority and exercise disciplinary authority to protect the flock; deacons do not share this task. As described, the task of a deacon does not involve the sort of teaching and exercising of authority which 1 Timothy 2:11–12 reserves to men. With this understanding of the office of the deacon, therefore, there is no violation of biblical restrictions on authority if women serve as deacons. This fact does not authorize the appointment of women deacons, but it does remove a problem which many face when they think of women deacons. *Other understandings of the office of deacon*, it must be re-emphasized, *may include types of authority which would reserve the office to men.* During the discussion which follows, further reasons for adopting the definition of the diaconate which I have preferred will emerge. If we are going to avoid confusion, it is important to keep in mind the view of the diaconate which I have adopted above.

2. Elders, deacons and women

Our preceding discussion has pointed out that the responsibilities of elders are such that they are within that area of teaching and authority reserved by Paul to men. The qualifications for elders (*episkopoi*, 'bishops' or 'overseers') reflect this. The office is specifically for men as indicated by the requirement that they have but one wife. It should be noted, however, that one woman married to two men would have been unthinkable and would therefore not require comment. The remainder of the set of qualifications is cast exclusively in male terms. I conclude that the teachings of 1 Timothy 2 and the qualifications of 1 Timothy 3 restrict the office of elder (bishop, presbyter) to men only.

1 Timothy 3:11 mentions a group of 'women' (*gynaikes*) who have become the centre of much controversy. Their significance is derived from the fact that they appear in the midst of a discussion of the qualifications necessary for the office of deacon. Are these women wives of the deacons mentioned, or of the elders mentioned previously; or are they themselves deacons? Paul's actual wording is ambiguous. *Gynaikes* means 'women', but that is the standard word used to speak of wives as well. Its definition is therefore dependent upon considerations relating to the context and to other biblical instruction rather than to translation as such. The relevant verses read as follows:

> [8]Deacons, likewise, are to be men worthy of respect, sincere, not indulging in much wine, and not pursuing dishonest gain. [9]They must keep hold of the deep truths of the faith with a clear conscience. [10]They must first be tested; and then if there is nothing against them, let them serve as deacons. [11]In the same way, wives/women are to be women worthy of respect, not malicious talkers but temperate and trustworthy in everything. [12]A deacon must be the husband of but one wife and must manage his children and his household well. [13]Those who have served well gain an excellent standing and great assurance in their faith in Christ Jesus (1 Tim. 3:8–13).

A number of factors make the mention of these women worthy of close attention. The basic options as to their identity are:

(1) they are women in general, (2) they are the wives of bishops and deacons, (3) they are wives of deacons, (4) they are themselves deacons, and (5) they are a group similar to but distinct from deacons.

It is virtually impossible that Paul interrupted a list of qualifications for deacons to list desirable attributes for women in general. We may dismiss the first option.

If he had the wives of deacons and elders in view, it is strange that he should place them in the midst of a discussion of deacons. They would more naturally follow the deacons. This option must be classed as unlikely but possible. It is more likely from their location that they would be wives of deacons. Other issues, however, raise questions about such an identification.

1. The location of the 'women' makes it unlikely that they include elders' wives. Yet it is strange that the wives of deacons should be singled out for close scrutiny and the wives of elders neglected.

2. If Paul intended to talk of wives, he could easily have made his intention clear by saying *'their* wives' or even *'the* wives'. Translations wishing to adopt the meaning 'wives' have generally supplied one of the two words. The biblical text offers no support for this.

3. Paul might have introduced the 'wives' in a manner similar to that which he used for the children in verse 4: 'having wives' (*gynaikas echontes*). He did not so choose.

4. Instead of using a pronoun which would have clearly shown the women to be wives ('their') or introducing them in a manner which showed them to be family members like the children ('having wives . . .'), Paul chose to introduce the women in a manner which set them parallel to the elders and deacons, implying a new, similar class of persons. He said, 'Women, likewise . . .' (*gynaikas hōsautōs*). The importance of this becomes clear when set alongside the introduction of the bishops (verse 2) and of the deacons (verse 8). He said, 'Elders must be . . .', 'Likewise, deacons (must be) . . .', 'Likewise, women (must be) . . .'. The relation between the three is clear. It is further strengthened by the fact that both the sentence introducing the deacons and the one introducing the 'women' have no verb of their own but presume the verb used to describe the elders: *dei*, 'must be'.

5. Consideration of the qualifications of the three classes shows a particular relation between the deacons and the women. All

three classes must be persons who hold public respect. This would naturally be important if they were to act on behalf of the church. The qualifications for the deacons include some elements which are distinctive and probably indicative of their particular role. The lists below compare the qualifications for the deacons and the 'women' of verse 11.

deacons:	women:
worthy of respect	worthy of respect
(*semnous*)	(*semnas*)
not double-tongued	not slanderers
(*mē dilogous*)	(*mē diabolous*)
not given to much wine	sober/temperate
(*mē oinō pollō prosechontas*)	(*nēphalious*)
not pursuing dishonest gain	trustworthy in all things
(*mē aischrokerdeis*)	(*pistas en pasin*)

The qualifications are point for point parallel. The final item in each list has to do with trustworthiness. In the case of the deacon it looks to his business life. In the case of the women, it looks to their handling of daily affairs and relationships, perhaps because few women were involved in business affairs.

The list for the deacons goes on after the first four items to require a firm commitment to the truths of the faith and that he be 'tested' (*dokimazesthōsan*) prior to being admitted to office. The word used for tested may simply mean 'examined'; it is, however, also used for a financial audit or examination. If the deacons were responsible for the administration of financial resources, the inclusion of an investigation of his financial affairs makes good sense. The fact that most women were not involved in financial affairs explains the lack of an audit for them.

3. Phoebe and the title 'deaconess': Romans 16:1

The combination of Paul's setting the women parallel to the elders and deacons as a distinct class and his setting out parallel lists of qualifications strongly suggests that the function of these women was parallel to that of the deacons. Why did he not simply call them deaconesses? In Paul's time the word did not exist. As we saw in the case of Phoebe, *diakonos*, the masculine form of 'deacon' or 'servant', was used for both men and women. The fact that

Paul used *diakonos* to introduce the men in 1 Timothy 3:8 explains the necessity of another word in verse 11 if he wished to turn attention to women deacons. All debate would have been settled if he had said 'women who are deacons' instead of 'women'; yet, if they had women deacons, it would have been quite unnecessary as everyone would have understood what he meant. Further, the expression *gynaikes diakonoi* would be clumsy. If they had a category of 'women' (perhaps 'women of the church'?) who corresponded to the deacons but were not called by that name it would be unnecessary to identify them more specifically than verse 11. The likelihood of such a group is somewhat lessened by the fact that these women appear in the middle of the discussion of deacons.

A final matter needs attention before we finish with 1 Timothy 3. After discussing the women of verse 11, Paul returns to the topic of deacons. Verse 12 sets out two additional requirements for deacons which parallel those needed for elders (being husband of one wife and managing their households well). Two points need to be made concerning these. 1. These requirements are uniquely applicable to men. Their position after the similar lists for deacons and women may be because they are distinctive in this sense. 2. Verse 13 uses an aorist participle, 'those who have served well' (*hoi kalōs diakonēsantes*). It is not, therefore, looking at qualifications for but at performance in office. It has been suggested in various places, perhaps with good reason, that verses 12 and 13 have in view deacons who have served well and who, because of their outstanding character, might be considered for the election to the office of elder. If such a change of role is in view, it would explain the mention in verse 12 of these two qualifications which are also required of elders.

I conclude, then, that 1 Timothy 3:1–11 sets out qualifications for three groups of persons: bishops (elders), deacons and women who probably served as deacons as well. For this latter group the church soon coined the term 'deaconess' (*diakonissa*). Pliny seems to echo such usage in his letter to Trajan (AD 112) speaking of them by the Latin form *ministrae*. Verses 8–10 describe qualifications for men being considered as deacons. Parallel qualifications are given for the women in verse 11. Verses 12 and 13 comment further about persons who have served as deacons in terms appropriate only to men, possibly thinking of men who may be chosen for the office of elder. Verse 13 indicates by its aorist (past) tense that it is talking of performance in office; it is possible that verse 12 is as well.

D. CONCLUSIONS

In the light of our consideration of 1 Timothy 2 and 3, I conclude that Paul taught that the office of elder/bishop/presbyter was restricted to men. He felt that the creational pattern of male headship in both home and church required that women should not exercise spiritual oversight of the flock. They could not be in positions of authoritative teaching or exercising discipline over men. He grounded his view in the relationship of the man and his wife before the fall (although we have noted that it continued beyond it) rather than on relationships established as a result of the fall of Adam. He did not make any appeal to cultural factors such as the relative lack of education for women or the response which outsiders might have to women in positions of responsibility. The nature of his argument leaves virtually no room for modification of his conclusions as a result of alterations in cultural situations.

Conclusions concerning the office of deacon are different. If we understand the deacon's office to involve leading and representing the congregation in ministering to the physical needs of its poor and needy and in expressing Christian love through physical ministry to those outside, the office does not entail authority of the sort prohibited to women in 1 Timothy 2. The 'women' of 1 Timothy 3 are best understood as a group of persons set parallel to the bishops and deacons. They would most naturally be assumed to be women deacons. The example of Phoebe, who is identified in Romans 16:1 as a *diakonos* (deacon/servant) of the church in Cenchraea, lends positive (but not indisputable) support to this conclusion. 1 Timothy 3 does not specify the relation of the female deacons (or women) to the males.

In the lack of such information, each church which establishes women as deacons or in some parallel role must determine their specific responsibilities in the light of passages such as 1 Timothy 2.

9
Conclusions

The preceding chapters have surveyed the role of women in the Bible and in surrounding cultures. In this brief chapter we shall review some of the major observations which we have made and then consider guidelines for their application to various situations. Space makes it impossible to consider a large number of specific cases.

A. SUMMARY

Our opening chapters discussed the role of women in the Old Testament and in the neighbouring cultures of Assyria and Babylon. We observed that all three were patriarchal societies and that their social and legal structures presumed a tribe or clan rather than a nuclear family as the basic kinship unit. The Old Testament differed from contemporaneous cultures in its respect for the woman as an individual. In Israel women were not chattels and had rights which were closely guarded by the law. Although inheritance was passed through the male line, women could inherit in the absence of a male. In religious life, women participated in worship including the taking of vows and offering of sacrifice. In patriarchal times, the patriarch led in family worship. Under Mosaic law, the religious leadership was more closely restricted, only males of the Levite family of Aaron without physical deformity being allowed to serve as priests. Other males and all females were barred from the priesthood. In the social sphere, Israelite women were free to participate in social and commercial life, although they were subordinate authorities in the sense that their contracts were subject to their husbands' ratification. The role of women in civil life was more difficult to ascertain. We have examples of Deborah and Athaliah, a prophetess and a queen. Neither is condemned for her role. Deborah was divinely appointed. Examples of women in such roles are not numerous.

When we turned our attention to Judaism as it had developed in the time of Christ, we found that the subordinate role of women had led to their being viewed as inferior beings as well as subordinate ones. Concern for sexual impropriety led to an effort to restrict communication with women to a minimum. Women were frequently seen as seductive and prone to play upon men's weaknesses. Among the wealthy, and perhaps among the very pietistic, the effort to avoid women was accompanied by restricting them to the house and by veiling. These were, however, not generally practised. Within the home, wives were valued and often tenderly loved. In the religious sphere, the male leadership and the low estimate of women led to the conclusion that women could not and should not learn about religious affairs. Worship was something which they could attend, but it was sufficient that their husbands attend. Civil affairs were seen as strictly the responsibility of men.

Graeco-Roman culture was extremely diverse and was in transition at the time of Christ. The older Greek attitude saw women as inferior beings who were useful only for labour, pleasure or children. Among the Romans of the wealthier class women had a stronger position. They could inherit, were often educated, and were socially acceptable, even in the highest society. Lower class Roman society apparently granted women a more servile place and no education. The urban nature of relations between the Greek cities and their Roman rulers was such that the benefits enjoyed by the wealthy Roman women influenced the status of their Greek counterparts.

The place of women in the ministry of Jesus stands in marked contrast to the place granted them by his Jewish contemporaries. His gospel reached to all human beings alike. Women enjoyed a natural place among those to whom he ministered. He chose none to be among the twelve disciples, who became the twelve apostles after his death, but he was accompanied by a number of women who ministered to his needs and learned from him. There is no evidence of any condescension to women on his part. He considered that they needed his message as did the men.

A key to Jesus' thought about the relation of the sexes was found in his response to questions about divorce. Divorce, he said, was permitted by Moses because of the hardness of Israel's heart. The kingdom which he proclaimed called for a different pattern of life. With respect to divorce, he called for obedience to the creational pattern of permanent marriage, with divorce only in cases of marital infidelity.

Jesus also proclaimed a new situation. Some of his followers would be single for the sake of the kingdom. His teaching thus taught both permanent marriage commitment and permanent single status as consequences of the arrival of the kingdom and the power of God. This dual situation was not seen as permanent. In the resurrection, marrying and giving in marriage would cease and all would be as the angels. The time between Jesus' announcement of the kingdom's arrival and the resurrection thus became an interim with a unique renewal of creational patterns and the beginning of patterns which will be universal in the new creation.

Jesus did not discuss certain questions which are of great concern to the twentieth century. While he spoke clearly to the manner in which authority is to be exercised, he did not give instructions about the manner in which his followers should organize themselves as the church or about the structure of authority within their families. These tasks remained for the apostles under the guidance of the Holy Spirit.

The apostolic church manifests the same attitude toward women which marked Jesus' ministry. Women were incorporated in the body of believers. They were considered able to learn and were taught about the faith. Women played a very sizeable role in the expansion of the church. They were constantly in evidence in the churches and as companions and fellow-workers of missionaries such as Paul.

The early church reflected the structure of Jesus' teaching about the kingdom as well. They did not see the resurrection of Jesus as the initiation of the age when celibacy would be practised (although certain believers at Corinth came to such a conclusion). Marriage was held in high esteem and was considered a permanent commitment. Celibacy, too, was viewed as a valid course to which one might be called and for which one might be gifted. The status of the believer as a member of Christ's body did not call for a breaking of old stations in life, but for new patterns of conduct which would honour God and demonstrate his power to strengthen people to be progressively conformed to his image, to live godly lives. Among the people of God, during the time before the return of the Lord, certain 'headship' or authoritative relations will continue to exist. This authority, we noted, is always for the sake of serving those under authority, *not* for the pride of those in positions of leadership.

Within the marriage relation the Christian is called to reflect the relation of God and his people. For the husband this means imitating Christ in his loving commitment of his own self and of all his resources for the sake of his bride. The husband is to be head, for the sake of the bride. The apostolic church understood the calling of the wife to be the image of God and to join her husband in glorifying God through ruling the earth and demonstrating the power of God to renew lives. With respect to marital authority she was called to respond to her husband's leadership as the church does to Christ's.

The appointive headship of men was not only in marriage but also in the church. As in Eden, and also in Israel, men were called upon to lead in the religious sphere. While all believers joined in the worship and vocal praise of God and in mutual encouragement, only men were to act as elders with responsibility for the spiritual welfare of God's people. Elders were charged to foster the spiritual growth of the flock, to ensure the faithful teaching of the Word, and to exercise the authority of Christ's undershepherds for the sake of the flock. Activities which involved the exercise of such authority, or verged on it, were restricted to men. This did not close off other areas of service and activity to women. They ministered widely in the church to the needs of the people. Among the 'deacons', understood as persons appointed to represent and to lead the congregation in deeds of mercy, we find provision for the inclusion of women. Phoebe is very likely an example of a woman deacon. In activities not involving the authoritative teaching and disciplinary authority of the elder, sexual distinctions seem not to have applied.

If the New Testament congregation is compared with the patriarchal and Mosaic organization of God's people, we find that in both times God appointed certain of the males to lead his people. No females and not all males were included among those called to exercise religious authority. In patriarchal times the patriarch was priest for the clan; under Moses the family of Aaron was called to act as priests; in the church certain men are called to be elders. From the point of view of authority within the church, all men who have not been called to be elders are in exactly the same position as women. Thus, it would be wrong to say that women (*as a sex*) are generically subordinate to men (*as a sex*) with respect to ecclesiastical authority. The entire congregation (men and women) is to honour God's calling of *certain* men to shepherd (nurture and teach) his flock. The entire flock is likewise called upon to receive the ministrations of certain persons (male and female deacons) who have been called by God to lead and to represent the flock in meeting physical needs. We note that nurture, teaching and ministering to others are not reserved exclusively to such officers. That which is distinctive is their formal role and responsibility.

In the churches of the first century, as in our modern churches, there were problems in the relationships of believers. Jealousy, anger, fraud, abuse and pride were all found. The Corinthian church, in particular, is a good example of such problems. The women wanted to reject any differences from the men. Some groups were drunken at the communion service while their neighbours had so little that they were still thirsty. Many were jealous of the 'high-profile' charismatic gifts (tongues, prophecy, *etc.*) of others. Others were depressed and felt that they did not really belong because they lacked such gifts or performed no 'really useful' function in the body. Paul's words to his fractured congregation reprimand their pride and their wrong assessments of what is an 'important' role in the body. They point the proud and quarrelsome Corinthians to the true purpose of their many gifts and callings: the building up of the body of Christ. Paul's words form a suitable closing to our discussion of the roles of women and men in the body of Christ. He said,

[4]There are different kinds of gifts, but the same Spirit. [5]There are different kinds of service, but the same Lord. [6]There are different kinds of working, but the same God works all of them in all men. [7]Now *to each one the manifestation of the Spirit is given for the common good* . . . . [11]All these are the work of one and the same Spirit, and *he gives them to each man, just as he determines.* [12]The body is a unit, though it is made up of many parts; and though all its parts are many, they form one body. So it is with Christ. [13]For we were all baptized by one Spirit into one body – whether Jews or Greeks, slave or free. . . . [14]Now the body is not made up of one part but of many. If the foot should say,

'Because I am not a hand, I do not belong to the body', it would not for that reason cease to be part of the body. . . . [18]But in fact *God has arranged the parts in the body*, every one of them, *just as he wanted them to be*. . . . [21]The eye cannot say to the hand, 'I don't need you!' . . . [22]those parts of the body that seem to be weaker are indispensable. . . . [24]God has combined the members of the body. . . [25]so that there should be no division in the body, but its parts should have equal concern for each other. [26]If one part suffers, every part suffers with it; if one part is honoured, every part rejoices with it (1 Cor. 12:4–7, 11–14, 18–22, 24–26).

. . . [7]who makes you different from anyone else? What do you have that you did not receive? And if you did receive it, why do you boast as though you did not? . . . [19]You are not your own; [20]you were bought at a price. Therefore honour God with your body (1 Cor. 4:7; 6:19–20).

B. APPLYING WHAT WE HAVE LEARNED

As was noted before, Christian ethics, the doing of what is pleasing to God and right for man, involves norms, situations and motivations. If all three are not in line, an answer or course of action is not fully right. Consider, for instance, a situation having the right norm (moral standard), the right motive, but misunderstanding the situation: I want my child to do that which is right by confessing his theft of a toy, but he does not. Finally I punish him for his theft and for his unwillingness to confess – only to discover later that he did not really do it. With the right norms and with the best of intentions (motives) I have done wrong. We can all invent or remember similar situations with errant norms or motivations.

We should note here that our knowledge will always be less than total and our actions therefore will always involve less than total understanding. This does not mean that all our conclusions are completely wrong, for generally we have sufficient knowledge to make a valid judgment. It does mean that we must walk humbly and carefully. It also means that there will be 'grey areas' in which our perceptions will differ from those of others or in which a lack of information will make precise decisions impossible and provisional decisions necessary. We shall conclude our study of biblical role relationships with consideration of some areas in the relation of men and women in which problems of preception or definition enter the picture.

1. What does 'headship' entail?

Our discussion of headship has centred, to a large degree, on the question of authority. It is, however, a major mistake to restrict the biblical teaching to 'the right to command' or to be 'top of the chain of command'. If so reduced, it is quickly dehumanizing and also unworkable. *Biblical headship and authority are for the sake of building up others.* We have noted Christ's instructions that the leaders of his followers must be servants of all. Leadership involves the responsibility to take action for the sake of others rather than the right to command others for one's own benefit.

A further problem arises from the 'right to command' idea. Authority to lead and to direct automatically includes the necessity to delegate authority. If I am directed to clean the floor, I have authority to take the steps needed to achieve that end. If the one exercising authority comes to feel that *all* authority must reside with himself, he must make *all* the decisions and even take *all* the actions! This, of course, rapidly becomes absurd. In practice authority must be delegated. The debate is about how much may be delegated to whom and under what conditions.

Consider, for instance, the division of labour and the delegation of responsibility in the exercise of 'marital authority'. A counsellor often sees couples struggling over issues related to 'headship' or power. Some men feel that their 'authority' is undercut if they are not asked what meals are to be served and what washing powder is to be used. They wish to hold all the reins, frequently crush their families and are seldom able to participate freely in family life. Any initiative on the part of others threatens their relatively fragile sense of control. Such headship is crippling to a family and to a marriage relation. The husband cannot hope to exercise his 'command' in every area and soon finds himself occupied at every turn with the defence of his status. The more thorough he is in his 'control' the more exhausted he will be from trying to be an expert everywhere and the more his family will feel alienated from him.

Headship modelled after Christ's must take into account the *needs* and *abilities* of those for whose sake decisions are made. It is the husband's responsibility to take initiative but not to do it all. The abilities and activities of the woman of Proverbs 31, for instance, show the extent to which authority may be delegated without challenge to 'headship'. Any effort to make all decisions or to make them independently undercuts real headship or leadership. Others are involved and a finite husband simply cannot be an expert in every area. While the responsibility to see that matters are dealt with and that others are nurtured, as well as ultimate responsibility for the decision, are his, he needs to seek the counsel of his wife and family and often to defer to their wisdom. His leadership should foster their full and free expression of their individual gifts. This ought not to be seen as an abdication of his responsibilities, but as effective fulfilment of them. Christ does not guide his church without paying the closest attention to the needs, desires and abilities of his people. The prayer life of virtually every husband will show his confidence that this is so. The husband's relation to his family should reflect a similar involvement.

Christ's role as husband of his church entails more than decision making. He is intimately involved with his people and is an *example* to them. The husband who understands his role only in terms of providing money and giving orders fails to be to his family as Christ is to the church. He must be immediately alongside them, if he is to know their growing abilities and changing interests. He must join his wife in preparing his children to be godly adults and he must know her if he is to love her as Christ does his church. Headship demands involvement. Involvement demands time. This is especially important in the twentieth century when we have so many distractions. It has been reported that the average American family spends 38 minutes each week in significant interaction. The average child spends less time than that with each of its parents. Fathers spend less time than mothers with the children. Biblical headship requires better performance than this. Effective leadership requires the ability to be an example, a model. Paul, the apostle with apostolic authority to command (1 Cor. 14:37), did not consider the giving of orders to be the fulfilment of his task. He also called upon his congregations to imitate his example as he imitated Christ (1 Cor. 11:1).

This is not the place to discuss particular jobs and tasks which might be assumed by the husband or by the wife. Other books explore such issues. It is, however, worth noting that there are *no particular tasks* which the New Testament assigns as 'men's work' or as 'women's work' within the marital sphere. The circumstances of a family may cause reassignments of tasks. It is not by certain actions but by a basic relationship that leadership is exercised. In the course of living, however, certain actions are soon associated with certain roles (*e.g.* the all-too-common but disastrous pattern: Daddy always reads the Bible; that is 'men's work'. Mother always prays; that is 'women's work'!). Such associations may have a positive value, but we need to beware of setting up wrong associations. The New Testament calls upon the husband to model Christ's headship, but does not spell out the tasks of that headship in detail. This suggests that it is not the husband's tasks but his initiative, example, leadership and responsibility which are in view. Each home and each culture must relate the husband's and wife's role to specific tasks – and be wary of 'canonizing' certain traits or tasks as exclusively male or female when the Scripture does not do so. Custom and tradition have a valuable role to play, but they must not be allowed to become absolute or to stand alongside the Scripture as a rule for faith and life.

2. What does it mean to 'teach or exercise authority over a man'?

When we turn from marital headship to headship in the church, we find that roles are somewhat more defined. The New Testament does give indication of the responsibilities of elders in the teaching, guiding, nurturing and shepherding of the flock. We have seen that the elders must be reliable men who understand the faith and are able to communicate it effectively (teach). Elders who teach and rule well were to be specially honoured. Clearly theirs was the *primary* responsibility to ensure that the flock learned the message of the gospel and its application to life. Well and good. But how much division of labour and delegation of authority is entailed in their task? Were the elders to be the *only* ones teaching? We saw that 1 Corinthians 14:26 assumes that everyone and anyone might bring a 'word of instruction' when the congregation met. Was everyone therefore a 'teacher' in the same sense that elders were? Obviously not. We are faced with a continuum or scale of 'teaching activities'. The same may be said for the admonition of false teachers or of those whose lives deny their profession of faith (church discipline).

Consider, for instance, the following, absurdly detailed, but often debated options relating to the scale of teaching. From 1 Corinthians 14:26 we conclude that a woman might bring a two-minute 'word of instruction' for the assembly. Few would argue against this in a 'sharing time' in modern churches. This is one end of the scale. At the other end let us place the decision of the elders of the congregation concerning an issue such as the deity of Christ. If a controversy arose within the church over this issue, the elders might 'teach' the congregation what the Scriptures say. In many churches they might also discipline members who rejected the teaching of the Word, commitment to which is involved in membership. Ultimately they might even put some out of the fellowship. This would surely qualify as the sort of thing which Paul prohibited to women in 1 Timothy 2:11–12 when he said they might not 'teach or exercise authority over a man'. With these two extremes defined, let us fill in a few points between. 1. Could a woman take five minutes to speak her 'word of instruction'? 2. Could she have fifteen minutes to do it (approaching sermon length)? 3. Could a man who was not an elder have the fifteen-minute time period? (Is that 'teaching'? Would that not undercut the elder's role?) 4. Could a woman be asked to share words of instruction for ten minutes on each of three weeks (regular 'teaching')? 5. Could a woman missionary (perhaps one of Paul's fellow-workers or Prisca) be asked to speak for a half-hour about God's work among the Gentiles and the way in which Paul confronted his opponents (this amounts to preaching about the material in Acts)? 6. Could she do so for eight weeks in a Sunday school class (woman Sunday school teacher)? 7. Could a woman who had worked with Paul be asked by the elders to testify about what Paul had said on a debated issue (is this participating in an act of discipline)? 8. Could she be asked to relate Paul's views on a regular basis (effectively making her the 'teacher' about Paul's message)?

This list is no doubt 'pedantic' but is intended to show the extent to which we are dealing with a continuum with space for 'grey areas' as well as black and white.

The Scripture does not speak *directly* to any of the items in our list except the extremes. Differences will exist regarding the points between. These differences will have to do with our understanding of the Scriptures and with the significance of the acts discussed within our individual points of view and our particular ecclesiastical tradition. Value-judgments must be made at each point. How are these value-judgments to be made? We shall use this set of possible involvements of women as a test case and example. The principles and applications which we apply to them can be transposed to other similar issues.

On the basis of the studies in this book I would propose the following biblical principles to guide the activity of women in the church and the following considerations as guidelines for evaluating where we should draw lines within grey areas. I am keenly aware that any brief formulations, even after hundreds of pages of development, lack the sort of qualifications which would prevent them from being misused. That which follows is intended to foster discussion, not to provide 'rules' which would cut discussion off. I have tried to indicate clearly where my own value-judgments enter in. *The formulations which follow are offered with the sure conviction that they are subject to wooden misuse, caricature and distortion. They are, nevertheless, offered, in the hope that they will prove useful.*

a. Biblical principles

1. The marriage relationship entails the self-sacrificing headship of the husband and the responsive submission of the wife. Practices which signify abdication or rejection of these roles ought not to be adopted.

2. The creational pattern of divinely appointed, representative male leadership in the teaching, ruling and nurturing of the people of God is to continue until the Lord returns. Activities and roles which reject or undercut this ought not to be entered into.

3. The restrictions which apply to the office of the elder do not apply to other ecclesiastical activities, including the diaconate (as understood in this book). Women and men serve on like footing outside the office of elder. Recent discussions of the priesthood of all believers have done much to call attention to the possibilities open to all congregational members. Church renewal movements, lay ministries and the mobilization of laypersons have all helped to overthrow ideas of clericalism which, in some communions, relegated virtually all but the clerics to a situation of pew-warmers.

4. Both the Old and the New Testaments show that the appointive headship of certain men does not apply outside of marriage and the church. In social and civic life there is no restriction on the roles of the sexes.

5. The exercise of leadership and authority must be marked by the attitude which Jesus required: 'the greatest among you shall be like the least and the one who rules like the one who serves'

(Lk. 22:26). Jesus is head over all things *for the sake of* the church (Eph. 1:22–23). Christian leadership and authority must actively reflect his example. Ascertaining biblical norms does not ensure right action. In addition to norms, we must have godly motives of love for God and for our neighbours. Harsh, cruel or holier-than-thou imposition of right conclusions is dishonouring to God and reprehensible in men. To speak the truth without visible love is to fail in our calling. The principles set out above can become ugly, cruel rules used to crush rather than to build up God's people. They ought not to be so used. *Corruptio optima pessima est.*

b. Guidelines for applying biblical principles

We have discussed norms (biblical principles) and motivation as crucial elements in faithful biblical ethics. A third aspect must also be taken into consideration: the actual situation. As in all aspects of life, principles alone do not describe reality. Each situation combines many actual details in a unique way. Faithful application of biblical principles requires that each distinctive situation be carefully assessed. An example from physics helps. Many of us learned rules governing the motion of a billiard ball when struck by another billiard ball. In first-year physics, those rules are set up to deal with ideal billiard balls in a vacuum on a table without friction. We have no such tables. If we are going to deal with real billiard balls on real tables we must find out (among other things) how air resistance, the surface of the table and the elasticity of the balls affect their behaviour upon impact. If we make foolish assumptions in these areas, we shall have the right guidelines but the wrong results.

When we seek to apply biblical principles, a similar set of considerations apply. We must take what steps we can to ensure that we truly understand both the situation with which we are dealing and the full range of biblical principles which should be brought to bear. We cannot succeed in billiards or physics without careful work and reflection. The application of ethical principles with people is more important still and worthy of our most careful attention.

The following guidelines are useful in assessing the context of any sort of action in a 'grey area'. They are formulated with the question of women's activities in church in mind. Examples of their application follow. Each guideline is formulated in two ways in order to highlight the element of personal evaluation necessary and to help to limit possible misuse. The first formulation of each guideline is prohibitive, the second permissive. The guidelines by no means exhaust the list of relevant considerations. They do, however, provide a usable frame from which to approach issues at hand.

1. Scriptural instructions:
   a. Prohibitive: *Does Scripture expressly prohibit the activity?*
   b. Permissive: *Does Scripture expressly permit the activity?*
2. Realities and definitions:
   a. Prohibitive: *Does the activity effectively overthrow a biblical norm or motive, but escape censure on a technicality of definition?*
   b. Permissive: *Is the activity in fact in keeping with the obvious purpose of Scripture, but prevented by a technicality of human definition?*
3. Perceptions:
   a. Prohibitive: *Is the activity likely to be misunderstood or perceived in such a way that it leads to confusion or becomes a stumbling-block?*
   b. Permissive: *Can the activity be explained sufficiently that it is not likely to be wrongly perceived or to become a stumbling-block?*

c. Examples

We shall consider the application of the guidelines to four specific examples which illustrate important points.

Example 1:

Situation: A charismatic church devotes a portion of each service to prophecy. Men and women prophesy. After each one, the congregation explores the message of the prophet and the elders render a judgment on the validity of the message.

Question: May the women join in the examination of the prophets?

Guidelines: 1. *Scriptural instructions*: Our first example is biblical. Paul answered its question in the negative in 1 Corinthians 14:33b–35. We need go no further, but it is worth while to do so for the sake of practice in applying our conclusions.

2. *Realities and definitions*: We are not entirely certain what the

women of 1 Corinthians 14 were actually doing. If they were rendering judgment, as such, on the prophets, then they were 'exercising authority over a man'. They were effectively over-throwing a biblical norm. The prohibitive guidelines 1a and 2a would then clearly apply. If the women were not 'officially' rendering judgment, but were in fact doing so by 'questions' and comments which voiced judgment (I judge this a serious likelihood in the vociferous Corinthian congregation which judged Paul: 1 Cor. 4:1–5), then we would conclude that they were effectively overthrowing a biblical norm, although they were not 'technically' exercising authority over men. Once again, prohibitive formulation 2a applies.

3. *Perceptions*: Paul directed that women with real questions should ask them at home (or elsewhere) but not in the judging of the prophets. We surmised that he wished to guard their right to learn and also to avoid the appearance of having women judge men. In effect, Paul applied prohibitive guideline 3a.

We find this same sort of reasoning in his handling of the question of meat offered to idols in 1 Corinthians 8 and 10 and in Romans 14. In these passages Paul sought to educate his congregation about situations in which some of them held unnecessary scruples about eating certain foods. He asked those who were 'stronger' and did not have the unnecessary scruples to abstain from such foods when their eating might tempt the weaker brothers to violate their consciences by eating. If Paul's educational discussion succeeded in teaching the weaker brothers that their scruples were unnecessary, it would become unnecessary for the strong to abstain.

This points the way to possible changes in our ideas about which ecclesiastical activities are appropriate for women or for non-elders. Those activities which are associated *by custom* with the activities of elders, *but need not be*, are open to change. If, in such cases, the congregation were taught to view the activities in a new light and not to associate them with the exercise of the elder's role, then there would be freedom for women or for non-elders to participate in them.

Consider, for instance, the reading of the Scripture during the worship service. In some churches this task is strongly identified with the authority of an elder. *If* we judge that it need not be so, *and if* the congregation were taught to view it in such a light, then anyone would be free to read Scripture in the service. This amounts to moving from the situation of prohibitive guideline 3a to that of permissive guideline 3b.

Example 2:

Situation: A well-known and well-educated Christian woman is asked to address a local congregation about the role of women in the church. Her teaching is well known to the elders, who approve of it. She is given a half-hour during the Sunday worship service for her talk. The pastor follows her talk with the usual (brief) sermon.

Question: May she 'teach' in this way?

Guidelines: 1. *Scriptural instructions*: Whether we judge that Scripture expressly prohibits this exercise will depend in part on our assessment of Paul's statement that women may not 'teach or exercise authority over men' (1 Tim. 2:12). It is my judgment that this instance is not really a border-line case and is not prohibited. Some may disagree and apply guideline 1a.

2. *Realities and definitions*: It is my opinion that the sharing and teaching under discussion does not in fact place the woman in the role of an elder. Her teaching has no authority apart from the approval of the elders. She is not seeking to enforce her teaching with discipline and is not assuming the elders' responsibility of ensuring that the flock is taught true doctrine (although we shall assume that what she teaches is true doctrine). Her participation in the worship service is still within the bounds of the priesthood of all believers. I therefore do not apply guideline 2a. I recognize that some will disagree. Paul did not forbid women to bring any teaching whatsoever. We have seen that all may bring a word of instruction. What he spoke of was the continuing, authoritative teaching which structures the faith of the church. A half-hour talk would not do this. Any acceptable person may address the congregation.

Let us assume for a moment that someone in the flock objects to the woman speaker on the grounds that *any* speaking to a congregation is a form of teaching and that *only* elders should teach. Thus only elders should speak publicly in church meetings. *As articulated*, this view is defective in that 1 Corinthians 11:5 and 14:26 contradict it. It is a good example of the problem pointed to in guideline 2b: a human definition overthrows a biblical purpose.

Other objections might be raised to a woman speaking, but this one is invalid. It does, however, point to the issue raised in guideline 3: how people perceive an action.

3. *Perceptions*: In some congregations a long speech by a woman would be understood as an assumption of the elder's role (apply guideline 3a). In such cases she should not speak without adequate preparation of the congregation, which would effectively make guideline 3b applicable. Such preparation would not necessarily entail the whole-hearted approval of all members, but would require the education of them and a serious, loving effort to persuade them by searching the Scriptures with them. In congregations which are used to guest speakers and which are able to distinguish such talks as this woman gives from an elder's task, only the possible effect on guests need be considered at length.

Example 3:
Situation: The woman 'teacher' lives near the church and is invited to become the teacher of the Sunday morning adult Bible class which is studying Christian doctrine. This class is the primary avenue of instruction for the congregation.

Question: May she take on the responsibility of preparing and teaching the lessons for this adult class?
Guidelines: 1. *Scriptural instructions:* It is my judgment that the responsibility for the regular, official instruction of the people of God in the doctrines of the faith belongs to the elders. It is authoritative teaching within the definition of 1 Tim. 2:12. As set out, the task offered to this woman teacher should not be given to any but an elder. If there are competent elders, they are the ones to do this teaching. As set out, I would apply guideline 1a to this situation. Guidelines 2a and 3a would also apply.

2. & 3. *Realities and definitions: Perceptions:* The situation described may be made somewhat more complex by introducing a few additional factors. Let us suppose that there are not enough qualified elders. Who will teach the people? The elders might decide to appoint and supervise non-elder teachers. By maintaining effective supervision and awareness the elders might fulfil their responsibilities to ensure faithful teaching without actually doing all of it. In this case it would be important that the non-elder teachers be clearly under the guidance of the elders. Given that fact, it would make no difference what the gender of the

appointed teacher is. Neither women nor men so appointed would necessarily prejudice the role of the elders. This potentially confusing and ambiguous situation would need to be handled with care and with clarity.

It should be noted that the issue raised by the appointment of a woman to teach the class is essentially the same if a non-elder man is appointed. There is less chance of confusion in the case of a man, but either would be taking up a responsibility for the official structuring of the faith of the people, a job which is the responsibility of the elders except in extraordinary circumstances. If a non-elder man is appointed and proves both gifted for teaching and otherwise qualified by his life to serve as an elder, it would be an obvious question whether the Holy Spirit has not called him to the office of elder. Women with equivalent gifts may and should use them to spread and to share the gospel, but not in the situation under discussion.

We should consider the situation of a woman missionary or of a woman or a man who is not an elder in a situation in which there are no elders (*e.g.* China after Mao's take-over or Uganda under Idi Amin). Such a situation is much like that of Prisca and Aquila in the education of Apollos (Acts 18:24–26). Prisca was involved in teaching Apollos, but did not take an elder's public role. In the absence of a church structure the Word should nevertheless be taught. Care needs to be taken, however, that such decisions and practices are clearly understood (guideline 3) and do not lead to wrong church structures. They should lead to the establishment of biblical church structures. I suspect that Prisca would have been an outstanding elder. Her gifts were not wasted, but it is certain that she was not an elder in a Pauline church! The modern church must develop and use the resources of all its members – and do so in a biblical manner.

I conclude that women and men who are missionaries should by all means teach the faith. Their activities in this area need not be equivalent to adopting an elder's role. The end result of their work should be the establishing of a strong biblical church with its own government. With the establishment of such a church, the initial teaching role of the outside missionary, regardless of sex, changes. The local elders assume the teaching responsibilities for their flocks. The time of transition from a mission work to a church with no missionaries present is one which needs thoughtful definition of roles to prevent confusion.

Example 4:

Situation: A group of students begin to meet together regularly for Bible study. The study prospers and soon there are a number of such groups. In some, a single person teaches each time. In others, the leadership rotates from member to member. Over time a campus-wide organization is formed with elected officers and ultimately paid staff members who co-ordinate activities and teach.

Question: Can women students teach the studies and serve as staff members?

Guidelines: 1. *Scriptural instructions:* Paul does not permit women to teach with authority in the worship or congregational setting (1 Tim. 2:11–12). He does permit any member of the congregation to bring a word of instruction or an insight (1 Cor. 14:26) and all believers are to join in encouraging one another in the faith. This process of ministering to one another's needs and encouraging one another in the faith is naturally a part of the priesthood of all believers. We are called to share our understanding of the Word with one another. If a woman shares in or leads a study group, it is a valuable contribution to the body of Christ.

2. *Realities and definitions:* The situation in view is not quite as simple as an informal Bible study. The students have established regular teachers and even staff personnel who are involved in structured instruction in the faith. Do these activities begin to place a woman in the sort of position which will in fact infringe upon that which is in fact the responsibility of elders? The answer to this question is complex, and needs to be answered at several levels.

a. Para-church organizations. I have posed the question in a manner which calls attention to the role of a woman in the instruction. The same problem would confront a man who begins to be involved in the regular structuring of the faith of believers. The leaders and staff members of the Christian fellowship have begun to teach others. Some Christians believe that such para-church organizations are not legitimate, precisely because they do what the church should do (evangelize, teach, shepherd) without being a church or formally responsible to a biblical church government. The dangers of such an organization are clear.

As we consider, for example, the campus Christian fellowship as a para-church organization we must ask carefully whether it is replacing the church or 'doing what the church should do'. All

Christians are to spread the gospel and to encourage one another in the faith. This is the job of the church, but not the exclusive job of the organized church. I see no wrong in the organization of support agencies to reach areas which are difficult for the church to reach. If they begin to supplant the church, the problem which they pose has nothing to do with the role of women. It must be confronted at the level of the debate over the legitimacy of para-church organizations.

b. Women leaders. The leaders of the campus fellowship are very much involved in discipling and teaching other believers. Their teaching, however, has no formal authority or church discipline behind it. It is, technically, advice and counsel from one believer to another. Whether men or women, the staff workers are not elders. From this point of view they are not violating Paul's teaching. It should, however, be carefully noted that if the students and staff begin to regard the campus fellowship as their primary fellowship and to substitute the instruction and views of the staff workers for the instruction of the church, the staff workers begin to function as elders. To the extent that this takes place, the definition of the fellowship changes. It begins to become, *de facto*, a church. Its problem would not be that it had women teaching, but that it was becoming what it should not be. With regard to the matter of realities and definitions, then, I would conclude that it is quite appropriate to have women staff workers and student leaders in support agencies. They have a perfectly natural and appropriate role to play in such situations. That role in no way jeopardizes that of ecclesiastical elders.

3. *Perceptions*: In many modern churches the role of the elder is poorly defined and understood. The function of a staff worker or Bible study leader may well be indistinguishable from that of a pastor or elder to many believers. This danger is inherent in the establishment of a para-church organization. The remedy for it is clearly not the prohibition of women staff workers. The solution must lie either in the disbanding of such organizations or in the education of the congregation. It does not seem likely to me that many will confuse women staff workers with elders. I suppose it is possible that those who are used to learning from women staff workers could come to question the biblical teaching concerning the eldership. It seems to me that careful biblical teaching is more than a sufficient response to this possibility.

C. AN EXERCISE

The examples which I have worked through provide some idea of the way in which I would apply the principles worked out in this book to situations confronting the Christian community today. I have tried to show where individual value-judgments enter the picture. I invite you to try the principles and guidelines on the various teaching situations which were mentioned on pages 240–242. Once you have done so, share your conclusions with a couple of others. If you do, you will gain a good idea of the effectiveness of your grasp of the biblical material and, I suspect, a good idea of the places where your own value-judgments enter into your conclusions.

D. FINAL REMARKS

This chapter has reviewed the findings of our study of the relation of women and men in the Scriptures and has considered the application of our conclusions to two areas of particular concern to the church at the end of the twentieth century. The nature of the topic itself has drawn our attention, especially in the latter chapters of the book, to matters to authority and headship in the man/woman relationship. It is right and good that we should consider the relationship of men and women in the body of Christ; but these things are not ends in themselves. We should willingly receive Paul's teaching that 'the body is a unit, though it is made up of many parts; and though its parts are many, they form one body' (1 Cor. 12:12); yet we must realize that God did not assemble that body and give gifts to its members so that we may quarrel or pass our time contemplating who shall be greatest in the kingdom. He has done these things so that both men and women, joint heirs of the gracious gift of life, may use all their talents and gifts in his service to spread his kingdom and to call humans of all sorts from death to new life in Jesus Christ. This book is written in the hope that a more precise understanding of the Scripture's teaching about the relation of women and men will help the members of Christ's body to be more effective in the service of Jesus Christ who calls Jew and Gentile, slave and free, male and female to be one in himself.

Appendix:
Veiling practices in Judaism and Graeco-Roman culture of the first century

Veiling practices of the first century are of particular concern to students of the New Testament because the apostle Paul refers to veiling in 1 Corinthians 11:2–16. The exegesis of this passage which is offered in this book follows the general line which I took in an article published in 1973.[1] The materials in this appendix are intended to provide background information to help people grasp the social context to which Paul spoke. Graeco-Roman customs are not subject to great debate; therefore the appendix treats them only briefly. The difficulty of assessing Jewish practice results in a more lengthy discussion of it. This appendix incorporates certain material from chapter 3; the conclusions reached here are incorporated in the main body of the book in the discussion of Judaism in chapter 3 and in the discussion of 1 Corinthians 11 in chapter 7.

The investigation of Jewish veiling practices in the time of Christ is made very difficult by the lack of specific graphic information such as sculpture or art, by the lack of precision in the terminology used to refer to veiling, and by later Islamic practices. The evidence available to us concerning Jewish practice stems largely from Talmudic and other late sources. The question to be asked is whether these may legitimately be presumed to represent Palestinian practice in the time of Christ. A majority of students of the field have assumed so without reflection. A close look at the evidence, however, suggests that they may be mistaken. Our discussion of the subject will be divided into the following sections: (A) the seclusion of women: a test case in which we find that the testimony of many of the witnesses is misleading about typical Jewish practices in New Testament times; (B) Graeco-Roman evidence about veiling in the time of Christ; (C) Jewish evidence about veiling; (D) conclusions drawn from the evidence. The Jewish evidence

---

[1] J. Hurley, 'Did Paul Require Veils?', *Westminster Theological Journal*, 35 (1973), pp. 190–220.

examined will include sources from time periods ranging from the Old Testament to the early Middle Ages.

A. THE SECLUSION OF WOMEN: A TEST CASE

An examination of Jewish sources from the first century appears to indicate that Jewish women were secluded or cloistered in their homes and kept out of contact with men. In support of this thesis may be offered certain commonly cited passages from Philo, and 4 Maccabees.

In his discussion of Jewish law, *De Specialibus Legibus*, Philo comments on the place of men and women in Judaism. His discussion is intended to explain the wisdom of Judaism to Greek audiences. He says,

> Market places and council halls and law-courts and gatherings and meetings where a large number of people are assembled, and open-air life with full scope for discussion and action – all these are suitable for men both in war and in peace. The women are best suited to the indoor life which never strays from the house, within which the middle door is taken by the maidens as their boundary, and the outer door by those who have reached full womanhood (*De Spec. Leg.* iii.169).

This passage provides us with Philo's view of what is appropriate. Elsewhere he gives us indication that it is not just a matter of theory. In his description of the end of Flaccus, prefect of Alexandria and Egypt from AD 32 to AD 37, Philo comments on the invasion of a Jewish house by a group of soldiers. The Jews were indignant

> that their women kept in seclusion, maidens confined to the inner chambers, who for modesty's sake avoided the sight of men, even of their closest relations, were displayed to eyes, not merely unfamiliar, but terrorizing . . .' (*In Flaccum*, 89).

The Jewish writer of 4 Maccabees also wrote in about the first century. His work sets out a Stoic view of life, atttributing it to Jews who by reason control emotion and are thus able to endure suffering and much trial. On the lips of a pious woman whose faith has permitted her to endure watching the execution of her seven sons, he puts the following comment, 'I was a pure maiden and left not my father's house, and I kept guard over the rib which became woman's body' (4 Macc. 18:7–8).

Some commentators have built from these passages (and others which might be cited) and from Talmudic passages which stress the importance of not talking to women and of women not going outside 'uncovered' (*e.g.* mKet. 7.6; mAb. 1.5) to the conclusion that Jewish women of the first century were cloistered or secluded. More judicious commentators have followed the lead of men such as Jeremias, noted contradictory evidence elsewhere, and concluded that, while seclusion may have been the practice of Alexandria (as evidenced by Philo and the writer of 4 Maccabees, who both were Alexandrian) and of the wealthy or Hellenized in Palestine (*cf.* 3 Macc. 1:18), it is not likely to have been a practice which was rigorously followed by the peasants.[2] This conclusion is manifestly correct, as the New Testament records attest. Large numbers of women were not cloistered but circulated freely in Palestine during the time of Jesus. Here then is a test case in which we find that the ideals of piety promoted by the Talmud and even contemporary sources prove to be misleading if taken as representative of the common practice. Is the veiling of women to be placed in the same category? Before we can answer this, we must consider a variety of sources of information.

B. GRAECO-ROMAN VEILING PRACTICES

First-century Palestine had been ruled by foreigners for large parts of the preceding three centuries. Under the successors of Alexander the Great (d. 330) she had been introduced to Greek ways, which made deep inroads into certain classes of society. The Romans began their rule some sixty years before Christ. Their cultural influence was much less than that of the Greeks because the Jews never embraced distinctively Roman culture as they did Greek. We may not freely assume that Greek or Roman customs provide valid illustrations of Palestinian customs. We must, however, take

---

[2] J. Jeremias' work, *Jerusalem*, is the most commonly cited English work in this area. He follows Strack and Billerbeck, *Kommentar zum Neuen Testament*, and J. Leipoldt, *Die Frau in der antiken Welt und im Urchristentum* (Leipzig, 1955) in assuming that the Palestinian Jews veiled and secluded their women and that the rural practice was much looser than the urban. Interestingly Jeremias offers no evidence of full veiling from the actual period under consideration. His point of departure is Pesikta Rabbati 26, a post-Islamic text from somewhere between the late sixth and the tenth century.

them into account as they will have been known by the Jews, who maintained not only political but also extensive commercial relations with both Greek and Roman cities.

Greek and Roman relics available to us cover a time-span which reaches more than a full three centuries to either side of the birth of Christ. Veiling customs and hair-styles can be discovered by simply looking at the heads of the figures portrayed. Such relics make it plain that both Greek and Roman culture knew unveiled women.[3] By the New Testament era the two cultures were quite similar. J. Balsdon remarks of the typical Roman woman, 'her *palla* [a large rectangular shawl] might cover her head, but by Augustus' time . . . it was a matter of indifference whether women pulled the *palla* up over their heads or not'.[4] Greek remains reveal a similar situation. The Roman *palla* was called a *himation* in Greek. Graeco-Roman culture did not require the wearing of veils.

A further observation, however, is in order before leaving Graeco-Roman practice. While it is clear that veiling customs were a matter of indifference for Greeks and Romans of the first century, it would appear that coiffure, hair-style, was not. Remains show that both boys and girls wore their hair either free or in one or two simple braids. Roman custom gave the men and boys relatively short hair, while Greek men had somewhat longer hair, sometimes reaching shoulder length. Adult women of both cultures, on the other hand, had long hair which was drawn up on or behind their heads in various styles. Women are not shown with their hair loose and flowing. In literature, however, dishevelled hair is a sign of despair, or mourning.[5] Balsdon remarks, 'in the [days of the Roman] republic, younger women dressed their hair in simple style, drawing it to the back of the head to form a simple knot, which was thrust through with a pin'.[6] In the later periods this simplicity was lost to ornamentation even for the younger women. From early times, the older women ornamented their hair with more complex hair-styles and cloth strips. By the time of Christ styles had become more ornate and decorations more expensive. Remarking on these decorations, Balsdon says,

---

[3] Among the best sources of information available are E. Potter, M. Albert, E. Saglio, 'Coma', in C. Daremburg and E. Saglio (eds.), *Dictionnaire des Antiquités Grecques et Romaines* (Paris, 1887), vols. 1, 2, and L. Wilson, *The Clothing of the Ancient Romans* (Baltimore, 1932).
[4] J. P. V. D. Balsdon, *Roman Women*, p. 252.
[5] W. van Unnik, 'Les Cheveux desfaits des femmes baptisées' in *Vigiliae Christianae*, I (1947), p. 88.
[6] J. P. V. D. Balsdon, *Roman Women*, p. 252.

the simple strips of rough wool, emblem of chastity and symbol of the honour due to a married woman, which originally enclosed the mass of the *tutulus* [the mass of hair drawn together on the head], changed to linen or silk ribbons in bright colours. In a variety of shapes and sizes, they were placed in the hair, in differing styles. When they were of precious metals, fringed with gold, held firm by pins or little gold buckles embroidered with pearls or other precious stones, they lost all utilitarian character, and passed into the category of jewels.[7]

A well-known bust of Julia, daughter of Titus, who led the overthrow of Jerusalem in AD 70, provides an example of the elaborate hair-styles which were worn at the Roman court in the first century and set the styles for elsewhere. Balsdon remarks on the bust,

> This was the time when, one must assume, hours upon end were devoted to the curling-tongs. . . . Curl climbs on top of curl and over the forehead there arose something which at its best looked like the *chef d'oeuvre* of a master pastry cook and, at its worst, like a dry sponge. At the back the hair was plaited, and the braids arranged in a coil which looks like basketwork. The towering splendour was to be viewed from one direction only, the front, and women must have manoeuvred at social gatherings, to keep out of view the ridiculous anti-climax which the back of their heads constituted.[8]

Other statues and portraits provide examples of other styles which include some with simple waves, others with complex braids, and still others so complicated that they are thought to be wigs. The elaborate styles were matched by elaborate ornamentation. Gold, jewels and pearls were worn on the body, in the ears and on the hair. In his *Natural History* (9) the elder Pliny complained of the vast sums being spent on such items. T. G. Tucker provides the following description of hair-styling.

> It might have a parting or no parting; it might be plaited over the head and fastened by jewelled tortoise-shell combs, or by pins of ivory, silver, or bronze with jewelled heads . . . it might

---

[7] *Ibid.*, pp. 255–256.
[8] *Ibid.*, p. 256; *cf.* illustration, p. 240.

be carried to the back and rest in a knot on the neck, where it was bound with ribbons; it might be piled into a huge pyramid or 'towers of many stories', so that it often looked tall in front and appeared quite a different person at the back; it might be encased in a coloured cloth or in a net of gold thread. . . .[9]

Styles at the Roman court were not uniform but were ornate. They no doubt set patterns which were emulated throughout the society, much as the styles of our movie stars and 'high society' set patterns today.

From what we have seen thus far of Roman styles it is easy to see how a woman's hair was at the same time a mark of her dignity and a potential show-place for her wealth or vanity. In our examination of Assyrian culture, we found that the 'veil', which was never clearly described, functioned as a symbol of rank and dignity. As Balsdon points out, the hair of Roman women served the same function. In view of its significance for Roman and Greek women, we must ask, in our examination of the veiling customs among the Jews, whether a woman's hair played any symbolic role for them.

C. JEWISH VEILING CUSTOMS

In our review of women's roles in the Old Testament we saw that the Israelites did not practise veiling as we usually think of it. In this section we shall look once again at Old Testament materials before considering later Jewish practice.

1. Old Testament veiling reconsidered

In our previous discussion we argued from numerous examples that the faces of women in the Old Testament were visible to men. From this we deduced that they were not wearing veils of the Islamic sort. Tamar, who played the prostitute with Judah, was the only exception (Gn. 38). We know little about that situation save that her face was covered as she sat by the road soliciting and that it did not seem strange to Judah, who never saw her face although he made love to her. Her garments were not her usual widow's clothes. Whether they were typical of a harlot, we do not know. From this event we dare not generalize.

---

[9] T. G. Tucker, *Life in the Roman World of Nero and St. Paul*, p. 311.

The Roman *palla* or shawl which was discussed above offers a new possibility. Perhaps the Israelites knew such a garment as a veil for women. Its use would explain the visibility of women's faces as the garment covered only the top of the head. The available texts give us no information about such a piece of clothing. If, with reservations, we may draw from later Near Eastern practice, we note that both men and women are known to have used such wraps to protect their heads from the sun. In practical situation then both sexes used garments like the *palla*. One name for them in Greek is *peribolaiōn*, which means 'a thing thrown around'. The word parallels our English term 'wrap'. Another, generally lighter garment which served this purpose was the *himation*.

The lack of any Old Testament legislation concerning the wearing of a veil of any sort speaks as forcefully against assuming universal veiling of women as does the evidence of women whose faces were visible. Any veiling which took place was a matter of custom rather than biblical requirement. Archaeology has provided us with very little of help in identifying Hebrew practice. There is, however, a monument of Sennacherib's which shows captive Hebrew women wearing garments like the Roman *palla* or the Greek *himation* which are draped over their heads and extend to their feet.[10] This relief demonstrates that Hebrews of that period knew such garments and that they did not practise total veiling after the Islamic style. What it does not tell us is why the women had their shawls up. Was it the sun on the journey or the social setting which motivated them? Whatever the case, we must once again conclude that there is no basis upon which to assert that the Old Testament knows veiling as a common practice.

If, instead of the veil, we consider hair, there are things to be learned from the Old Testament. The way in which one wore his or her hair was of importance in the Old Testament. The shaving of the head was a cause of great shame (2 Sa. 10:4–5; Is. 3:17; 7:20; Je. 7:29). Long or dishevelled hair also had a significance. Hebrew response to something which was a cause of great regret, sorrow or repentance involved tearing of the clothes and letting the hair fly loose (sometimes with dirt or ashes upon it), or even cutting it off. Thus, death called forth mourning, which was signified by

---

[10]Paterson, *Assyrian Sculptures, Palace of Sennacherib*, pl. 71–73, cited by M. Jastrow in 'Veiling in Ancient Assyria', in *Revue Archéologique*, 5th series, XIV (1921), p. 229, n. 3.

wailing and lack of care for the self; clothes were torn for sorrow and the hair let loose and dirt put on it or it was cut off (Lv. 21:5, 10–12; Dt. 14:1; Jos. 7:6; 1 Sa. 4:12; Is. 15:1–3; Je. 7:29; 16:6). Thus Joshua and the people tear their clothes, weep and put ashes on their heads when Achan's sin led to their defeat at Ai (Jos. 7:6). Likewise Josiah began mourning when the book of the law was read to him and he realized the sin of Israel (2 Ki. 22:11). God responded to his actions through Huldah, saying, 'because your heart was penitent, and you humbled yourself . . . and . . . rent your clothes and wept . . . I also have heard you' (2 Ki. 22:19, RSV).

Dishevelled hair was a universal Near Eastern sign of mourning. Hebrew culture used long hair in other ways as well. As a highly visible sign, it set its wearer off from others. The leper, the Nazirite, the suspected adulteress and perhaps the warrior all wore long hair. Leviticus 13:45 directs that the leper wear torn clothes, let his hair hang loose (parû'),[11] cover his upper lip (with his garment), and cry, 'Unclean, unclean'.[12] Even at a distance he was recognized as distinct and to be avoided.

In the case of the Nazirite, it was the sign of a vow of special dedication to God. During the time of his dedication he might not touch wine or grape products and might not become ceremonially unclean by touching dead persons, even if they were of his own family. Numbers 6:5 instructs, 'During the entire period of his vow of separation no razor may be used on his head. He must be holy [dedicated or set apart from that which is common] until the period of his separation to the LORD is over; he must let the hair of his head grow long (gadēl pera').' The long hair of the Nazirite shows him to be set apart from others by dedication to God rather than by unclean disease, as was the leper. At the end of the time of his vow, the Nazirite brought offerings to the Lord and cut off his locks, which were offered to the Lord in the fire. Women, as men, might become Nazirites.

The priests who served the Lord were forbidden, as was the Nazirite, from entering into mourning rites. In Leviticus 10:6 Aaron and his remaining sons are forbidden to let their hair hang loose ('al tipra 'û) as a sign of mourning for the two who died by

---

[11] Cf. F. Brown, S. Driver and C. Briggs, A Hebrew and English Lexicon of the Old Testament (Oxford, 1966), pp. 828–829 for the range of meaning of the term.
[12] Cf. C. Keil and F. Delitzsch, Biblical Commentary on the Old Testament, 2, Pentateuch (Grand Rapids, n.d.), pp. 352–353, 382.

the Lord's hand. A more general prohibition, of the same sort but for the high priest, is found in Leviticus 21:10 (*lō' yip̄ra'*). Ezekiel 44:20 calls for holiness on the part of the priests in the new temple. They are commanded neither to shave their heads, nor to let their locks grow (*ûp̄e ra' lo'*), but rather to trim their hair. The dedication of the priest to God meant that he could not enter into the usual signs of mourning.

In each of the examples cited above, the Hebrew root *pr'* is used to indicate hair hanging loose or dishevelled. In a related meaning it can be used of other situations in which things are 'let loose', 'unsheathed' or 'uncovered', for instance Exodus 32:25 where Aaron 'let loose' the people before the idolatrous calf. The reference here is either to chaos or possible to 'uncovering' or to nakedness in sacred sexual acts.

There is one other important passage in which the verb *pr'* is used of hair hanging loose, Numbers 5:18. This is found in the chapter which precedes the intructions for the Nazirite and which gives instructions for the administration of the 'bitter-water' rite for a woman suspected of adultery. The priest was told to place the woman before the Lord and to unbind her hair or lay bare her head (*ûpārah e't ro'š*). The letting loose of her hair sets the woman apart. She is not sacredly dedicated as the Nazirite, but is suspected of being unclean as the leper, except in a moral sense. Having let her hair loose, the priest gave her the 'bitter water' to drink. If the water did not cause swelling and bodily deterioration, the woman was cleared of the charges and returned to her home, presumably putting her hair up once again. The fact that the woman's hair was let loose necessarily presumes that it was previously put up in some manner, and that that would be a typical style for women. The sign of her shame was not the removing of her veil (although this would be done if she were wearing one), but the loosing of her hair.

I draw the following conclusions from the evidence reviewed: 1. The Old Testament never commanded the veiling of women in any fashion. 2. Its narrative portions give no indication of general veiling of women after the Muslim fashion (total coverage save the eyes) or even of over-the-hair veiling, although there is evidence that Hebrew women taken captive by Sennacherib wore shawls over their heads for a reason unknown to us. 3. The bitter-water rite of Numbers 5:18 calls for the loosing of hair rather than the stripping of a veil. It presumes that a woman's hair would be somehow put up, indicating that this style was probably the general practice. From these conclusions it would seem likely that Hebrew customs, as reflected in the Old Testament, were quite close to those of Greece and Rome in the time of Christ and that a woman's hair was a sign of her dignity and honour. A veil might perhaps re-emphasize this.

2. Veiling in Josephus

Josephus provides us with an account of the bitter-water ceremony in his *Antiquities*. A certain amount of care has to be exercised about this particular work as it was very much an apologetic effort and is in error in numerous details. Josephus published his first edition of the work in AD 93–94, more than twenty years after the destruction of the temple, but within the life of persons who might have actually observed the ceremony. The relevant text reads:

> One of the priests stations her [the suspected woman] at the gates which face the Temple and, after removing the veil [*to himation*] from her head, inscribes the name of God upon a skin [parchment]; he then bids her declare upon oath that she has done her husband no wrong. . . .[13]

Josephus' account neglects various elements of the rite as required in Numbers 5. He does not, for instance, mention the loosing of the woman's hair, which is prescribed in Numbers and described in other accounts. It is valuable for our purposes, however, to note that the garment removed from the woman's head is the *himation*, which corresponds to the Roman *palla* and is a rectangular shawl. Josephus' text, therefore, bears witness to head veiling, but not facial veiling in this public situation.

3. Veiling in the Mishnah

The 'tractates' of the Mishnah represent digests of rules for Jewish life as brought together towards the end of the second century AD, evidently by Rabbi Judah the Patriarch. Much of their teaching stems from earlier days, some regulations originating before the destruction of the temple in AD 70 and perhaps even before the time of Christ. The Mishnah is only broadly organized and shows clearly the efforts of the rabbis to adapt Jewish life to the loss of

[13]*Antiquities*, iii. 270, trans. H. St. J. Thackeray (London, 1930).

the temple and the Jewish state. It does mention veiling and hair at several points. Examination of some of these passages offers limited insight into the practices of that time.

In a passage discussing evidence which proved that a woman had married as a virgin rather than as a widow or as a divorced woman, the Mishnah comments, '. . . if there are witnesses that she went forth [to the marriage] in a litter and with her hair unbound . . . (mKet. 2.1)' she must be considered to have married as a virgin. This passage uses the Hebrew verb *pr'* to describe the girl's hair. We deduce from this that married women did not wear their hair loose but rather put it up. When we examine the evidence of the Talmud, we shall see that Judaism came to use the verb *pr'* to mean 'to take off a covering and let the hair flow loose'. It is easy to see how this could come about since it was necessary to take off any covering to get to the hair and since a derivative meaning meant 'uncover'. The two have been conflated. It is possible that the Mishnah is using the verb in this conflated fashion, although the more traditional meanings would be equally satisfactory. The same observation applies to mKet 7.6, which grants divorce without financial settlement for the offence of going out with the hair unbound. The Mishnah is not clear about veiling customs, but reflects serious concern about either the veiling or hair-style of married women.

4. Veiling in the Talmud

The Babylonian Talmud is an extended commentary on the Mishnah which was prepared over a period of several centuries. The date of its final form is generally placed in the late fifth or sixth century AD. It incorporates a wealth of diverse material from various eras and is therefore difficult to evaluate with respect to the date of a given tradition. We shall examine a few passages concerning veiling and hair-style.

An instructional passage for our purposes is the Talmud's discussion of the Mishnah about going outside without having the hair bound up (mKet. 7.6; bKet. 72a, b). The Talmud quotes the Mishnah at the start of the discussion: 'These are divorced without receiving their Kethubah: A wife who transgresses the law of Moses or Jewish practice' (mKet. 7.6). The Mishnah uses going outside with 'uncovered head' as an example of violation of Jewish practice: 'And what [is a transgression of] Jewish practice? Going out with head 'uncovered' (*r̀sh prw'*) (mKet. 7.6). The Mishnah's explicit view of the nature of the offence as a violation of Jewish practice rather than a Pentateuchal obligation is particularly significant when it is compared with the Talmud's view. After citing the Mishnah account, the Talmud comments,

> [Is not the prohibition against going out with] an uncovered head Pentateuchal; for it is written [in Numbers 5:18] *and he shall uncover the woman's head*, and this, it was taught at the school of Rabbi Ishmael, was a warning to the daughters of Israel that they should not go out with uncovered head (*bprw' r's*)? Pentateuchally it is quite satisfactory [if her head is covered by] her work basket; according to Jewish practice, however, she is forbidden [to go out uncovered] even with her basket on her head (bKet. 72a, b).

The following points should be noted:

1. The school of Rabbi Ishmael apparently interpreted the verb *pr'* to refer to unveiling the head rather than loosing the hair. This allowed them to apply the Numbers passage in which *pr'* is used to the case at hand and thus to make veiling a Pentateuchal rather than a customary obligation.

2. This interpretation caused a conflict with the teaching of the Mishnah, a completely unacceptable situation. The rabbis were therefore forced to discover a way in which they could explain the apparent contradiction.

3. They did so by explaining that, while even a basket satisfied the Pentateuchal regulation, Jewish custom demanded *more* covering. Thus it was going out without *adequate* covering which violated Jewish practice.

4. The coverings under consideration were almost surely not after the Islamic pattern, as a woman with a basket over the face could not see where she was going. A shawl draped over the head could be imitated by putting a basket over the hair.

The school of Rabbi Ishmael lacked any texts requiring veils and has in fact taken advantage of two meanings of the word *pr'*. In this discourse the term relates to uncovering while in Numbers 5 it certainly included and perhaps exclusively meant loosing the hair. That the Talmud knows *pr'* as 'loosing the hair' is made clear by its discussion of administering the bitter-water rite of Numbers 5. Sotah 8a says,

. . . what is the object of the text [of Numbers 5] declaring, 'and let the hair of her head go loose (*pr'*)'? It teaches that the priest undoes her hair (*str*).

In this passage there can be no confusion concerning the meaning of *pr'* as the verb *str*, translated 'undoes her hair', means 'unravel' or 'tear down'. It is not her veil but her hair-do which is being discussed. This is made more clear still a few lines later when the rite itself is described:

> she [the adulteress] wound a beautiful scarf about her head for him [the adulterer], therefore a priest removes her *cph* [headgear of some sort] and places it under her feet. . . . She plaited her hair for him; therefore the prist undoes (*str*, tears down) her hair (bSotah 8b, 9a).

It is not clear what the *cph* was; it may have been a cap or a veil or any other sort of headgear. It is clear, however, that her head was bare when the priest undid or 'tore down' her hair (*str*), *and that is what Sotah 8a said corresponded to the rite of Numbers 5*. We conclude, therefore, that the school of Rabbi Ishmael was taking advantage of a possible meaning of *pr'* and knew full well that the action called for by Numbers 5:18 was the loosing of the hair rather than simply the removing of a veil.

Rabbi Ishmael's pun was not intended to establish a debated point with regard to the necessity of coverings. All parties conceded the appropriateness of head-coverings. The debate was with respect to the Pentateuchal nature of the obligation. Numerous rabbinical texts could be adduced to demonstrate that head coverings were expected. We shall look at only three.

In the Jerusalem Talmud, Tractate Yoma, 1.1, in a section discussing the purity of the high priest, there is a brief remark about Kamhith, a woman who was said to have had seven sons who become high priests:

> 'What good works have you done?' the sages asked her. 'I swear,' she replied, 'that the rafters of my house have not seen my hair nor the border of my shirt (so great was her modesty and chastity)' (jYoma 1.1).

The text is unrealistic in its idealization of the woman's modesty and chastity, but makes its point very well. It was clearly an ideal at that time that women should cover their hair as an expression of modesty. It should be noted, in addition, that the text gives us another bit of information. Kamhith did not refer to her face as hidden, but rather to her hair as veiled. This corresponds well with our earlier observations about head rather than facial veiling among the Jews.

As part of a discussion of vows, the Babylonian Talmud (bNed 30a) makes the following remark, assuming it as self-evident: 'Men sometimes cover their heads and sometimes do not; but women's hair is always covered, and children are always bareheaded.' By the time this was written a covering was an assumed fact of life for women. Men covered their heads for prayer or as a sign of respect for the holy.

If we look at another passage we can learn more about what sort of hair coverings were and were not in view in the Talmud. Tractate Shabbath discusses obligations for the sabbath day. Chapter 6 of the tractate discusses what people may wear on the sabbath. The opening section (6.1) describes a number of facial and head ornaments for women which may not be worn outside on the sabbath. From the prohibition we may infer that the ornaments might be worn on other days and that this fact makes total veiling unlikely, because it would seem pointless to wear facial ornaments and hair ornaments if they were to be covered by a complete veil from the time of leaving the house. Section 6 of the same chapter says that 'Arabian women may go out [on the sabbath] wearing a veil (r'lwt).' The corresponding Arabic word (ra'l) describes a veil which covers all but the eyes of its wearer.[14] The fact that the veil was *not* considered an ornament for Arabian Jewesses but *was* for others argues forcefully that Arabian Jewesses were customarily veiled and that others were not.

One final comment is in order before we turn to the Pesikta Rabbati and draw conclusions concerning Jewish veiling customs. It has been observed that, although Islamic literature has a fairly detailed vocabulary about veiling practices, Judaism lacks any technical terminology for it.[15] Analogy suggests that this reflects

---

[14] R. de Vaux makes this point in his useful article, 'Sur le voile des femmes dans l'Orient ancien', *Revue Biblique* 44 (1935), pp. 397–412; cf. p. 403.

[15] Krauss (*Talmudische Archaeologie*, 1, p. 189) cites Low to this effect. Jastrow ('Veiling in Ancient Assyria', p. 229) expresses the opinion that the veil is not mentioned among the Jews in the Talmudic period. It would appear that he has somewhat overstated the case.

a relative lack of interest in the topic. The extreme care with which the rabbis debated details, for instance, concerning bathing after menstruation (bNid. 66a–67b) provides a good example of a topic which was of importance to them. If veiling was restricted to a hair covering or was not an issue, we can understand the lack of detail about it.

5. Post-Talmudic veiling: Pesikta Rabbati

The Pesikta Rabbati is a collection of Jewish discourses regarding the Scriptures which has been dated variously between the late sixth and the tenth centuries of this era. Its teachings are judged, at various points, to derive from the Talmudic period and perhaps even earlier.[16] Piska 26 contains a saying, attributed to (but obviously not really derived from) the prophet Jeremiah, in which a high priest administers the bitter-water rite of Numbers 5 to a woman suspected of adultery. When the woman was brought to him for the ritual cup of bitter water, 'he bared her head, disarrayed her hair, held out the cup – saw that she was his mother!' It would seem that the veil which the woman wore hid her face from her son at the time of her arrival and that beneath the veil, she wore her hair done up in some manner.

This account was written in Palestine after the Islamic conquest and seems to project backwards to the time of Jeremiah the total veiling imposed by the prophet Muhammad upon his followers. This is a good example of historical anachronism. We have seen evidence that the Hebrews did not veil in Jeremiah's time and scholarly studies have shown that full veiling, although practised in some parts of Arabia, was not generally practised in the Near East until enforced by Islam. Among the Bedouin it never did succeed; many of their women remain unveiled.[17] The Jews of Palestine moved from their over-the-head veiling to the Islamic fashion as a matter of necessity after Islamic conquest, but probably without much protest. By the time of the Pesikta the older customs had been forgotten and the current practices were simply projected onto former remarks about 'veils'. It would seem quite likely that a similar process produced Talmudic assumptions about the necessity of veiling in earlier times. In the case of Rabbi Ishmael, this has obviously happened. By assuming that the veiling

---

[16] For a recent discussion of the dating of the Pesikta, see W. Braude, *Pesikta Rabbati* (London, 1968), pp. 20–26.

[17] The evidence is well presented by de Vaux in 'Sur le voile', pp. 398–403.

practices of his day applied in patriarchal times, he was able to use a biblical text from patriarchal Israel, which required the loosing of hair and which presumed the necessity of having the hair up, to demonstrate the necessity of having a covering upon the tied-up hair. It is more likely that the Hebrews of Numbers 5 had customs like the Bedouin than like those of Rabbi Ishmael.

D. CONCLUSIONS

The following observations, drawn from our survey of Near Eastern veiling customs, helps us in answering our questions about coiffure and veiling in the first century of this era.

1. Evidence taken from first-century and rabbinic sources must be carefully weighed before being accepted as reflective of general Palestinian practice in the first century. A study of evidence for the seclusion of women showed that, in an effort to promote their cause, first-century writers sometimes presented practices of the wealthy or ideals of the pious such as the seclusion of women as though they were the common practice. The Talmudic authors likewise sought to promote their ideals. This sometimes led them to overstate their case or to read the pious practices of the day back into the past. It is therefore possible that veiling evidence from the Talmud or even then contemporary writers may overstate its case by making a pious view appear a general practice.

2. Graeco-Roman practice of the day, as evidenced by art and literature, did not include mandatory veiling of any sort. Facial veiling was unknown and whether or not women pulled their shawls (*palla*, Latin; *himation* or *peribolaiōn*, Greek) over their heads was a matter of indifference.

3. Graeco-Roman custom was concerned with the coiffure of women. Loose and hanging hair was a sign of mourning. A woman's hair was generally dressed with great care. It was frequently braided and decorated, sometimes with very costly ornaments. The dressed hair was a sign of rank and dignity.

4. The Old Testament includes no requirements of veiling for women, although it presumes that their hair will be put up (Nu. 5:18). The inferential evidence from the Old Testament precludes full facial veiling but it is not incompatible with veiling by drawing a shawl over the head. Evidence from a monument of Sennacherib (705–681 BC) witnesses such a veil, although its purpose is unclear.

5. Loose hair was a sign of separation among the Hebrews. Mourning, leprosy, Nazirite vows, suspicion of adultery and repentance all called for such a coiffure.

6. Josephus, a contemporary of Paul, testifies explicitly to the practice of drawing the *himation* over the head as a veil.

7. The evidence of late second-century Mishnah is difficult to assess. Its use of the Hebrew word *pr'*, which meant loosed hair in the Old Testament, is ambiguous and may include unveiling it as well. Such a broadening of the meaning of the term is easily understood as any covering must be removed if hair is to be loosed.

8. The evidence of the Talmud indicates that by somewhere between the third and the sixth century it had become the practice of Jewish piety for women to go outside with a shawl drawn over their heads. Full facial veiling was not the practice of Talmudic Jews.

9. The Talmud uses the Hebrew word *pr'* to refer both to removing a covering and to loosing hair.

10. By the time of the Pesikta Rabbati, after the Islamic conquest, the Jews of Palestine understood veiling according to the Islamic practice of full facial veiling and projected this practice backwards as they read the older history and as they made illustrations from it.

From the ten observations above, the following five conclusions relevant to the question of Jewish veiling practices in the time of Jesus may be drawn.

1. The Old Testament assumes that a woman's hair will be put up; it nowhere requires or even illustrates the veiling of women as a general custom. This applies to full facial veiling and to veiling with a shawl over the head. The latter custom may, however, have existed.

2. There is almost no likelihood that the Jews of the time of Christ practised the full facial veiling of women after the pattern of Islam.

3. It is possible that it was the practice of Jewish piety in that era for women to wear a shawl over the head when out of doors.

4. In less wealthy areas and in areas of weaker tradition, more lax piety, or of either Greek or Roman influence, it is likely that veiling by a shawl would have been a matter of either indifference or neglect.

5. Among Jews, Greeks and Romans alike loosed hair was a

sign of distress and not a hair-do for adult women. Women of all three societies put their hair up and decorated it in various, sometimes expensive, ways. Their hair, so done, was a sign of their dignity and honour.[18]

---

[18] The evidence above has been gathered without reference to New Testament texts. This has been done because they were dealt with in chapter 7 and could be held to represent Christian traditions. It is my opinion, however, that they support the conclusions drawn here.

Bibliography

The bibliography is divided into the following four sections to facilitate the location of pertinent information:

A. Works relating to the cultural background of the Bible and of the church.

B. Selected technical articles on specific topics.

C. Selected book-length treatments of the role of women.

D. Other useful books and articles

A. WORKS RELATING TO THE CULTURAL BACKGROUND OF THE BIBLE AND OF THE CHURCH

Arnold, F. X., *Woman and Man: Their Nature and Mission* (Herder, New York, 1963).

Balsdon, J. P. V. D., *Roman Women, their history and habits* (Bodley Head, London, 1962).

de Boer, P. A. H., *Fatherhood and Motherhood in Israelite and Judean Piety* (Brill, Leiden, 1974).

Daniélou, Jean, *The Ministry of Women in the Early Church* (Faith Press, London, 1961).

Dayton, Donald W. and Lucille S., 'Women as Preachers: Evangelical Precedents', *Christianity Today*, 23 May 1975.

Epstein, L. M., *Sex Laws and Customs in Judaism* (Bloch, New York, 1948).

Forster, W., *Palestinian Judaism in New Testament Times* (Oliver and Boyd, London, 1964).

Goodwater, L., *Women in Antiquity: An Annotated Bibliography* (Scarecrow Press, Metuchen, NJ, 1975).

Gryson, R., *The Ministry of Women in the Early Church* (Liturgical Press, Collegeville, Minn., 1976).

Jastrow, M., 'Veiling in Ancient Assyria', *Revue Archéologique*, 5th series, 14, 1921, pp. 209–238.

Leipoldt, J., *Die Frau in der antiken Welt und im Urchristentum* (Koehler and Amelang, Leipzig, 1954).

Loewe, R., *The Position of Women in Judaism* (SPCK, London, 1966).

Meyer, C. R., 'Ordained Women in the Early Church', *Chicago Studies*, 4, 1965, pp. 285–308.

Osborne, G. R., 'Hermeneutics and Women in the Church', *Journal of the Evangelical Theological Society*, 20, 1977, pp. 337–352.

Pratt, Dwight M., 'Woman', *International Standard Bible Encyclopedia* (Chicago, 1915).

Schlier, Heinrich, 'Kephalē' in Kittel, G. (ed.), *Theological Dictionary of the New Testament*, 3 (Eerdmans, Grand Rapids; hereafter *TDNT*), pp. 673–681.

Stagg, E. and F., *Woman in the World of Jesus* (Westminster Press, Philadelphia, 1978).

Swindler, L., *Women in Judaism: The Status of Women in Formative Judaism* (Scarecrow Press, Metuchen, NJ, 1976).

Tucker, T. G., *Life in the Roman World of Nero and St. Paul* (Macmillan, London and New York, 1910).

van Unnik, W. C., 'Les cheveux defaits des femmes baptisées', *Vigiliae Christianae*, 1, 1947, pp. 77–100.

de Vaux, Roland, 'Sur le voile des femmes dans l'orient ancien', *Revue Biblique*, 44, 1935, pp. 397–412.

Williams, N. P., *The Ideas of the Fall and of Original Sin* (Longmans, London, 1927).

Yamauchi, E. M., 'Cultural Aspects of Marriage in the Ancient World', *Bibliotheca Sacra*, 135, 539, 1978, pp. 241–252.

B. SELECTED TECHNICAL ARTICLES ON SPECIFIC TOPICS

Adinolfi, M., 'Il velo della donna e la rilettura paolina di I Cor. II, 2–16', *Revista Biblica*, 23, 1975, pp. 147–173.

Barre, M. L., 'To Marry or to Burn: *pyrousthai* in I Cor. 7.9', *Catholic Biblical Quarterly*, 36, 1974, pp. 193–202.

Bedale, Stephen, 'The Meaning of *kephalē* in the Pauline Epistles', *Journal of Theological Studies*, 5, 1954, pp. 211–215.

Bruce, F. F., *'All things to All Men'. Unity and Diversity in New Testament Theology* (Eerdmans, Grand Rapids, 1978), pp. 82–99.

Buchler, A., 'Das Schneiden des Haares als Strafe der Ehebrecher bei den Semiten', *Wiener Zeitschrift für die Kunde des Morgenlandes*, 19, 1905, pp. 91–138.

Carle, P.-L., 'La femme et les ministères pastoraux selon l'Ecriture', *Nova et Vetera*, 47, 1972, pp. 161–187.

Carle, P.-L., 'II. La femme et les ministères pastoraux d'après la tradition', *Nova et Vetera*, 47, 1972, pp. 263–290.

Carle, P.-L., 'III. La femme et les ministères pastoraux. Etude théologique', *Nova et Vetera*, 48, 1973, pp. 17–36.

Carle, P.-L. 'IV. La femme et les ministères pastoraux. Réflexion théologique (suite et conclusion)', *Nova et Vetera*, 48, 1973, pp. 262–285.

Cerling, C. E., Jr., 'Women Ministers in the New Testament Church?' *Journal of the Evangelical Theological Society*, 19, 1976, pp. 209–215.

Cope, L., 'I Cor. 11:2–16: One Step Further', *Journal of Biblical Literature*, 97, 1978, pp. 435–436.

Daube, D., 'Concessions to Sinfulness in Jewish Law', *Journal of Jewish Studies*, 10, 1959, p. 121.

Davis, J. J., 'Some Reflections on Gal. 3:28, Sexual Roles, and Biblical Hermeneutics', *Journal of the Evangelical Theological Society*, 19, 1976, pp. 201–208.

Feuillet, A., 'Le signe de puissance sur la tête de la femme. I Cor. 11, 10', *Nouvelle Revue Théologique*, 95, 1973, pp. 945–954.

Feuillet, A., 'L'homme "gloire de Dieu" et la femme "gloire de l'homme" (1 Cor. XI, 7b)', *Revue Biblique*, 81, 1974, pp. 161–182.

Feuillet, A., 'La Dignité et le rôle de la femme d'après quelques textes pauliniennes: comparaison avec l'Ancien Testament', *New Testament Studies*, 21, 1975, pp. 157–191.

Hommes, H. J., 'Let Women be Silent in the Church', *Calvin Theological Journal*, 4, 1969, pp. 5–22.

Hooker, Morna D., 'Authority on her head. An Examination of 1 Cor. XI. 10', *New Testament Studies*, 10, 1964, pp. 410–416.

Hurley, James B., 'Did Paul Require Veils or the Silence of Women? A Consideration of 1 Cor. 11:2–16 and 1 Cor. 14:33b-36', *Westminster Theological Journal*, 35, 1973, pp. 190–220.

Jaubert, A., 'Le voile des femmes (1 Cor. xi. 2–16)', *New Testament Studies*, 18, 1972, pp. 419–430.

Jebb, S., 'A Suggested Interpretation of I Ti. 2:15', *Expository Times*, 81, 1970, pp. 221–222.

Knight, G. W., 'The Number and Function of the Permanent

Offices in the New Testament Church', *Presbyterian*, 1, 1975, pp. 111–116.

de Merode, M., 'Une Théologie Primitive de la femme?' *Revue Théologique Louvensis*, 9, 1978, pp. 176–189.

Moody, D., 'Charismatic and Official Ministries. A Study of the New Testament Concept', *Interpretation*, 19, 1965, pp. 168–181.

Murphy–O'Connor, J., 'The Non-Pauline Character of 1 Corinthians 11:2–16', *Journal of Biblical Literature*, 95, 1976, pp. 615–621.

Murray, John, *Divorce* (Presbyterian & Reformed Pub. Co., Philadelphia, 1961).

Oepke, A., *'anēr'*, *TDNT*, 1, pp. 360–364.

Oepke, A., *'gunē'*, *TDNT*, 1, pp. 776–789.

O'Donovan, O.M.T., 'Towards an Interpretation of Biblical Ethics', *Tyndale Bulletin*, 27, 1976, pp. 54–78.

Scaer, D. P., 'The Office of the Pastor and the Problem of Ordination of Women Pastors', *Springfielder*, 38, 1974, pp. 123–133.

Schüssler-fiorenza, E., 'Women in Pre-Pauline and Pauline Churches', *Union Seminary Quarterly Review*, 33, 1978, pp. 153–166.

Spencer, A. D. B., 'Eve at Ephesus (Should Women be Ordained as Pastors According to the First Letter to Timothy 2:11–15)', *Journal of the Evangelical Theological Society*, 17, 1974, pp. 215–222.

Stahlin, Gustav, *'Asthenēs'*, *TDNT*, 1.

Stendahl, Krister, *The Bible and the Role of Women* (Fortress Press, Philadelphia, 1966).

Vos, G., *Biblical Theology* (Eerdmans, Grand Rapids, 1948).

Walker, W. O., Jr., '1 Corinthians 11:2–16 and Paul's Views Regarding Women', *Journal of Biblical Literature*, 94, 1975, pp. 94–110.

Waltke, B. J., '1 Cor. 11:2–16: An Interpretation', *Bibliotheca Sacra*, 135, 537, 1978, pp. 46–57.

Williams, M. J., 'The Man/Woman Relationship in the New Testament', *Churchman*, 91, 1977, pp. 33–46.

C. SELECTED BOOK–LENGTH TREATMENTS OF THE ROLE OF WOMEN

Adeny, Walter F., *Women in the New Testament* (Nesbit, London, 1901).

Baltensweiler, H., 'Die Ehe im Neuen Testament', *Abhandlungen zur Theologie des Alten und Neuen Testaments*, Band 52 (Zurich, 1967).

Boldrey, R. and J., *Chauvinist or Feminist? Paul's View of Women* (Baker Book House, Grand Rapids, 1976) formerly published as 'Woman in Paul's Life', *Trinity Studies*, 22, 1972 (Trinity Theological Seminary, Deerfield, Ill.).

Brunner, Peter, *The Ministry and the Ministry of Women* (Concordia, St Louis, 1971).

Charles, R. H., *The Teaching of the New Testament on Divorce* (Williams and Norgate, London, 1921).

Delling, G., *Paulus' Stellung zu Frau und Ehe* (W. Kohlhammer, Stuttgart, 1931).

Elliot, Elisabeth, *Let Me Be A Woman* (Tyndale House, Wheaton, Ill., 1976).

Ford, J. M., 'Biblical Material Relevant to the Ordination of Women', *Journal of Ecumenical Studies*, 10, 1973, pp. 669–694.

de Fraine, J., *Women in the Old Testament* (St Norberts Abbey Press, De Pere, Wisc., 1968).

Hurley, James B., *Man and Woman in 1 Corinthians* (unpublished Ph D thesis, Cambridge University, 1973).

Jewett, Paul K., *Man as Male and Female* (Eerdmans, Grand Rapids, 1975).

Kähler, Else, *Die Frau in den paulinischen Briefen* (Gotthelf, Zurich, 1960).

Knight, George W. III, *The New Testament Teaching on the Role Relationship of Men and Women* (Baker Book House, Grand Rapids, 1977).

Kosnik, A., *Human Sexuality: New Directions in American Catholic Thought* (Paulist Press, New York, 1977).

Maertens, T., *The Advancing Dignity of Woman in the Bible* (St Norberts Abbey Press, De Pere, Wisc., 1969).

Mollenkott, Virginia R., *Women, Men, and the Bible* (Abingdon Press, Nashville, 1977).

Pape, Dorothy R., *In Search of God's Ideal Woman: A Personal Examination of the New Testament* (Inter-Varsity Press, Downers Grove, Ill., 1976).

Ryrie, Charles, *The Place of Women in the Bible* (Moody Press, Chicago, 1968).

Sapp, S., *Sexuality, the Bible and Science* (Fortress Press, Philadelphia, 1977).

Scanzoni, Letha and Hardesty, Nancy, *All We're Meant to Be: A Biblical Approach to Women's Liberation* (Word, Waco, Tex., 1974).

Thrall, M. E., *The Ordination of Women to the Priesthood* (SCM, London, 1958).
Tiemeyer, Raymond, *The Ordination of Women* (Augsburg, Minneapolis, 1970).
Wijngaard, J. N. M., *Did Christ Rule Out Woman Priests?* (Mayhew-McCrimmon, Great Wakering, 1977).
Zerbst, Fritz, *The Office of Woman in the Church* (Concordia, St. Louis, 1955).

D. OTHER USEFUL BOOKS AND ARTICLES

Aldunate, J. Bulness, 'Three Submissions and Continual Renewal', *Concilium*, 39, 1968, pp. 45–68.
von Allmen, J. J., *Pauline Teaching on Marriage* (Faith Press, London, 1963).
Babbage, Stewart Barton, *Christianity and Sex* (Inter-Varsity Press, Downers Grove, Ill., 1963).
Bailey, D. S. *Sexual Relation in Christian Thought* (Harper, New York, 1959).
Baldwin, J. G., 'A Response to G. Wenham', *Churchman*, 93, 1979, p. 54.
Bainette, H., 'Coarchy: Partnership and Equality in Man-Woman Relationship', *Review and Expositor*, 75, 1978, pp. 19-24.
Barrois, G., 'Women and the Priestly Office According to the Scriptures', *St Vladimirs Theological Quarterly*, 19, 1975, pp. 174–192.
Bartle, D. L., 'A Biblical Perspective on Homosexuality', *Foundations*, 20 (Rochester, NY, 1977), pp. 133–147.
Bliss, K., *The Service and Status of Women in the Churches* (SCM, London, 1952).
Blum, G. G., 'The Office of Woman in the New Testament', *Churchman*, 85, 1971, pp. 175-189.
Boucher, M., 'Some Unexplored Parallels to 1 Cor. 11.11–12 and Gal. 3.28: the N.T. on the Role of Women', *Catholic Biblical Quarterly*, 31, 1969, pp. 50–58.
Bruce, M. and Duffield, G. E., *Why Not? Priesthood and the Ministry of Women* (Marcham Books, Appleford, Berkshire, 1976).
Caddeo, L., 'Le "diaconesse" ', *Ricerche Bibliche e Religiose*, 7, 1972, pp. 193–210.
Caird, G. B., 'Paul and Women's Liberty', *The Bulletin of the John Rylands Library*, 54, 1972, pp. 268–281.

278

Chilton, B. D., 'Opening the Book: Biblical Warrants for the Ordination of Women', *Modern Churchman*, 20, 1977, pp. 32-35.

Christenson, Larry, *The Christian Family* (Fountain Trust, Esher, Surrey, 1971).

Collins, R. F., 'The Bible and Sexuality', *Biblical Theology Bulletin*, I. 7, 1977, pp. 149–167; II. 8, 1978, pp. 3–18.

Drane, J. W., 'Tradition, Law and Ethics in Pauline Theology', *Novum Testamentum*, 16, 1974, pp. 167–178.

Dumais, M., 'Couple et sexualité selon le Nouveau Testament', *Église et Théoligie*, 8, 1977, pp. 42–72.

Ford, P. J., 'Paul the Apostle: Male Chauvinist?' *Biblical Theology Bulletin*, 5, 1975, pp. 302-311.

Fraser, David and Eloise, 'A Biblical View of Women: Demythologizing Sexogesis, *ThNN*, 21, 1975.

Giles, Kevin, *Women and their Ministry* (Dove, East Malvern, 1977).

Graham, R. W., 'Women in the Pauline Churches: A Review Article', *Lexington Theological Quarterly*, 11, 1976, pp. 25–34.

Hall, B., 'Paul and Women', *Theology Today*, 31, 1974, pp. 50–55.

Hamann, H. P., 'The New Testament and the Ordination of Women', *Lutheran Theological Journal*, 9, 1975, pp. 100-108.

Harper, J., *Women and the Gospel* (Christian Brethren Research Fellowship, Pinner, Middlesex, 1974).

Hull, W. E., 'Woman in Her Place: Biblical Perspectives', *Review and Expositor*, 72, 1975, pp. 5–17.

Hunt, Gladys, *Ms. Means Myself* (Zondervan, Grand Rapids, 1972).

Isaksson, A., *Marriage and Ministry in the New Temple: A Study with Special Reference to Mt. 19:3–12 and 1 Cor. 11:3–16* (Gleerup, Lund, 1965).

Kurzinger, J., 'Frau und Mann nach 1 Kor. 11.11f.', *Biblische Zeitschrift*, 22, 1978, pp. 270–275.

Lampe, G. W. H., 'Church Tradition and the Ordination of Women', *Expository Times*, 76, 1965, pp. 123–125.

Legrand, L., 'Women's Ministries in the New Testament', *Biblebhashyam*, 2, 1976, pp. 286–299.

Lightfoot, N.R., 'The Role of Women in Religious Services', *Restoration Quarterly*, 19, 1976, pp. 129–136.

Lindsell, Harold, 'Egalitarianism and Biblical Infallibility', *Christianity Today*, 26 March 1976, pp. 45–46.

Lindsell, Harold, *The World, the Flesh and the Devil* (Cannon, Washington, DC, 1973).

Loewen, H., 'The Pauline View of Women', *Direction*, 6, 1977, pp. 3–20.

Longstaff, T. R. W., 'The Ordination of Women: A Biblical Perspective', *Anglican Theological Review*, 57, 1975, pp. 316–327.

Marucci, C., 'La donna e i ministeri nella Bibbia e nella tradizione', *Rassegna di Teologia*, Naples, 17, 1976, pp. 273–296.

Menoud, P. H., 'Saint Paul et la femme', *Revue de Théologie et de Philosophie*, 19, 1969, pp. 318–330.

Mettinger, T. N. D., 'Eva och revbenet – Manligt och kvinnligt i exegetisk belysning' (Eve and the Rib – Male and Female in the Light of Exegesis), *Svensk Theologisk Kvartalskrift*, 54, 1978, pp. 55–64.

Mollenkott, Virginia, Foreword to P.K. Jewett's *Man as Male and Female* (Eerdmans, Grand Rapids, 1975).

Moore, P. (ed.), *Man, Woman, and Priesthood* (SPCK, London, 1978).

Pagels, E. H., 'Paul and Women: A Response to Recent Discussions', *Journal of the American Academy of Religion*, 42, 1974, pp. 538–549.

Pousset, E., 'L'homme et la femme de la création à la réconciliation', *Lumière et Vie*, 21, 106, 1972, pp. 60–74.

Pretlove, J., 'Paul and the Ordination of Women', *Expository Times*, 76, 1965, p. 294.

Reumann, J., 'What in Scripture Speaks to the Ordination of Women?' *Currents in Theology and Missions*, 44, 1973, pp. 5–30.

Sakenfeld, K. D., 'The Bible and Women: Bane or Blessing?' *Theology Today*, 32, 1975, pp. 222–233.

Sapp, S., 'Biblical Perspectives on Human Sexuality', *Duke Divinity School Review*, 41, 1976, pp. 105–122.

Scroggs, Robin, 'Paul: Chauvinist or Liberationist?' *The Christian Century*, 15 March 1972, p. 307.

Scroggs, Robin, 'Paul and the Eschatological Woman', *Journal of the American Academy of Religion*, 40, 1972, pp. 283–303.

Scroggs, Robin, 'Paul and the Eschatological Woman: Revisited', *Journal of the American Academy of Religion*, 42, 1974, pp. 532–537.

Stein, D., 'Le statut des femmes dans les lettres de Paul', *Lumière et Vie*, 27, 139, 1978, pp. 63–85.

Trible, P., *God and the Rhetoric of Sexuality: Overtures to Biblical Theology* (Fortress Press, Philadelphia, 1978).

Weeks, N., 'Of Silence and Head Covering', *Westminster Theological Journal*, 35, 1972, pp. 21–27.

Wenham, G.J., 'The Ordination of Women: Why is it so diverse?' *Churchman*, 92, 1978, pp. 310-319.

Index of biblical references

Index of extra-biblical sources

Subject index